**SERIES
IN
HUMAN
RESOURCE
DEVELOPMENT**

THE
1989 ANNUAL: DEVELOPING HUMAN RESOURCES

(The Eighteenth Annual)

Edited by
J. WILLIAM PFEIFFER, Ph.D., J.D.

UNIVERSITY ASSOCIATES, INC.
8517 Production Avenue
San Diego, California 92121

Printed in the United States of America

Published by
University Associates, Inc.
8517 Production Avenue
San Diego, California 92121
619-578-5900

University Associates of Canada
4190 Fairview Street
Burlington, Ontario L7L 4Y8
Canada

University Associates International
Challenge House
45-47 Victoria Street
Mansfield, Notts NG18 5SU
England

PREFACE

The contents of this eighteenth volume of the *Annual* series again indicate that the field of human resource development (HRD)—which incorporates training, career development, personnel, management development, and organization development functions—continues to flourish and grow. The changes in the title of the *Annual* over the last eighteen years reflect the evolution of HRD as well as the intention of University Associates to remain at the cutting edge of this field.

From the outset the central purpose of the *Annual* has been to keep readers aware of and involved in the current developments in the field. To achieve this purpose, each year the contents of the *Annual* are selected and edited to reflect these developments as we at UA perceive them. For several years now the HRD function in most organizations has become steadily more and more visible and has exerted a stronger and more valuable influence in such endeavors as strategic planning. The individual pieces selected for this *Annual* serve as further evidence of the progress and richness of the field today. They not only serve as cause for optimism about the future of HRD; they also offer food for thought about the needs and requirements of that future.

In this year's *Annual*, the Lecturette, Theory and Practice, and Resources sections again are integrated into a single Professional Development section. This format, initiated in 1984, allows greater flexibility in selection and facilitates a more coherent overview of what is occurring in the HRD field.

In the Instrumentation section, University Associates intends to continue to publish practical measurement devices that are useful for trainers, consultants, and managers. Moreover, as has been the case in the last several *Annuals*, both the theoretical background for each instrument and practical suggestions for its administration and application are included. These added features should make the instruments easier to use and should increase their value to our readers. Those people who intend to submit instruments and other materials to the *Annual* are advised to take these standards into account.

There are several aspects of the *Annual* series that have not changed in the last several years, nor will they change in the future. One is a continuing bias that the *Annual* be strongly user oriented, that everything in it be potentially useful to the professional trainers, consultants, facilitators, and managers who read it. The content of this *Annual* focuses on increasing each reader's professional competence and, therefore, his or her impact on the field of HRD. In keeping with this objective, users are allowed to duplicate and modify materials from the *Annuals* for *educational and training* purposes, so long as the credit statement found on the copyright page of the particular volume is included on all copies. However, if University Associates materials are to be reproduced in publications for sale or are intended for large-scale distribution (more than one hundred copies in twelve months), *prior written permission* is required. Also, if a footnote indicates that the material is copyrighted by some source other than University Associates, no reproduction is allowed without the written permission of that designated copyright holder.

We at University Associates continue to solicit materials from our readers—especially materials with a clear organizational focus and those that reflect the changing nature of the HRD field. The success of the *Annual* as a clearing house for HRD professionals depends on the continual flow of materials from our readers. We encourage and welcome the submission of structured experiences, instruments, and articles, including both innovative methods and tried-and-true procedures. Our guidelines for contributors are available from the Editorial Department at the San Diego address listed on the copyright page of this volume, and submissions should be sent to the managing editor at the same address.

I want to express my sincere appreciation to the dedicated people at University Associates who have made this year's *Annual* an object of pride for me: Carol Nolde, senior editor and project manager; Marian Prokop, editor; Mary Kitzmiller, managing editor; Arlette C. Ballew, developmental senior editor; Jennifer Bryant, editorial assistant; Jacqueline Pickett, typographer; and Judy Whalen, typesetter. I also wish to thank Beverly Byrum, Ph.D., whose review of the structured experiences from a facilitator's perspective has, for several years now, enhanced their usefulness immeasurably. As always, I am especially grateful to our authors—our peers and colleagues—for sharing their professional ideas, materials, and techniques.

J. William Pfeiffer

San Diego, California
November, 1988

About University Associates

University Associates is engaged in publishing, training, and consulting in the broad field of human resource development (HRD). UA has earned an international reputation as the source of practical publications that are immediately useful to today's facilitators, trainers, consultants, and managers. A distinct advantage of these publications is that they are designed by practicing professionals who are continually experimenting with new techniques. Thus, UA readers benefit from the fresh but thoughtful approach that underlies UA's experientially based materials, resources, books, workbooks, instruments, and tape-assisted learning programs. These materials are designed for the HRD practitioner who wants access to a broad range of training and intervention technologies as well as background in the field.

UA's practical, applied, theory-based approach is evident in its training and consulting activities as well. Its experienced trainers and consultants conduct training programs in both the public and private sectors, train trainers, and consult with organizations and communities to solve human and organizational programs. Activities include workshops on fundamental and current topics in human resource development and organization development, as well as workshops that are customized to meet specific client needs. In addition, professional certification is offered by the UA Graduate School through its intern program in laboratory education and its master's degree in human resource development.

The wide audience that UA serves includes training and development professionals, internal and external consultants, managers and supervisors, and those in the helping professions. For its clients and customers, University Associates offers a practical approach aimed at increasing people's effectiveness on an individual, group, and organizational basis.

TABLE OF CONTENTS

---

*See Structured Experience Categories, p. 5, for an explanation of numbering.

GENERAL INTRODUCTION TO THE 1989 ANNUAL

The 1989 Annual: Developing Human Resources is the eighteenth volume in the *Annual* series. The series is, and will continue to be, a collection of practical and useful materials for professionals in human resource development (HRD), materials written by professionals for their colleagues. As such, the series continues to provide a publication outlet for HRD professionals to share their experiences, their viewpoints, and their procedures with their professional colleagues on a world-wide basis.

Following the changes made in the *Annual* format in 1984, there are now three rather than five sections: Structured Experiences, Instrumentation, and Professional Development. The Professional Development section combines the Lecturettes, Theory and Practice, and Resources sections that appeared in the first twelve volumes of the series. Over the years, some of the distinctions among those three categories had become blurred; it also seemed that some of the materials in those sections would be more useful if placed elsewhere in the volume. The arrangement we now use relates the published pieces more logically and conveniently and allows us more flexibility in meeting the needs and interests of practitioners in the growing field of HRD.

There is, however, one aspect of the series that has not changed in this volume of the *Annual:* the quality of content. As has been the case from the inception of the series, the materials for the 1989 *Annual* have been selected for their quality of conceptualization, applicability to the real-world concerns of HRD practitioners, relevance to today's HRD issues, clarity of presentation, and ability to provide readers with assistance in their own professional development. In addition to using the aforementioned criteria for selecting valuable tools, we were also able to choose structured experiences that will create a high degree of enthusiasm among the participants and add a great deal of enjoyment to the learning process. As in the past few years, readers will notice a greater focus on organizational issues, which reflects the fact that more and more of our readers are organizationally based or are consultants and trainers for organizations. Thus, there is a need for more structured experiences that have organizational relevance or that can be used with intact groups, especially work groups. A description of the structured experiences that we selected for this volume is given in the "Introduction to the Structured Experiences Section."

The order of the structured experiences in the 1989 *Annual* is dictated by the categorization scheme of our *Structured Experience Kit* and the *Reference Guide to Handbooks and Annuals.* We believe that this order will prove to be more logical and easier to use for our readers, particularly those who regularly use structured experiences in their work and who select them from the *Reference Guide* or the *Structured Experience Kit.*

The Instrumentation section of this *Annual* contains three new paper-and-pencil, instrumented-feedback scales, questionnaires, or inventories. These three, which are both interesting and useful, are described in the "Introduction to the Instrumentation Section."

The Professional Development section is intended to assist readers of the *Annual* in their own professional development. As usual, the articles in the 1989 *Annual* cover a broad range of issues that confront HRD professionals today. These articles are described in the "Introduction to the Professional Development Section."

The editor and the editorial staff continue to be surprised by and pleased with the high quality of materials submitted. Nevertheless, just as we cannot publish every manuscript that is submitted, readers may find that not all of the articles we publish are equally useful to them. We actively solicit feedback from our readers in order that we may continue to select manuscripts that meet their needs.

We follow the stylistic guidelines established by the American Psychological Association, particularly with regard to the use and format of references. Potential contributors to University Associates' publications may wish to purchase copies of the APA's *Publication Manual* from: Order Department, American Psychological Association, 1200 Seventeenth Street, N.W., Washington, DC 20036. University Associates also publishes guidelines for potential UA authors. These guidelines were revised in 1986, were published at the end of the Professional Development section of the 1987 *Annual*, and are also available from the University Associates editorial department.

Biographies of *Annual* authors are published at the end of each structured experience, instrument, and professional development article; and at the end of each *Annual* is a list of contributors' names, affiliations, addresses, and telephone numbers. This information is intended to contribute to the "networking" function that is so valuable in our field.

INTRODUCTION TO THE
STRUCTURED EXPERIENCES SECTION

Experiential learning continues to gain wider support in the training and development community. There is a greater understanding that adult-learning processes are different from those of younger learners and that vehicles for learning other than the traditional lecture need to be used in order to promote adult learning. The use of structured experiences, probably the most frequently used of the experiential-learning strategies, has grown accordingly.

The 1989 *Annual* continues to provide a balance of materials. Several of the structured experiences in this section can be used for a variety of purposes in different settings; however, in selecting structured experiences for publication in this volume, we gave precedence to those that could be used in organizational settings.

In the past we have attempted to cross-reference the materials in the *Annuals* and the series of *Handbooks* and to publish (at the end of each structured experience) suggestions for "similar structured experiences," "suggested instruments," and "lecturette sources." With the 1987 *Annual* we discontinued this process, for several reasons. In response to a questionnaire, our sample of readers indicated that the cross-references were not being used as frequently as we had anticipated. In addition, because older volumes do not reflect material in later volumes, the cross-referencing in any particular volume is incomplete as soon as a later volume is published. Finally, the *Reference Guide to Handbooks and Annuals,* which is revised periodically, is apparently much more beneficial to our readers. It provides the type of help that the cross-referencing was originally intended to give. With each revision, the *Reference Guide* is completely updated and provides an easy way to select appropriate material from *all* of the *Annuals* and *Handbooks.*

Readers of past *Annuals,* and those familiar with other University Associates publications, will note that the structured experiences are presented in an order that reflects their classification into categories, according to their focus and intent. A list of the six major categories and their subcategories can be found immediately following this introduction, and an explanation of the categorization scheme can be found in the "User's Guide" to the *Structured Experience Kit,* in the discussion beginning on page 19 of the *Reference Guide to Handbooks and Annuals* (1988 Edition), and in the "Introduction to the Structured Experience Section" of the 1981 *Annual.*

The structured experiences in the 1989 *Annual* represent five of the six major categories: Personal, Communication, Group Characteristics, Group Task Behavior, and Organizations. "The Art of Feedback" is used to teach the feedback process and its value to members of an intact work group. "The Girl and the Sailor" allows participants to practice identifying and clarifying values and to see how values affect relationships and decisions.

The next structured experience, "What's Legal?," develops the participants' awareness of legal issues in connection with interviewing applicants for employment.

"Four Factors" acquaints the participants with Rosenthal and Jacobson's (1968) four-factor theory of leader influence on follower behavior and gives the participants an opportunity to analyze case studies illustrating the four factors.

"Control or Surrender," the first of two structured experiences concerning problem solving and awareness, introduces the members of an intact work group to a method for changing the way in which they perceive problems and allows them to apply this method to a predefined group problem. "Marzilli's Fine Italian Foods" illustrates the impact of assumptions on problem solving, introduces the participants to the concept of strategic thinking, and encourages them to suspend assumptions while they practice strategic thinking.

Two structured experiences deal with group feedback. "America's Favorite Pastime" identifies team roles and helps members of an intact work group to share their perceptions of one another by determining which roles are fulfilled by which members. "It's in the Cards" also allows members of an intact work team to share their perceptions of one another and addresses the members' perceptions of the team as a whole and the team's relationship to the organization.

"The Candy Bar" introduces the participants to various power strategies. It acquaints them with seven bases of power and offers them an opportunity to experience and compare the effects of strategies associated with the seven bases.

The last three structured experiences represent the Organizations category. "The Impact Wheel" introduces the members of an intact work group to a tool for identifying the effects and ramifications of events in their work lives. "The Robotics Decision" introduces the participants to the strategic assumption surfacing and testing (SAST) process (Mason & Mitroff, 1981) and offers them a chance to use this process in solving a sample problem. The final structured experience, "City of Buffington," allows the participants an opportunity to practice interviewing for the purpose of obtaining information for diagnosing organizational problems.

All structured experiences in this *Annual* contain a description of the goals of the activity, the size of the group(s) that can be accommodated, the time required to do and *process*[1] the activity, the materials and handouts required, the physical setting, step-by-step directions for facilitating the experiential task and discussion phases of the activity, and variations of the design that the facilitator might find useful. As always, all of the structured experiences are complete; the content of all handouts is provided within the design.

REFERENCES

Mason, R.O., & Mitroff, I.I. (1981). *Challenging strategic planning assumptions.* New York: Wiley Inter-Science.

Rosenthal, R., & Jacobson, L. (1968). *Pygmalion in the classroom.* New York: Holt, Rinehart and Winston.

---

[1]It would be redundant to print here a caveat for the use of structured experiences, but HRD professionals who are not experienced in the use of this training technology are strongly urged to read the "Introduction to the Structured Experiences Section" of the 1980 *Annual* or the "Introduction" to the *Reference Guide to Handbooks and Annuals* (1988 Edition). Both of these articles present the theory behind the experiential-learning cycle and explain the necessity of adequately completing each phase of the cycle in order to allow effective learning to occur.

STRUCTURED EXPERIENCE CATEGORIES

449. THE ART OF FEEDBACK: PROVIDING CONSTRUCTIVE INFORMATION

Goals

I. To develop the participants' understanding of how to give and receive feedback.

II. To offer the participants an opportunity to practice giving and/or receiving feedback.

III. To develop the participants' understanding of the impact of receiving feedback.

IV. To develop the participants' understanding of how the feedback process can help an individual or a work group to improve functioning.

Group Size

All members of an intact work group. A generally well-functioning group should be able to complete this structured experience without any major difficulties. However, because this feedback process poses a degree of risk, the facilitator is advised to ensure that the group is ready to handle it. If preparation is necessary, a trust-building activity can be useful.

Time Required

Approximately two and one-half hours.

Materials

I. One copy of the principles handout for each participant.

II. One copy of the guidelines for feedback on peer behavior for each participant.

III. One copy of the guidelines for feedback on subordinate behavior for each participant.

IV. One copy of the guidelines for feedback on supervisor behavior for each participant.

V. Two pencils and two clipboards or other portable writing surfaces to be used by the group spokespersons (see Steps IV and X) and by the supervisor (see Step VII).

Physical Setting

A room in which the participants can work without distractions. A separate area should be provided so that one to three of the participants can work on tasks outside the main meeting room (see Steps IV, VII, and X).

Process

I. The facilitator introduces the activity by explaining the goals, distributes copies of the principles handout, and leads a discussion on the handout content. (Twenty minutes.)

II. *Feedback Round 1:* Each participant is given a copy of the guidelines for feedback on peer behavior. The facilitator asks for a volunteer who is willing to receive feedback from his or her peers on the three activities listed on this handout. The peers are told that they have fifteen minutes to prepare appropriate feedback and that they should select a spokesperson to give this feedback; they are given a pencil and a clipboard or other portable writing surface for the spokesperson's use. Then the facilitator and the supervisor leave the room with the volunteer so that they can coach the volunteer on how to receive the upcoming feedback. (Fifteen minutes.)

III. The facilitator, the supervisor, and the volunteer return to the main meeting room. The facilitator asks the spokesperson to give the group's feedback to the volunteer. The remaining participants are told to listen carefully to determine whether the spokesperson and the volunteer follow the principles for giving and receiving feedback, respectively. (Ten minutes.)

IV. The facilitator assists the participants in evaluating the feedback, how it was given, and how it was received. First the spokesperson and the feedback recipient critique themselves; then the remaining participants are invited to contribute suggestions for ways in which the feedback process might have been improved. (Fifteen minutes.)

V. *Feedback Round 2:* Each participant is given a copy of the guidelines for feedback on subordinate behavior. The facilitator asks for a volunteer subordinate who is willing to receive the supervisor's feedback on the three activities listed on the handout. The facilitator tells the supervisor that he or she has ten minutes to prepare appropriate feedback responses about the volunteer's effectiveness in the three activities and gives the supervisor a pencil and a clipboard or other portable writing surface; then the supervisor leaves the room to complete the task. The facilitator stays in the main meeting room with the remaining participants and leads a discussion on how the volunteer can best receive the feedback. (Ten minutes.)

VI. The supervisor is invited to return to the main meeting room and to give feedback to the volunteer. The remaining participants are instructed to listen and determine whether the supervisor and the volunteer follow the principles for giving and receiving feedback, respectively. (Ten minutes.)

VII. The group evaluates the feedback, how it was given, and how it was received. First the supervisor and the subordinate critique themselves; then the remaining participants offer comments. (Ten minutes.)

VIII. *Feedback Round 3:* Each participant is given a copy of the guidelines for feedback on supervisor behavior. All participants except the supervisor are instructed to work as a group to determine appropriate feedback for their supervisor with regard to the three activities listed on the sheet. The participants are also told to select a spokesperson to give this feedback to the supervisor (a different person from the one selected in Step II); the first spokesperson is told to give the pencil and clipboard or other portable writing surface to the new spokesperson. The facilitator tells the participants that they have ten minutes to complete this task, leaves the room with the supervisor, and coaches the supervisor on how to receive the upcoming feedback. (Ten minutes.)

IX. The facilitator and the supervisor return to the main meeting room. The spokesperson gives the group's feedback to the supervisor while the remaining participants listen and determine whether the principles for giving and receiving feedback are being followed. (Ten minutes.)

X. The group evaluates the feedback, how it was given, and how it was received. First the spokesperson and the supervisor critique themselves; then the remaining participants offer comments. (Ten minutes.)

XI. The facilitator leads a concluding discussion by asking the following questions:

1. How did you feel while giving feedback? How did you feel while receiving feedback? Which would you rather do and why?

2. What interactions occurred among the members while determining what feedback to give? What patterns of giving and receiving feedback developed during the three feedback rounds?

3. What generalizations can be made about the effect of constructive feedback on the individual who receives it? What generalizations can be made about the effect on the work group that receives feedback?

4. How can the effect of feedback improve individual functioning? How can it improve group functioning?

XII. The facilitator suggests that the participants keep their copies of the handout on principles of feedback and refer to them from time to time to refresh their understanding of the feedback process. The facilitator also suggests that the participants repeat this process periodically to improve group functioning.

Variations

I. The feedback rounds may be presented in a different order: (1) supervisor as recipient, (2) subordinate as recipient, and (3) peer as recipient. This order works well when subordinates are more accustomed to giving feedback to their supervisor than to one another. Also, this design alternative offers the advantage of allowing the supervisor to model the appropriate receiving of feedback.

II. In addition to the feedback provided by the spokesperson during the peer-feedback step, each participant may be asked to provide the recipient with individual feedback.

III. The activity may be continued by repeating the feedback process for each participant who has not yet received feedback. Feedback may be given either by the supervisor or by a peer.

IV. At the conclusion of the activity, the facilitator may assist the participants in developing an action plan covering (1) what they will do with the feedback they heard and (2) what they can do in the future with the feedback process.

V. To shorten the activity, one focus may be chosen: supervisor, subordinate, or peer.

Submitted by Stephen C. Bushardt and Aubrey R. Fowler, Jr. This structured experience is based on "Teacher Evaluation: An Experiential Exercise in Giving and Receiving Feedback" by S.C. Bushardt and Aubrey R. Fowler, Jr., 1987, in *On the Cutting Edge of Management: Theory and Practice* (Proceedings of the Twenty-Fourth Annual Meeting of the Eastern Academy of Management) (p. 225) by N.J. Beutell and D.J. Lenn (Eds.).

Stephen C. Bushardt, D.B.A., is a professor of management in the College of Business Administration at the University of Southern Mississippi in Hattiesburg. He is also actively involved in consulting and training in the health care industry. His research focuses primarily on performance evaluation, reward systems, and motivation. Dr. Bushardt has published articles in a number of journals, including Group and Organization Studies, Leadership and Organizational Development Journal, Journal of Business Communication, Personnel Administration, Journal of Business Strategies, and Management World.

Aubrey R. Fowler, Jr., Ph.D., is an associate professor of management and the chairman of the Department of Marketing and Management at the University of Central Arkansas in Conway. He also has taught at the University of Southern Mississippi, Idaho State University, Drake University, and Nicholls State University in Louisiana. Dr. Fowler has published in a variety of management-related journals and has research interests in the areas of performance and employee evaluation. He has consulted widely with small businesses and is a member of the Academy of Management.

THE ART OF FEEDBACK
PRINCIPLES

Definitions of Feedback

Constructive feedback is information that helps people to decide whether their behaviors have had the intended effects.

Positive feedback is information that reinforces desired behaviors and encourages repetition of those behaviors by communicating that they had the intended effects.

Negative feedback is information that discourages behaviors by communicating that they did not have the intended effects.

Principles of Giving Feedback

1. Be sure that your intention is to be helpful.
2. If the recipient has not asked for feedback, check to see whether he or she is open to it.
3. Deal only with behavior that can be changed.
4. Deal with specific behavior, not generalities.
5. Describe the behavior; do not evaluate it.
6. Let the recipient know the impact that the behavior has on you.
7. Use an "I statement" to accept responsibility for your own perceptions and emotions.
8. Check to make sure that the recipient understood your message in the way you intended it.
9. Encourage the recipient to check the feedback with other people.

Principles of Receiving Feedback

1. When you ask for feedback, be specific in describing the behavior about which you want the feedback.
2. Try not to act defensively or rationalize the behavior at issue.
3. Summarize your understanding of the feedback that you receive.
4. Share your thoughts and feelings about the feedback.

THE ART OF FEEDBACK
GUIDELINES FOR FEEDBACK ON PEER BEHAVIOR

The peer is to be given feedback on how effective he or she is at the following activities:

1. Contributing during team meetings

2. Supporting and encouraging other team members

3. Working for the good of the team (instead of just for himself or herself)

THE ART OF FEEDBACK
GUIDELINES FOR FEEDBACK ON SUBORDINATE BEHAVIOR

The subordinate is to be given feedback on how effective he or she is at the following activities:

1. Completing work accurately and on time

2. Working without close supervision

3. Problem solving with fellow team members

THE ART OF FEEDBACK
GUIDELINES FOR FEEDBACK ON SUPERVISOR BEHAVIOR

The supervisor is to be given feedback on how effective he or she is at the following activities:

1. Communicating expectations and task instructions

2. Listening when a subordinate presents a problem

3. Praising a subordinate or providing suggestions for improvement when appropriate

450. THE GIRL AND THE SAILOR: VALUE CLARIFICATION

Goals

  I. To provide an opportunity for the participants to practice identifying and clarifying values.

 II. To develop the participants' awareness of some of the factors that affect their own value judgments as well as those of others.

III. To demonstrate how values affect relationships as well as personal and group decisions.

Group Size

Any number of subgroups of five to seven participants each.

Time Required

Approximately two hours.

Materials

  I. A copy of The Girl and the Sailor Case History Sheet for each participant.

 II. A pencil for each participant.

III. A sheet of newsprint prepared in advance with the following questions written on it:

  1. What values seemed to underlie the choices that were made?

  2. What similarities in members' values became apparent? What differences became apparent? How do you account for the similarities and differences?

  3. What feelings did you experience when someone agreed with your values? What feelings did you experience when someone disagreed with them?

  4. How did differences in values affect relationships among the members of your subgroup? How did these differences affect the effort to achieve consensus?

  5. What conclusions can you draw about the effects of values on decisions? What generalizations can you make about the effects of values on relationships with others and on teamwork?

 IV. A sheet of newsprint and a felt-tipped marker for each subgroup.

  V. Newsprint and a felt-tipped marker for the facilitator's use.

 VI. Masking tape.

Physical Setting

A room large enough so that the subgroups can work without disturbing one another. During Step II each subgroup should be placed near a wall so that a sheet of newsprint can be displayed within the view of all of its members.

Process

I. The facilitator introduces the activity and its goals.

II. The participants are assembled into subgroups of five to seven each and are given copies of The Girl and the Sailor Case History Sheet and pencils.

III. The facilitator asks the participants to read the case history sheet and to work individually to complete the task instructions at the end of the handout. (Ten minutes.)

IV. The members of each subgroup are instructed to share their rankings, disclosing their rationales and articulating their associated values and beliefs as clearly as possible. The facilitator emphasizes that during this sharing no one is to express an opinion regarding another member's decisions or beliefs; requests for clarification are the only permissible comments. (Fifteen minutes.)

V. Each subgroup is given a sheet of newsprint, a felt-tipped marker, and masking tape. The facilitator explains that the members of each subgroup are to spend twenty minutes trying to reach a consensus regarding the ranking of any or all of the characters. If a consensus is reached, one member should be appointed to record the decisions on newsprint and post the newsprint on the wall in view of all the subgroup members; if no consensus is possible, nothing is posted. (Twenty minutes.)

VI. The facilitator posts the newsprint that was prepared in advance with questions written on it (see the Materials section, III) and explains that each subgroup is to incorporate them into a discussion of reactions to the activity. (Twenty minutes.)

VII. The total group is reconvened for sharing of answers to the questions posted during the previous step. (Ten minutes.)

VIII. New subgroups of three or four participants each are assembled. Each participant is asked to identify and discuss with fellow subgroup members one or two significant factors that influence his or her judgment in assessing similar situations involving value conflicts. (Fifteen minutes.)

IX. A volunteer from each subgroup reports to the total group on typical factors that were identified during the previous step. (Ten minutes.)

X. The facilitator summarizes the general themes expressed in the subgroup reports and then elicits comments from the participants regarding possible applications of their learnings. The following questions are asked:

1. What are some value conflicts that you are presently experiencing?

2. How can you use what you have learned from this activity to deal more productively with those value conflicts?

3. How can you use this information to improve a situation at work? What will be your first step?

4. What consequences do you expect from taking that first step? How will you manage those consequences?

Variations

I. To shorten the activity, Steps VIII and IX may be eliminated. In Step X the participants may be asked simply to offer statements about back-home applications.

II. Steps VII and VIII may be combined, with the processing taking place in the total group.

III. To heighten the experience of value conflict, the subgroups may be told that they *must* arrive at a consensus on the ranking of characters in the case history sheet.

IV. After Step VI the participants may be asked to form dyads on the basis of dissimilar values. Within each dyad one partner explains his or her point of view while the other partner engages in active listening; the listening partner does not respond with his or her personal viewpoints until the speaking partner has finished the explanation. Then the partners switch roles and repeat the process. This variation promotes understanding of others' values.

This structured experience is an adaptation of "Louisa's Problem: Value Clarification" (Structured Experience 283) by C.E. Amesley, 1981, in *The 1981 Annual Handbook for Group Facilitators* (pp. 13-15) by J.E. Jones and J.W. Pfeiffer (Eds.), San Diego, CA: University Associates, and of "The Promotion: Value Clarification" (Structured Experience 362) by J.L. Mills, 1983, in *A Handbook of Structured Experiences for Human Relations Training*, Volume IX (pp. 152-158), by J.W. Pfeiffer (Ed.), San Diego, CA: University Associates. The case of the girl and the sailor is part of the folklore of value clarification; the version adapted here is from "Cog's Ladder: A Process-Observation Activity" (Structured Experience 126) by G.O. Charrier, 1974, in *The 1974 Annual Handbook for Group Facilitators* (pp. 8-12), by J.W. Pfeiffer and J.E. Jones (Eds.), San Diego, CA: University Associates.

THE GIRL AND THE SAILOR
CASE HISTORY SHEET

The Dilemma

A ship sank in a storm. Five survivors scrambled aboard two lifeboats: a sailor, a girl, and an old man in one boat; the girl's fiance and his best friend in the second.

That evening the storm continued, and the two boats separated. The one with the sailor, the girl, and the old man washed ashore on an island and was wrecked. The girl searched all night in vain for the other boat or any sign of her fiance.

The next day the weather cleared, and still the girl could not locate her fiance. In the distance she saw another island. Hoping to find her fiance, she begged the sailor to repair the boat and row her to the other island. The sailor agreed, on the condition that she sleep with him that night.

Distraught, she went to the old man for advice. "I can't tell you what's right or wrong for you," he said. "Look into your heart and follow it." Confused but desperate, she agreed to the sailor's condition.

The next morning the sailor fixed the boat and rowed her to the other island. Jumping out of the boat, she ran up the beach into the arms of her fiance. Then she decided to tell him about the previous night. In a rage he pushed her aside and said, "Get away from me! I don't want to see you again!" Weeping, she started to walk slowly down the beach.

Her fiance's best friend saw her and went to her, put his arm around her, and said, "I can tell that you two have had a fight. I'll try to patch it up, but in the meantime I'll take care of you."

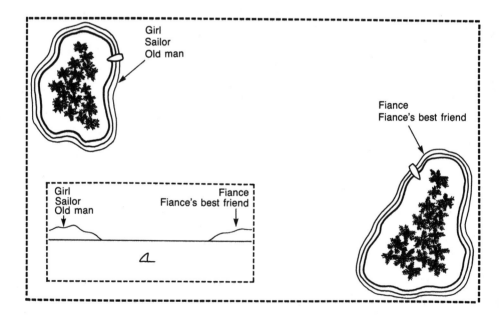

Task Instructions

Rank order the following characters from *1* (the person you liked best or valued most) to *5* (the person you liked or valued least):

_____ The sailor

_____ The girl

_____ The old man

_____ The girl's fiance

_____ The fiance's best friend

451. WHAT'S LEGAL?: INVESTIGATING EMPLOYMENT-INTERVIEW QUESTIONS

Goals

I. To develop the participants' awareness of legal issues in connection with interviewing applicants for employment.

II. To assist the participants in identifying legal and illegal employment-interview questions and in determining why they are legal or illegal.

III. To give the participants an opportunity to practice devising legal employment-interview questions.

Group Size

Twelve to thirty participants in subgroups of four or five.

Time Required

Approximately two hours and forty-five minutes.

Materials

I. One copy of the What's Legal? Case Study Sheet for each participant.

II. One copy of the What's Legal? Clarification Sheet for each participant.

III. One copy of the What's Legal? Suggested Interview Questions for each participant.

IV. A pencil and a clipboard or other portable writing surface for each participant.

V. A newsprint flip chart and a felt-tipped marker for each subgroup.

VI. A newsprint flip chart and a felt-tipped marker for the facilitator's use.

VII. Masking tape for posting newsprint.

Physical Setting

A room large enough so that the subgroups can work without disturbing one another. Movable chairs should be provided.

Process

I. The facilitator begins the activity by introducing the goals and then emphasizes the importance of employment interviewing in light of current trends:

"Due to the threat of potential legal problems such as lawsuits, fewer and fewer organizations are willing to provide either positive or negative feedback regarding former employees. Consequently, it becomes all the more important to develop and ask reliable questions during an employment interview. These questions and the responses they elicit may be the only route open for assessing the potential of a job candidate."

II. The facilitator briefly summarizes the process of the entire activity.

III. Each participant is given a copy of the case study sheet, a pencil, and a clipboard or other portable writing surface. The facilitator explains the instructions for completing the sheet, emphasizing that the first step is to complete the Individual Evaluation column for each of the twenty questions. The participants are instructed to begin their individual work and to stop and wait for further instructions after they have completed this first step. (Fifteen minutes.)

IV. After all participants have completed their work, they are assembled into subgroups of four or five members each. The facilitator states that within each subgroup the members are to discuss their individual responses on the case study sheet and then agree on subgroup responses (including reworded questions where applicable) and record the subgroup information on their individual sheets. Each subgroup is also instructed to select a spokesperson to report the subgroup decisions to the total group. Then the participants are told to begin. While they work, the facilitator monitors their progress and periodically apprises them of the remaining time. (Forty minutes.)

V. The facilitator calls time, asks the subgroups to stop their work, and reconvenes the total group. Each question is dealt with separately in this fashion:

1. The spokespersons report their subgroups' decisions about whether the question is legal or illegal and whether it can be reworded. (Specific rewording is *not* reported.)

2. The facilitator records the subgroups' findings on newsprint. Then, after all spokespersons have reported, the facilitator gives the "correct" answer and the rationale (from the clarification sheet); records the "correct" answer on newsprint; and suggests a possible rewording, if applicable.

After all responses have been shared and recorded on newsprint, the facilitator distributes copies of the clarification sheet and suggests that the participants keep this handout for future reference. (Thirty-five minutes.)

VI. The facilitator leads a discussion by asking the following questions:

1. What reactions did you have to this experience? What did you discover?

2. What common opinions did you find in your subgroup? What were the differences of opinion?

3. What generalizations can we make about legal interview questions? What generalizations can we make about illegal questions?

4. How can you avoid asking illegal questions during your own hiring processes? What is one thing you can do to ensure the legality of interview questions in your own organization?

(Twenty minutes.)

VII. The subgroups are reassembled, and the facilitator gives each a newsprint flip chart and a felt-tipped marker. Each subgroup is instructed to select a recorder to record the members' ideas while they devise a list of *five* legal employment-interview questions that could be used to obtain useful information for a number of different jobs. As the subgroups work on this task, the facilitator remains available to assist as needed and periodically lets the participants know how much time is remaining. (Ten minutes.)

VIII. The recorders are asked to post their sheets of newsprint in an area of the room where these sheets can be seen by all participants. The facilitator reviews all questions and leads a discussion of them, eliciting opinions about their legality and phraseology. (Approximately twenty-five minutes.)

IX. The facilitator distributes copies of the handout of suggested interview questions and leads a discussion of the handout contents, comparing these contents with the questions generated by the participants in the previous step. During this discussion the facilitator emphasizes the importance of focusing on job-related issues during an employment interview. The participants are encouraged to keep these handouts for future reference.

Variations

I. To save time, the subgroup evaluations and sharing of results (Step IV and part of Step V) may be eliminated. In addition, the facilitator may administer the case study sheet in two halves, covering the "correct" responses and leading a discussion after the participants have completed each half. This alternative allows the facilitator and the participants to note improvements in their learning and their understanding of the legal principles involved.

II. At the end of the activity, the facilitator may offer to combine all the legal questions generated by the participants into a master list and to distribute or send copies of the list to the participants at a later date.

III. After the participants have developed legal questions, they may assemble into dyads and conduct interviews based on these questions.

Submitted by Robert J. ("Jack") Cantwell.

Robert J. ("Jack") Cantwell is the training officer for the Personnel Office of the DeKalb County Government in Decatur, Georgia. He also serves as an internal consultant on organization development projects. Previously he held the position of senior management trainer for ARAMCO in Saudi Arabia. His special interests include organization development and cross-cultural training and development, and his area of expertise is use of the Myers-Briggs Type Indicator in organizational settings.

WHAT'S LEGAL?
CASE STUDY SHEET

Background and Instructions

John Richards is the recruitment manager for the personnel department of a county government. Recently John has become aware of a problem concerning the employment-interview questions asked by members of his staff and other departments. He has received complaints from job candidates about the fact that some departments focus their interviews almost entirely on previous work experience, while other departments concentrate on the likelihood that the candidate will "fit in around here." Consequently, in an effort to standardize the interviewing process, John has prepared the following list of twenty questions that each interviewer should ask every candidate.

Read each of the twenty questions and place a check mark in the appropriate blank in the *Individual Evaluation* column to indicate whether the question is:

1. Legal;

2. Illegal and cannot be reworded so that it is legal (or should not be reworded because there is no bonafide rationale for asking it); *or*

3. Illegal and can be reworded, assuming that there is a bonafide rationale for trying to elicit the information implied by the question.

If you decide that the question is illegal and can be reworded, write your suggested rewording in the space provided for that purpose. (Subgroup evaluations will be completed later.)

Questions to Be Evaluated

1. How old are you?

Individual Evaluation	Subgroup Evaluation	
_____	_____	Legal
_____	_____	Illegal; cannot/should not be reworded
_____	_____	Illegal; can be reworded as follows:

2. Have you ever been arrested?
   Individual   Subgroup
   Evaluation   Evaluation

   _____   _____   Legal

   _____   _____   Illegal; cannot/should not be reworded

   _____   _____   Illegal; can be reworded as follows:

3. Do any of your relatives work for this organization?
   Individual   Subgroup
   Evaluation   Evaluation

   _____   _____   Legal

   _____   _____   Illegal; cannot/should not be reworded

   _____   _____   Illegal; can be reworded as follows:

4. Do you have children, and if you do, what kind of child-care arrangements do
   you have?
   Individual   Subgroup
   Evaluation   Evaluation

   _____   _____   Legal

   _____   _____   Illegal; cannot/should not be reworded

   _____   _____   Illegal; can be reworded as follows:

5. Do you have any handicaps?
   Individual   Subgroup
   Evaluation   Evaluation

   _____   _____   Legal

   _____   _____   Illegal; cannot/should not be reworded

   _____   _____   Illegal; can be reworded as follows:

6. What are the address and telephone number where you can be reached?
   Individual   Subgroup
   Evaluation   Evaluation

   _____   _____   Legal

   _____   _____   Illegal; cannot/should not be reworded

   _____   _____   Illegal; can be reworded as follows:

7. Are you married?
   Individual   Subgroup
   Evaluation   Evaluation

   _____   _____   Legal

   _____   _____   Illegal; cannot/should not be reworded

   _____   _____   Illegal; can be reworded as follows:

8. Where were you born?

Individual Evaluation	Subgroup Evaluation	
_____	_____	Legal
_____	_____	Illegal; cannot/should not be reworded
_____	_____	Illegal; can be reworded as follows:

9. What organizations do you belong to?

Individual Evaluation	Subgroup Evaluation	
_____	_____	Legal
_____	_____	Illegal; cannot/should not be reworded
_____	_____	Illegal; can be reworded as follows:

10. Have you ever been convicted of a crime?

Individual Evaluation	Subgroup Evaluation	
_____	_____	Legal
_____	_____	Illegal; cannot/should not be reworded
_____	_____	Illegal; can be reworded as follows:

11. Do you get along well with other men/women?

Individual Evaluation	Subgroup Evaluation	
_____	_____	Legal
_____	_____	Illegal; cannot/should not be reworded
_____	_____	Illegal; can be reworded as follows:

12. Have you ever worked under a different name?

Individual Evaluation	Subgroup Evaluation	
_____	_____	Legal
_____	_____	Illegal; cannot/should not be reworded
_____	_____	Illegal; can be reworded as follows:

13. What languages can you speak and/or write fluently?

Individual Evaluation	Subgroup Evaluation	
_____	_____	Legal
_____	_____	Illegal; cannot/should not be reworded
_____	_____	Illegal; can be reworded as follows:

14. What experience, if any, have you had in the military?

Individual Evaluation	Subgroup Evaluation	
_____	_____	Legal
_____	_____	Illegal; cannot/should not be reworded
_____	_____	Illegal; can be reworded as follows:

15. What is your spouse's income?

Individual Evaluation	Subgroup Evaluation	
_____	_____	Legal
_____	_____	Illegal; cannot/should not be reworded
_____	_____	Illegal; can be reworded as follows:

16. What make, year, and model is your car?

Individual Evaluation	Subgroup Evaluation	
_____	_____	Legal
_____	_____	Illegal; cannot/should not be reworded
_____	_____	Illegal; can be reworded as follows:

17. This is a hectic office. Can you keep up with the younger people here?

Individual Evaluation	Subgroup Evaluation	
_____	_____	Legal
_____	_____	Illegal; cannot/should not be reworded
_____	_____	Illegal; can be reworded as follows:

18. Do you have any medical problems that would prevent you from performing your job duties?

Individual Evaluation	Subgroup Evaluation	
_____	_____	Legal
_____	_____	Illegal; cannot/should not be reworded
_____	_____	Illegal; can be reworded as follows:

19. How long have you lived in this city/state?

Individual Evaluation	Subgroup Evaluation	
_____	_____	Legal
_____	_____	Illegal; cannot/should not be reworded
_____	_____	Illegal; can be reworded as follows:

20. What experience have you had in . . .?

Individual Evaluation	Subgroup Evaluation	
_____	_____	Legal
_____	_____	Illegal; cannot/should not be reworded
_____	_____	Illegal; can be reworded as follows:

WHAT'S LEGAL?
CLARIFICATION SHEET

> Important: The following evaluations of the twenty questions are intended to provide clarification rather than to serve as strict legal interpretations. The reader should note that employment law is continually in flux and that appropriate legal counsel should be engaged before formalizing these or any other employment-interviewing concepts into organizational guidelines. In addition, the Equal Employment Opportunity Commission (EEOC) of the Federal Government can provide useful information about the legalities involved.

Legal questions are those that can be shown to be directly related to performance on the job. *Illegal* questions are those that have no direct bearing on job performance and that might imply some kind of prejudice (against race, creed, national origin, sex, handicaps, and so forth). An organization whose employees ask illegal questions during employment interviews can be subject to a variety of legal penalties. Consequently, anyone interviewing job applicants would be well advised to become acquainted with the legal principles involved. Also, it is a good idea for an interviewer to test potential interview questions in these ways:

- Would I ask this question of a white person?
- Would I ask it of a man?
- Would I ask it of an American-born citizen?
- Would I ask it of a physically able person?

Unless the answer is "yes" in every case, it might be advisable not to ask the question.

1. *How old are you?*
   This question is legal but inadvisable. An applicant's date of birth or age can be asked, but it is essential to tell the applicant that Federal and state laws prohibit age discrimination. It is a good idea to avoid focusing on age, except in those cases in which an occupation requires extraordinary physical ability or training and a valid age-related rule is in effect.

2. *Have you ever been arrested?*
   This question is illegal unless an inquiry about arrests is justified by the specific nature of the business. Questions about arrests are generally considered suspect since they may tend to disqualify minority groups. Convictions should be the basis for rejection of an applicant only if their number, their nature, or how recent they are renders the applicant unsuitable. The interviewer should tell the applicant that a conviction record should not necessarily preclude employment. (See also the clarification of Item 10.)

3. *Do any of your relatives work for this organization?*
   This question is legal if the intent is to discover situations involving nepotism.

If that is the case, the interviewer may say something like "We have a policy against nepotism here. Do you have any relatives working for the organization?"

4. *Do you have children, and if you do, what kind of child-care arrangements do you have?*

   Both parts of this question are illegal; they should not be asked in any form because the answers would not be job related. In addition, they might imply sex discrimination.

5. *Do you have any handicaps?*

   This question is illegal as phrased here. An applicant does not have to divulge handicaps or health conditions that do not relate reasonably to his or her fitness to perform the job. (See also the clarification of Item 18.)

6. *What are the address and telephone number where you can be reached?*

   This question is legal if the intent is to learn how to notify the applicant in the event that he or she has been hired. Note that the question does not ask where the applicant lives; therefore, it would not be likely to be construed as eliciting information about the applicant's socioeconomic status or ethnic background.

7. *Are you married?*

   This question is illegal and should not be reworded. Marriage has nothing directly to do with job performance. In addition, the question might have sexual overtones or might imply a prejudice for or against a particular marital status.

8. *Where were you born?*

   This question is illegal and should not be reworded. There is no bonafide rationale for asking it, and it might indicate discrimination on the basis of national origin.

9. *What organizations do you belong to?*

   As stated, this question is legal; it is permissible to ask about organizational membership in a general sense. However, it would be preferable to ask specifically about job-related or professional organizations. It is illegal to ask about membership in a specific organization when the name of that organization would indicate the race, color, creed, sex, marital status, religion, or national origin or ancestry of its members.

10. *Have you ever been convicted of a crime?*

    This question is legal but might be inadvisable. (In most cases convictions are a matter of public record.) The question is advisable if conviction of a crime *in and of itself* is germane to employment, but the interviewer should be aware that on a number of occasions it has been perceived as conveying a prejudice against minorities. An important point is that being arrested (held in custody) is not the same as being convicted (proven guilty after a legal trial). (See also the clarification of Item 2.)

11. *Do you get along well with other men/women?*

    This question is illegal; it seems to perpetuate sexism. However, if the objective in asking it is to determine whether the applicant gets along well with people in general, the question might be reworded as "How would you describe your style of communicating with others?" or "How would you describe your leadership style?"

12. *Have you ever worked under a different name?*
This question is legal if the purpose of asking it is to simplify record keeping. For example, people often change their names in Social Security records; and a prospective employer might want to know if an applicant has a work history under another name. To be on the safe side, the interviewer might preface the question by saying something like "For our Social Security records, ..."

13. *What languages can you speak and/or write fluently?*
Although this question is legal, it might be perceived as a furtive way of determining an individual's national origin. However, it is permissible to ask the question if the job involves language ability (for example, when the job of salesperson requires dealing primarily with customers who speak a particular language). It is not permissible to ask how any given language was learned.

14. *What experience, if any, have you had in the military?*
This question is legal if the purpose is to discover job-related skills or knowledge that may have been learned in the military, but questions about the specific skills or knowledge would be preferable.

15. *What is your spouse's income?*
This question is illegal and should not be reworded. The answer would not be directly job related.

16. *What make, year, and model is your car?*
This question is illegal. Presumably the reason for asking it is to determine whether the applicant would have difficulty in getting to work, and it is not permissible to delve into this issue. However, if the interviewer is merely concerned with whether the applicant could keep acceptable hours at work, he or she might legally say, "Our working hours are 9:00 a.m. to 5:00 p.m. Would you have any trouble meeting this work schedule?"

17. *This is a hectic office. Can you keep up with the younger people here?*
This question is illegal as stated; it indicates a possible age bias. However, it could be reworded as "How would you describe the way you manage stress/deal with a rapid pace in an organizational setting?"

18. *Do you have any medical problems that would prevent you from performing your job duties?*
This question is legal. It is permissible to ask about general or specific conditions of a physical, mental, or medical nature if those conditions would interfere with the applicant's ability to perform the job. (See also the clarification of Item 5.)

19. *How long have you lived in this city/state?*
This question is legal if the response information is to be used only for the purpose of record keeping (taxes or Social Security, for example). It would be a good idea for the interviewer to accompany the question with a statement indicating that purpose.

20. *What experience have you had in . . . ?*
This question is legal as long as it is job related.

WHAT'S LEGAL?
SUGGESTED INTERVIEW QUESTIONS

The following are some legal interview questions/probes that may be useful:

1. What is your definition of the job for which you are interviewing?
2. What would you expect to get out of this job?
3. What do you find most attractive about the job for which you are interviewing? What do you find least attractive?
4. What do you see as the most difficult task involved in the position for which you are interviewing?
5. What kind of job skills and experience can you offer us?
6. What do you know about our company?
7. Why do you want to work for our company?
8. What are your salary expectations?
9. What are your long-range career goals? How would you accomplish them in our company? How long would you expect to stay with our company?
10. How long would it take you to make a meaningful contribution to our company? What would be the nature of that contribution?
11. What do/did you like best about your present/previous position? What do/did you like least?
12. Why are you leaving your present job?
13. If I spoke with your current/previous boss, what would he or she say are your greatest strengths and weaknesses?
14. What do you consider to be your work-related strengths and weaknesses?
15. What do you consider to be your major accomplishments in your current (or previous) job?
16. What adjectives would you use to describe your relationships with your co-workers in your present/previous position? What adjectives would you use to describe your relationships with your subordinates? Explain.
17. In your present/most recent position, what problems did you identify that had been overlooked previously? How did you handle these problems?
18. Describe a situation in which your work was criticized and how you handled this situation.
19. What is your concept of an ideal work environment?
20. Which do you like better—working with figures or working with words? Explain.
21. How do you manage pressure or deadlines?
22. Would you rather initiate action or support those who initiate it? Explain. What qualities are necessary for the one you chose?

23. When the applicant has had supervisory experience and the position in question also entails supervision/management: How would you describe your management style?

24. When the applicant has had supervisory experience and the position in question also entails supervision/management: How many people do/did you supervise in your present/previous job?

25. When the applicant has had supervisory experience and the position in question also entails supervision/management: How do you think your subordinates perceive(d) you? How does their perception compare with the way you perceive yourself?

26. When the position entails supervision/management: What would you look for when hiring people?

27. When the applicant has had supervisory experience and the position in question also entails supervision/management: Have you ever had to fire anyone? If so, what were the circumstances and how did you handle the situation?

452. FOUR FACTORS: THE INFLUENCE OF LEADER BEHAVIOR

Goals

   I. To acquaint the participants with Rosenthal and Jacobson's (1968) four-factor theory explaining a leader's influence on followers and the effect of this influence on follower behavior.

   II. To give the participants an opportunity to analyze case studies showing how particular leader approaches to Rosenthal and Jacobson's four factors (climate, feedback, input, and output) can positively or negatively affect followers.

Group Size

   Four subgroups of four to six participants each.

Time Required

   Approximately one hour and forty-five minutes.

Materials

   I. One copy of the theory sheet for each participant.

   II. One copy of each case study (A, B, C, and D) for each participant.

   III. One copy of the analysis sheet for each participant plus one copy for each subgroup.

   IV. A pencil for each participant.

Physical Setting

   A room large enough so that the subgroups can work without disturbing one another. Ideally, a table and movable chairs should be provided for each subgroup; however, if tables are not available, clipboards or other portable writing surfaces may be substituted.

Process

   I. The facilitator introduces the goals of the activity.

   II. The participants are given copies of the theory sheet and are instructed to read this handout. (Five minutes.)

III. The facilitator leads a discussion of the handout content, clarifying ideas as necessary. The participants are invited to share examples from their own experience of the ways in which leader behavior affects follower productivity. (Fifteen minutes.)

IV. The participants are assembled into four subgroups. The facilitator gives a different set of case study sheets to each subgroup. (In one subgroup each member receives a copy of case study A; in another subgroup, each member receives case study B; in the third, each receives case study C; and in the fourth, each receives case study D.) The facilitator also gives each participant an analysis sheet and a pencil and then states that each participant is to work independently to complete the analysis of the assigned case study. (Fifteen minutes.)

V. The facilitator asks the participants to stop their work. The members of each subgroup are instructed to discuss their analyses and to arrive at a consensus on each item of the analysis sheet. The facilitator asks each subgroup to select a reporter to record the consensus responses on a separate analysis sheet and to report these responses later to the total group; each subgroup is given a new copy of the analysis sheet for the reporter's use. The subgroups are informed that they have twenty minutes to complete the task and are told to begin. (Twenty minutes.)

VI. After twenty minutes the facilitator reconvenes the total group and asks the reporters to take turns reading their case studies and sharing the contents of their analysis sheets. Before each reporter begins, the facilitator distributes copies of the pertinent case study to all of those who do not yet have copies so that the participants can follow along as the reporter reads. At the conclusion of each report, the participants are asked to share their reactions to the case and/or to the subgroup's analysis; then the facilitator reviews the specific leader behaviors in the case that can be associated with Rosenthal and Jacobson's factors. (Thirty minutes.)

VII. The facilitator leads a concluding discussion by asking these questions:

1. What were your personal reactions to the leader in your case study? Would you have reacted the way you predicted that the followers would react? How did you feel about your subgroup's consensus report?

2. What viewpoints similar to yours were shared in your subgroup? What different viewpoints were shared? How did the subgroup work with the situation to arrive at consensus? How did Rosenthal and Jacobson's four factors operate in your subgroup? How was your motivation affected? How was your productivity affected?

3. What have you learned about the four factors from the case studies? What have you learned from the experience of analyzing a case in your subgroup?

4. Which of the things you learned were consistent with what you know about your own leadership in your present position? Which were consistent with what you know about leadership in general in your company?

5. Which of the four factors might you choose to enhance in your own leadership style? How specifically would you do that?

Variations

I. The facilitator may lead a discussion of positive influencers who are well known and whose efforts had dramatic results on followers. It may enhance the discussion to show video clips of these leaders in action and to point out how the leaders behave with respect to the four factors.

II. The participants may be asked to share personal examples of how leader behavior toward followers (in terms of the four factors) affected bottom-line results.

III. If the activity is being used as part of a management-training program, within each subgroup the members may be asked (1) to share their own behavioral tendencies with regard to the factors of climate, feedback, input, and output and (2) to consider and discuss the consequences of these tendencies.

IV. Within each subgroup each member may be asked to think of a peak performer and a poor performer in a back-home work group, to describe to fellow members how each of them is currently treated by the group leader (in terms of the four factors), and to discuss ways in which changes in the leader's behavior toward each might lead to changes in follower behavior.

V. The participants may analyze the case studies first and then be presented with the information on the four factors.

VI. The participants may be asked to develop personal action plans for improving their own leadership behavior with regard to the four factors.

VII. At the conclusion of the activity, the participants may return to their subgroups to develop assessment tools by which they can gather feedback from their own followers about their behavior with regard to the four factors.

Reference

Rosenthal, R., & Jacobson, L. (1968). *Pygmalion in the classroom.* New York: Holt, Rinehart and Winston.

Submitted by William N. Parker.

William N. Parker is a training specialist with the management and professional development section of human resources at Virginia Power near Richmond, Virginia. A self-described "Situational Leadership® fanatic," he designs and delivers workshops on leadership, supervision, motivation, and the Myers-Briggs Type Indicator. Mr. Parker's special interests include the pursuit of excellence in both the workplace and the classroom.

FOUR FACTORS
THEORY SHEET

Robert Rosenthal and Lenore Jacobson (1968) have isolated four factors or areas in which leader behavior produces an impact on follower behavior:

1. *Climate.* Both verbal and nonverbal behaviors can be used by a leader to establish a climate that is warm, supportive, friendly, and accepting. Typical leader behaviors that contribute positively to climate include a pleasant tone of voice, frequent eye contact, smiles, and approving head nods.

2. *Feedback.* A leader can stimulate high follower performance by giving feedback that is frequent, specific, and tends to focus on what the follower is doing right. Specific feedback that is intended to help direct a follower toward greater task proficiency helps that follower to become more competent, successful, and self-confident.

3. *Input.* A leader can provide followers with resources of all types: time, written materials, people, coaching, training and development sessions, and supplies. These resources are offered to enhance the skills of followers and/or to enable them to accomplish their tasks effectively. A leader also can make a conscious effort to assign projects that are interesting, challenging, and visible within the organization.

4. *Output.* A leader can encourage followers to employ innovative, creative approaches; to collaborate in decision making; and to express points of view that are different from his or her own. While followers are experimenting, the leader offers assistance; helps to solve problems; and supports all results, including those that are less than superior.

The leader whose behavior follows these patterns is rewarded with followers whose performance, self-confidence, and enthusiasm for their tasks can well exceed minimum standards. On the other hand, the leader who fails to exhibit these behaviors may find followers to be apathetic and marginal producers.

Reference

Rosenthal, R., & Jacobson, L. (1968). *Pygmalion in the classroom.* New York: Holt, Rinehart and Winston.

FOUR FACTORS
CASE STUDY A: THE POWER STATION

John Applegate has been an operator in a power station for five years. He has just been assigned to Frank Fleming's shift. Frank has heard through casual conversation with his fellow supervisors that John is essentially a below-average performer; in fact, several other supervisors have told Frank that they do not want John on their shifts.

When John reports to Frank for the first time, Frank extends a hearty handshake and a genuine welcome and then tells John specifically what he will receive from Frank in terms of direction and support to help him be successful on the job. John is urged to use Frank as a resource whenever he has questions or ideas about better ways of doing things. Finally, Frank talks about the high performance standards of the shift and expresses confidence in John's ability to meet those standards.

At the end of John's first day on Frank's shift, Frank asks John to his office, praises him for his performance in the operational areas in which he has met or exceeded standards, and then points out the areas in which John needs to improve. After collaborating with John to develop specific steps for improvement, Frank once again expresses confidence in John's ability to be a high performer.

FOUR FACTORS
CASE STUDY B: XYZ TOOL & DIE

Jim Green is the production floor supervisor at XYZ Tool & Die. He supervises over one hundred assemblers who work on the company's day shift assembling cabinets for computers. Recently he has noted a decline in productivity and an increase in the error rate. In order to improve performance, Jim posts a chart in the employee cafeteria. This chart lists the names of all employees as well as their daily performance (by number of computer cabinets assembled) and their error rates (by number of mistakes). Next to the chart Jim posts a magazine article about how the assemblers at ABC Tool & Die have managed to increase productivity with a smaller work force and more obsolete equipment.

Jim also begins to mention the names of the poorest performers at the weekly review meetings and to compare these people with the ABC assemblers. He implies that poor performers are dispensable.

FOUR FACTORS
CASE STUDY C: THE TEACHER'S AIDE

Lynn Lewis is the administrator of a nonprofit organization that works with local children and teachers to build their fine-arts education programs. She has recently hired several individuals who previously worked as classroom teacher's aides. Her intent was to have them do clerical tasks for her professional staff. However, one of these aides, Joan, has shown an exceptional talent for painting and sculpture. After a period of praising and supporting Joan's creative endeavors, Lynn asks Joan to design a program that will introduce preschool children to art; to help Joan obtain the necessary training, Lynn enrolls her in a child-development class at a local university.

Lynn sets up a weekly meeting with Joan to review what she is learning and how she might use it in the preschool art program. Together they brainstorm different methods of approaching and developing the project. Each time Joan suggests an approach that differs from the current fine-arts program, Lynn compliments her for her originality and asks her to figure out a way to integrate her idea with the organization's philosophy.

FOUR FACTORS
CASE STUDY D: THE NEW MARKETING BOSS

Wayne Smith is the newly appointed marketing manager for a large corporation. He is responsible for the activities of seven employees, all of whom have been with the company for several years and are experienced, creative, and competent in their jobs. Wayne calls his first meeting with the group an hour before the work day begins and "lays down the law" in an effort to appear strong and decisive. Standing at the head of the conference table, he tells all seven employees that they must account for their time by project and submit weekly reports of their activities. In addition, so that he can keep track of their breaks and their hours on the job, he installs a board on which employees sign in and sign out.

Sharon, the first employee who fails to sign out, receives a written memo from Wayne that reads "See me before work tomorrow. You failed to sign out after work yesterday!" When Sharon comes to Wayne's office the next morning, Wayne hands her a directive about signing in and out that includes disciplinary measures to be taken if the rules are not followed. When Sharon attempts to explain that she did not sign out because she worked late and the room containing the board was locked, Wayne cuts her off by saying, "Don't give me excuses. Just follow the rules. I make the decisions around here."

FOUR FACTORS
ANALYSIS SHEET

Instructions: After reviewing the case study you received, complete this sheet. Several sections present two options with blanks; when you are completing one of these sections, place a check mark in the blank that seems appropriate to you. Also jot down facts/comments supporting your assessment where indicated.

Overall Leader Treatment of Follower(s)

Positive _____   Negative _____

Rosenthal and Jacobson's Four Factors

1. Climate

Warm _____   Cool _____

Facts/Comments

2. Feedback

Frequent/Specific/   Infrequent/General/
Focuses on   Focuses on
"right" actions or success _____   "wrong" actions or error _____

Facts/Comments

3. Input

Much Information   Little/No Information
and Support Given _____   and Support Given _____

Facts/Comments

4. *Output*

Encouragement/
Opportunity Offered _____

No Encouragement/
Opportunity Offered _____

Facts/Comments

Predictions of Follower Reaction to Leader Behavior

1. Follower Confidence for the Task

High Confidence _____

Low Confidence _____

Reasons

2. Follower Motivation/Enthusiasm for the Task

Motivated/Enthusiastic _____

Demotivated/Apathetic _____

Reasons

3. Follower Productivity/Performance (Short Term)

High Productivity/
Performance _____

Low Productivity/
Performance _____

453. CONTROL OR SURRENDER: ALTERING APPROACHES TO PROBLEM SOLVING

Goals

  I. To introduce the participants to a method for changing the way in which they perceive problems.
 II. To assist the participants in developing action plans in which they apply their changed perceptions to a group-owned problem.
III. To assist the participants in synthesizing their individual action plans into a group approach to dealing with the problem.

Group Size

All members of an intact group assembled into subgroups of two or three. This structured experience is used when an intact group has a *predefined, internal problem* to consider.

Time Required

Approximately one hour and forty minutes.

Materials

  I. One copy of the Control or Surrender Theory Sheet for each participant.
 II. One copy of the Control or Surrender Problem Approach Sheet for each participant.
III. Newsprint prepared in advance with the predefined problem written at the top and followed by these incomplete sentences:

1. I want to _____

    but _____.

2. I can't _____

    because _____.

3. If it weren't for _____,

    I would _____.

4. I have to _____   _____

    because _____.

5. _____

     makes me _____.

IV. Blank paper and a pencil for each participant.

V. A newsprint flip chart and a felt-tipped marker.

VI. Masking tape for posting newsprint.

Physical Setting

     A room in which the subgroups can work without disturbing one another. A table should be provided for each subgroup, and a movable chair should be provided for each participant. If tables are not available, each participant should be given a clipboard or other portable writing surface.

Process

    I. The facilitator introduces the goals of the activity. The participants are given blank paper and pencils and are instructed to begin thinking about the predefined, internal problem facing the group. The facilitator posts the newsprint with the incomplete sentences (see Item III in the Materials section) and asks the participants to work individually to complete the sentences, using their own unique perceptions of the problem as a basis for their completions. The facilitator explains that later the participants will be asked to use these sentences as practice in viewing the problem in a new way. (Ten minutes.)

    II. The facilitator distributes copies of the Control or Surrender Theory Sheet and asks the participants to read this handout. (Five minutes.)

    III. The facilitator leads a brief discussion of the handout contents, clarifying as necessary and eliciting examples of control/surrender in problem-solving situations from the participants' own experience. (Ten minutes.)

    IV. The facilitator announces that before the participants practice viewing the group problem in a new way, they will have a chance to practice changing their viewpoints about a nonproblem situation. Then the facilitator delivers the following instructions in a quiet, soothing voice, pausing at intervals for the length of time indicated:

       1. Sit with your lower back against the chair, your feet flat on the floor, and your arms and hands open. *[Pause of ten seconds.]*

       2. Relax; close your eyes; and take three long, deep breaths. *[Pause of ten seconds.]*

       3. Focus your attention on your breathing. Don't change your breathing at all; just become aware of it. *[Pause of ten seconds.]*

       4. Relax further, and continue to focus on your breathing. Notice the precise points at which the breath starts to come in and starts to go out. *[Pause of thirty seconds.]*

       5. Without changing anything except your attention, act as if the air is breathing you. Give up the control of your breathing. Surrender. Let the air be the doer; let it reach itself into you and draw itself out. *[Pause of ten seconds.]*

6. Now, without changing anything except your attention, act as if you are the doer. Observe yourself as the one doing the breathing. *[Pause of ten seconds.]*

7. Now shift once again, and act as if the air is breathing you. This time notice if there is any change in your feelings when you shift from the controlling role to the surrendering role. *[Pause of ten seconds.]*

8. Switch again. Act as if you are breathing the air and you are in the controlling role. Notice the change in feeling. *[Pause of ten seconds.]*

9. Now relax, and think for a moment about the differences you observed in the two kinds of breathing experiences. *[Pause of ten seconds.]*

10. Now let your eyes open.

(Five minutes.)

V. The participants are instructed to form subgroups of two or three members each and to spend five minutes sharing perceptions of their experiences during the previous step. While the subgroups are sharing, the facilitator divides a sheet of newsprint into two columns, one headed "Control" and the other headed "Surrender." (Five minutes.)

VI. The facilitator asks the subgroups to stop and then invites the participants to share both their positive and negative feelings during each of the two breathing experiences, controlling and surrendering. As the participants report, the facilitator records responses in the appropriate columns without comment. (Ten minutes.)

VII. The facilitator instructs the participants to review their five sentence descriptions of the problem and to consider these sentences as "victim self-talk," the way that people talk to themselves when they feel relatively powerless about a particular situation. The participants are further instructed to make the following changes in their sentences, taking a few minutes after each to discuss in their subgroups how the change in wording causes a shift in the way the problem is perceived:

1. In the first sentence cross out the word "but," and substitute the word "and."

2. In the second sentence cross out the word "can't," and substitute the word "won't."

3. In the third sentence cross out what you wrote in the first blank, and substitute what you might be thinking, feeling, expecting, or doing that is interfering with solving the problem.

4. In the fourth sentence cross out the word "have," and substitute the word "choose."

5. In the fifth sentence cross out what you wrote in the first blank, and substitute the word "my" followed by whatever fits (see the first blank in the third sentence).

(Fifteen minutes.)

VIII. The facilitator distributes copies of the Control or Surrender Problem Approach Sheet and instructs the members of each subgroup to use this sheet to help one another design new approaches to the problem. The facilitator emphasizes that although the problem is owned by the entire group, each member's approach to it is individual; therefore, each member's sheet should reflect what action and/or personal responsibility he or she intends to take to solve the problem. (Twenty minutes.)

IX. The facilitator reconvenes the total group and leads a concluding discussion by asking the following questions:

1. What were the new actions, attitudes, and/or viewpoints that emerged from this process?

2. What were some of your thoughts and feelings as you switched your problem-solving approach to arrive at these new tactics?

3. How did your change of approach affect the other members of your subgroup? How did their changes affect you?

4. What can we conclude about the effect of switching problem-solving approaches on the way an individual views a problem? What about the effect of switching on the way a group views a problem? What about the effect on the problem itself?

5. How could the group synthesize the members' individual action plans to develop alternative approaches to the group's problem?

Variations

I. The activity may be used to address individual problems of the participants' own choice rather than a group-owned problem.

II. The facilitator may present the concept of control or surrender as a continuum along which one can move, depending on the situation.

III. The facilitator may connect the concept of control or surrender with brain-hemisphere theory, interpersonal communication, interpersonal conflict (fight or flight), social-styles theory, or stress management.

IV. After Step IX the participants may be asked to combine their action plans into a group action plan or a list of individual commitments to the group problem.

V. If the previous variation is used, the participants may be asked to speculate about the possible effects on the problem.

Submitted by Jim Ballard.

Jim Ballard is a developmental editor with University Associates, Inc., in San Diego, California. Active in the field of training for twenty-one years, he has published a total of twelve books for trainers and facilitators and formerly owned a consulting and publishing firm that specialized in how-to materials for teachers. Jim also conducts life-skills and self-esteem training for young people. His special interests include self-management, leadership, and using change as a means of empowerment.

CONTROL OR SURRENDER THEORY SHEET

The ability to change one's mind—to shift at will the way that something is viewed—is a skill that can be especially useful during times of rapid change. Often the way a person looks at a problem *is* the problem. Typically, having a problem means feeling the victim of it instead of the cause or source of it. In that state of mind, people do not experience their power to change things. This powerlessness reduces perceptual range and leads to tunnel vision. This is why in most situations the problem owner's ability to recognize the key dynamics of the situation is diminished.

In order to gain new power in a problem situation and a new perspective on the problem itself, it is a good idea to experiment with the priceless ability that all of us possess—the ability to change our minds. The phrase "change your mind" usually denotes something that happens after much consideration or after confronting irresistible evidence contrary to a long-held belief. In other words, it usually takes a long time. But there is another kind of mind changing that has different characteristics:

1. *It is fast.* It can be done at any time, in a moment.

2. *It is conscious.* It involves deliberate control of the mind and does not happen without an act of the will.

3. *It is inclusive.* It sees all possibilities, including the original mind-set, the opposite mind-set, and all the points of view between the two.

4. *It is noncommittal.* It involves suspending judgment or commitment to a particular point of view.

Everyone has experienced the occasional problem that seems to defy resolution. One approach that can be helpful is to employ a kind of mind changing that involves altering one's perspective and experimenting with a new perspective. As Einstein said, it is impossible to get out of a problem by using the same kind of thinking that it took to get into the problem. If one has been attempting to *control* the problem situation, one can make a conscious decision to reverse this perspective and *surrender* to the problem in order to see it differently. Surrendering does not mean permanently accepting the problem or its negative effects; instead, it means deciding to "let go" and stop working so hard to solve it. Letting go may have any of several positive results: the problem may resolve itself; someone else may come up with an acceptable or desirable solution; a good solution may even occur to the problem owner without any conscious effort. Sometimes the release of pressure opens up a number of possibilities. This perspective is based on the notion that in losing something or giving it up, one finds it or gets it back.

On the other hand, if one has been surrendering to the problem, one can decide to control it instead—again in order to see it differently. Controlling means taking a proactive rather than passive approach, working consciously to solve or resolve the situation as opposed to giving in or letting go. It can be invigorating to feel in charge of a problem situation, and it can be freeing as well. It becomes possible to discover previously unknown resources and to bring these resources to bear on the situation in a productive way.

Both control and surrender are viable ways to address a problem. Steadfast use of one approach or the other can limit creativity and options, whereas the ability to switch viewpoints from one to the other can expand opportunities.

CONTROL OR SURRENDER
PROBLEM APPROACH SHEET

My Approach to the Problem

1. So far my approach to the problem has been one of:

_____ Control

_____ Surrender

2. To help the group solve or resolve the problem, I will use the opposite approach:

_____ Control

_____ Surrender

3. The following opposite-approach tactics appeal to me:[1]

Control

_____ Look for new information.

_____ Do a force-field analysis.

_____ Get help in diagnosing.

_____ Confront a key player.

_____ State my needs clearly.

_____ Ask myself what I am doing that maintains the problem.

_____ Change my own behavior.

_____ Be more forceful/influential/persuasive.

_____ Gather support.

_____ Devise a strategy for removing power from opposing forces.

_____ Define the worst-case scenario.

_____ Bring in more muscle.

_____ Examine my own commitment to change.

---

[1]If you are unfamiliar with any terms in the following lists, ask your facilitator to clarify them for you.

_____ _____

_____ _____

_____ _____

Surrender

_____ Act as if the situation is the way it is for a reason.

_____ Ask myself what I would do if I *were* the problem (if I viewed the situation from "inside" the problem).

What would I say?

How would I view the situation and the people involved, including myself?

What positive effects would I, as the problem, have?

_____ Ask myself how the situation makes sense within a larger framework.

_____ Ask myself what I can learn from the situation and/or what the challenge is.

_____ Ask myself what would happen if I left the problem alone.

_____ Listen more to others.

_____ Practice serenity.

_____ Identify what good can come from the problem.

_____ _____

_____ _____

_____ _____

My Contract with Myself

1. I will change the way I view the situation by doing the following:

_____

_____

_____

_____

_____

2. I will change my emotional response/reaction/feelings with regard to the problem by doing the following:

_____

_____

_____

_____

_____

3. I will change my behavior by doing the following:

_____

_____

_____

_____

_____

_____

Signature

Witness: _____

Witness: _____

454. MARZILLI'S FINE ITALIAN FOODS: AN INTRODUCTION TO STRATEGIC THINKING

Goals

I. To help the participants to become more aware of the assumptions they make in solving problems.

II. To demonstrate the value of suspending assumptions while engaged in problem-solving efforts.

III. To introduce the participants to the concept of strategic thinking and to give them an opportunity to practice it.

Group Size

Fifteen to forty participants in subgroups of five to eight members each.

Time Required

Approximately one hour and thirty to forty-five minutes.

Materials

I. One copy of the Marzilli's Fine Italian Foods Case Study Sheet for each participant.

II. One copy of the Marzilli's Fine Italian Foods Guidelines for Strategic Thinking for each participant.

III. A newsprint flip chart and a felt-tipped marker for each subgroup.

IV. Masking tape for posting newsprint.

Physical Setting

A large room in which the subgroups can work without disturbing one another. Movable chairs should be provided.

Process

I. The facilitator announces that the participants will be working on a case study and then asks them to assemble into subgroups of five to eight members each.

An excellent source of background on strategic thinking is *Applied Strategic Planning: A How to Do It Guide* by J.W. Pfeiffer, L.D. Goodstein, and T.M. Nolan, 1986, San Diego, CA: University Associates.

II. Each participant is given a copy of the case study sheet and is asked to read the contents. (Five minutes.)

III. The facilitator explains that within each subgroup the members are to spend twenty-five minutes discussing the case and deciding, as a group, which of the two options presented is the better choice. The facilitator further explains that each subgroup should select a spokesperson to report the members' decision and their rationale to the total group. Then the subgroups are told to begin. (Twenty-five minutes.)

IV. At the end of the working period, the facilitator calls time, reconvenes the total group, and asks the spokespersons to take turns reporting the decisions and rationales. If some subgroups have chosen alternatives beyond the two mentioned in the case study, the facilitator simply accepts their decisions without asking for clarification or elaboration. (Two minutes per report.)

V. The facilitator gives each participant a copy of the guidelines for strategic thinking and leads a brief discussion of the contents of the handout. During the discussion the facilitator emphasizes how assumptions can govern planning options, points out the assumptions underlying the two options in the case study, defines strategic thinking as the search for opportunities in the environment, and provides examples of how to put each guideline into practice. (Ten minutes.)

VI. The participants are told to reconvene their subgroups and to open up their thinking about what Jim Marzilli's options might be. The facilitator explains that this task necessitates abandoning all restrictive assumptions, searching for opportunities, and generating as many options as possible. In addition, the facilitator tells each subgroup to select a recorder to record the subgroup's ideas and to present them later to the total group. Each subgroup is given a newsprint flip chart and a felt-tipped marker for the recorder's use. (Twenty minutes.)

VII. The facilitator tells the subgroups to stop their work, reconvenes the total group, and asks the recorders to take turns reporting. Each recorder posts his or her newsprint list at the beginning of the report; all lists remain posted for the duration of the activity. (Ten minutes.)

VIII. The facilitator concludes the activity with a discussion focused on the following questions:

1. How did your thinking change after the discussion of the guidelines for strategic thinking? What different feelings did you experience?

2. How did your subgroup's process change as a response to the guidelines? How would you describe the difference in results between the first and second discussions of Marzilli's options?

3. What generalizations can you draw about the effect of assumptions on problem solving? What generalizations can you draw about eliminating restrictive assumptions?

4. What are some of the assumptions you generally make in solving problems in your own work environment?

5. What is one new action you might take to reduce the effect of assumptions in your own problem-solving efforts?

Variations

I. Because the decision about the future of the business rests to a great extent on Jim Marzilli's values, the participants may be asked to assess these values during the course of the activity. (For further information, see Chapter 4, "Values Audit," in *Applied Strategic Planning: A How to Do It Guide.*)

II. In Step VII the facilitator may list the subgroup responses on newsprint in categories such as *products/services, locations, types of distribution,* and so on. Then the categories and their entries may be discussed.

III. After the discussion in Step VIII, the participants may be asked to generate (1) a list of assumptions they make that restrict problem solving and (2) a method to eliminate or reduce the effects of each assumption. Then they could share their lists and methods in subgroups and receive feedback from their fellow subgroup members.

IV. The facilitator may continue the activity by asking the participants to examine and discuss the viability of the options presented. During the discussion the facilitator should ask the participants to consider what information they would need in order to make a wise decision about what should happen to the Marzilli business. (For further information, see Chapter 7, "Performance Audit," in *Applied Strategic Planning: A How to Do It Guide.*)

V. The activity may be used with intact work groups as a warm-up to an actual planning or problem-solving effort.

VI. The case study may be used as a planning problem in a workshop on strategic planning. In this case the participants would be asked to design a planning process that would allow Jim Marzilli to make a wise decision about the future of the business. *Applied Strategic Planning: A How to Do It Guide* may be used as a model of the process to be followed, and the participants may be asked to discuss what they might do in each phase of strategic planning. The facilitator should note that continuing the strategic planning process in this fashion would require a great deal of additional time.

Submitted by Homer H. Johnson.

Homer H. Johnson, Ph.D., *is the director of the Center for Organization Development and of the Master's Program in Organization Development at Loyola University of Chicago. He consults in the areas of strategic planning, organizational change, and the creation of new ventures. He is the author of* The HRD Professional's Bibliography of Resources and References.

MARZILLI'S FINE ITALIAN FOODS
CASE STUDY SHEET

Marzilli's Fine Italian Foods is a grocery store founded in 1935 by Gino Marzilli and his wife Maria. In its early years the business provided Italian specialty grocery items to the residents of an Italian immigrant neighborhood in the center-city area. Gino and Maria were immigrants themselves. Gino's family ran a grocery store in Milan, Italy, and his own store had much of the flavor of Milan.

Over the years the business has been quite successful. In 1952 Gino and Maria bought a large building not far from the original store. The building was remodeled and provided them with a much larger store area plus an apartment to live in. In 1960 they also began producing homemade pasta and a series of high-quality sauces to be used with Italian foods. The recipes were developed by Maria, and the products are sold exclusively at the store and have continued to be quite popular.

Gino and Maria retired to Florida in 1972 and turned the business over to their only child, Jim Marzilli. Jim has been involved in the business all of his life. He is married, but his wife has not been involved in the business. They and their four children live in a southern suburb of the city.

Although the business remained very successful in the 1970s, more recently the sales revenues have shown a steady decline. Jim attributes this decline to several factors. Most important is the fact that most of the old Italian population has moved from the center-city area to the suburbs. These people are dispersed in five or six southwestern suburbs that are a forty- to sixty-minute drive from the old neighborhood. Thus, many of the store "regulars" shop infrequently at Marzilli's, although the store is crowded on Fridays and Saturdays, particularly before holidays and feast days.

The center-city neighborhood where the store is located is now populated by young professionals. Although some of them patronize the store, they purchase only a limited number of items, such as the bread and certain sauces. Jim feels that this is because their knowledge of Italian cuisine is limited, although many seem to be interested in Italian cooking.

Over the past year the business has been barely at the break-even point, and Jim feels it is time to do something about the situation. He would like the store to be the busy meeting place for Italians that it was in the 1950s but realizes that times have changed. He is 52 years old and does not want to retire or sell the business. Three of his four children now live out of town and are not interested in the business, but his youngest son Dom has expressed some interest. Dom lives in an apartment above the store and works downtown for a market-research firm. His wife June is a teacher and has helped in the store during rush times. Although June is not Italian, Jim says that she is almost as great an Italian cook as his mother. Dom and June have no children.

At this point Jim sees two basic options:

1. *Maintain the same line of products, but cut back on the number of employees and store hours.* Since much of the business comes from old customers who come on Fridays and Saturdays, Jim feels that he could maintain the same level of sales by being open only Tuesday through Saturday.

He now has six employees and thinks he could get along with four. The shorter hours and cutback of employees will cut costs; and if sales remain at about the same level, Jim thinks the business will be profitable in the coming years.

2. *Start adding "American" foods to attract more of the current neighborhood residents.* Thus, Marzilli's would become a neighborhood grocery store rather than an Italian specialty food store. Jim would retain some Italian foods to serve his old customers, but the store would gradually evolve into a neighborhood grocery store. There are no grocery stores within a four- or five-block radius, and Jim feels that he could pick up a lot of neighborhood trade.

Which of these two options would you recommend to Jim?

MARZILLI'S FINE ITALIAN FOODS
GUIDELINES FOR STRATEGIC THINKING

1. Keep loose; open up your thinking; keep an open mind.
2. Distinguish between the ends and means of planning so that you do not confuse *how* you accomplish your goals with *what* your goals are.
3. Ask questions that you may not have had the time to ask previously.
4. Focus on opportunities, not on resources.
5. Identify your assumptions. Concentrate on the "restrictive assumptions"—those that you assume cannot be changed—and change them.
6. Generate as many ideas as you can—the more the better. There is no such thing as a stupid idea. Some may prove better than others for the current situation, but you will not know which ideas are superior unless you express all that occur to you.

University Associates

455. AMERICA'S FAVORITE PASTIME: CLARIFYING ROLE PERCEPTIONS

Goals

I. To identify the various roles that exist in a team.

II. To provide a means for sharing the team members' perceptions of their roles.

III. To develop the members' awareness of their own contributions to the team as well as the contributions of fellow team members.

IV. To assist the team members in identifying ways to use their perceptions of their own and one another's roles to improve team functioning.

Group Size

All members of an intact work group.

Time Required

One hour and forty-five minutes to two hours.

Materials

I. A copy of the America's Favorite Pastime Position Sheet for each participant.

II. A pencil for each participant.

III. A newsprint version of the baseball diamond illustrated on the position sheet (prepared in advance). The titles of the twelve roles should be written on the newsprint, but the role descriptions should not.

IV. A newsprint flip chart and a felt-tipped marker.

V. Masking tape for posting newsprint.

Physical Setting

A room in which the team members can work comfortably and without interruptions. Movable chairs should be provided.

Process

I. The facilitator begins by stating that often people use baseball expressions to describe events at work: "She really hit a home run with that idea" or "When the meeting ended, I felt as if I'd been left stranded on second base" or "When the two of them started arguing, I felt as if I'd gotten caught in a squeeze play." The facilitator then says that the world of baseball and the world of work are related in other ways as well and begins a discussion about the similarities between a baseball team and a work team. During the discussion the facilitator emphasizes these similarities:

1. The team purpose is to win, and a variety of tasks must be carried out to accomplish that purpose.
2. The many different tasks that have to be carried out are distributed among the various "players," management, and support personnel.
3. Sometimes when members are missing or not functioning well, other team members cover for them and provide backup.
4. In addition to specifically assigned duties, the members have a number of general and supportive functions to perform.
5. Sometimes conflicts arise when members trip over one another in their attempts to carry out the same task, compete for the "best score," blame one another for not "making the catch," or "shake off" directions.
6. When members are uncertain of their roles, they sometimes hold back their contributions; when this happens, they "let the ball drop."

(Ten minutes.)

II. The facilitator introduces the goals of the activity and explains that the work team will be examining how it functions by comparing its various roles to those on a baseball team.

III. The facilitator distributes copies of the America's Favorite Pastime Position Sheet and reviews the twelve roles described on the sheet. As each role is discussed, the facilitator asks the participants to contribute any additional information about the responsibilities of that role, particularly those for which parallels can be drawn with a similar role in a work group. As contributions are made, the facilitator lists them on newsprint; a separate sheet of newsprint is completed and posted for each role. (Twenty minutes.)

IV. The facilitator distributes pencils, instructs each participant to work individually to make up an imaginary baseball team from the members of the work team, and provides the following guidelines for completing the task:

1. The roles on the position sheet should be assigned to team members who function in similar capacities.
2. The participants should base their decisions on individual members' tasks, authority, leadership abilities and functions, and personalities.
3. Not all twelve roles must be assigned; it is possible that some of the roles may not appear to be filled by anyone on the team.
4. More than one member may be assigned to one role, and each member may have more than one role; the decision depends entirely on each participant's perception of how the work team functions.
5. The participants should consider their own roles on the team and assign positions to themselves as appropriate.

After eliciting and answering questions, the facilitator tells the participants that they have ten minutes to complete the task and asks them to begin.

V. At the end of the ten-minute period, the facilitator calls time, asks the participants to assemble into a semi-circle in such a way that each person can see everyone else, and posts the newsprint diamond in front of the participants. The facilitator deals with each of the positions separately and asks the participants to call out the names of the members they have assigned to that position. All names are recorded in the appropriate areas on the newsprint diamond. After all positions have been covered, the facilitator asks the participants to take turns explaining why they assigned names as they did. (Thirty minutes.)

VI. The facilitator leads a concluding discussion by asking the following questions:

1. What were your feelings and thoughts while deciding which names to assign to the various roles?

2. How did you feel about the assignments you received from others? How did you feel about the explanations of these assignments? How do you feel about any discrepancies between your own perception of your role and your team members' perceptions?

3. What is it like to fill your role on the team as you see it?

4. What do the assignments say about the way in which your team functions? How clear are the roles of the team members?

5. When do the players on your team trip over one another in trying to play the same role or compete for the "best score" or blame one another for not "making the catch" or "shake off" directions? When and how is the ball being dropped because there is no team member to play a particular role? What do these circumstances suggest to you?

6. How are members credited, praised, or rewarded for the positions they fill? How can the team do a better job of crediting its members' accomplishments?

7. How are the team members critiqued or coached on improvement? How could that process be improved?

8. How do the members cover for one another and provide backup?

9. How do the members' role assignments help the team to fulfill its purpose or mission?

10. Which roles would you like to play? Which roles might represent avenues of growth for you?

11. What do you personally need or want to do to use what you have learned during this activity? What can you do to help your team improve its functioning?

Variations

I. This structured experience may be used to introduce a team-building session. The data from the activity then serve as a basis for further group work during the session.

II. As a follow-up to the last discussion question in the final step, the participants may be asked to draw baseball diamonds with ideal assignments of team members.

III. The baseball analogy may be used to examine external factors affecting the team. The following questions offer examples:
1. What cheerleaders does your team have?
2. Who is the batter you fear most?
3. Whom would you like to see in the bleachers? Who do you wish would stay home?

IV. The baseball analogy may be used to focus on team goals (What would "going for the pennant" mean?) or on relationships within the team (What would you like to say to the coach?).

V. If the team is small, basketball analogies may be used.

Submitted by Tim Hildebrandt.

Tim Hildebrandt *is a trainer/coordinator at Employment Services and Economic Security in Manitoba, Canada. He will be the team leader of two upcoming projects there, training managers in such areas as communication skills, motivation, and organizational behavior. Mr. Hildebrandt has been involved with adult education for nine years and has delivered training in various human service areas. His special interests include the development of reading and writing skills.*

AMERICA'S FAVORITE PASTIME
POSITION SHEET

Center Fielder
Throws long, travels
the farthest, looks
deep and wide

Left Fielder
Fields the hits
that are far out,
is good on grounders,
climbs the wall
to stop home runs

Right Fielder
Shifts with the
batter, fields
foul balls,
covers first base

Second Base
Relays the ball
from the outfield,
cuts off the
base runner

Shortstop
Makes the glamorous
catch, dives for
the line drive,
starts the double
play, covers second
base, is team
"hot shot"

Third Base
Moves in for the
fast play, is right
on top of things,
covers the bunts,
anticipates the play

First Base
Is first in line
for the hard throw,
has long reach,
must stay on feet

Pitcher
Starts the game,
raises the issues,
is excellent judge
of character,
glances over shoulder
for the "steal"

Manager/Coach
Directs, keeps on
track, analyzes plays,
plans for improvement,
makes connections,
reminds of goals

Water Person
Provides support
and maintenance

Catcher
Controls the traffic,
calls the plays,
captains the team
because he/she can
see the whole field

Umpire
Makes decisions,
judges fairness
of proceedings

456. IT'S IN THE CARDS: SHARING TEAM PERCEPTIONS

Goals

I. To help the participants to clarify how they perceive (1) themselves as team members, (2) their fellow team members, (3) the team as a whole, and (4) the team's relationship to the organization.

II. To offer the participants an opportunity to share their perceptions and to provide one another with feedback.

III. To assist the participants in working the issues surfaced during the activity.

Group Size

All members of an intact work team. *Note:* Because this activity involves a high degree of risk, it should be used after the team has completed several other team-building activities that involve less risk.

Time Required

Approximately three hours, depending on the size of the group.

Materials

I. A copy of the It's in the Cards Instruction Sheet for each participant.

II. At least as many decks of assorted kinds of playing cards (for example, tarot, Old Maid, jumbo, miniature, corporate, airline, round, patterned)[1] as there are participants.

III. Newsprint reproductions of the discussion questions in Step V. Before conducting the activity, the facilitator writes each of these questions on a separate sheet of newsprint.

IV. A newsprint flip chart and a felt-tipped marker.

V. Masking tape for posting newsprint.

---

[1] An excellent source of various cards is the *Best of Cards Catalogue,* which is available from U.S. Games Systems, Inc., 179 Ludlow Street, Stamford, CT 06902, phone (203) 353-8400.

Physical Setting

A large room in which the participants can work without disturbing one another. It is preferable that each participant be provided with a separate table and a movable chair and that the tables be placed well apart. However, if no tables are available and the participants are amenable, the participants may work on the floor. In Step III the facilitator may dump the cards either on the floor or on a table provided for that purpose.

Process

I. The facilitator explains the goals of the activity.

II. Each participant is given a copy of the instruction sheet. After the participants have read the handout, the facilitator elicits and answers questions about the task. (Ten minutes.)

III. The facilitator opens the packages containing the decks of cards, dumps the packages on one of the tables or on the floor, and emphasizes the following points:

1. Each participant should choose at least one card to represent each team member, including himself or herself; at least one card to represent the team as a whole; and at least one card to represent the total organization.

2. After selecting cards each participant should be seated at a separate table or in a separate area to create the representation.

3. The participants have thirty minutes to complete the task.

During the work period, the facilitator keeps the participants apprised of the remaining time. (Thirty minutes.)

IV. The participants are instructed to stop their work and to take turns sharing their representations. (The representations are left on the tables, and the total group moves around the room to view them one at a time.) The facilitator tells the participants that while a representation is being shown and explained, it is permissible to ask for clarification but not to express reactions, thoughts, or feelings. (Approximately five minutes per representation.)

V. The facilitator reveals and posts the following questions one at a time and leads a discussion based on these questions, recording participant responses for each:

1. How are you feeling at this moment?

2. What feelings, thoughts, reactions, or observations would you have liked to share while the representations were being shown and explained?

3. Which team members do you need to talk with as a result of this activity?

4. Now that you have viewed the different representations, what issues seem to be blocking the team and keeping it from functioning as well as it might?

5. What can you do to help the team improve its functioning?

6. What can the team do to contribute more to the organization?

7. What can the team do to improve the organization's perception of the team?

(Thirty minutes.)

VI. The facilitator assists the team members in reviewing the issues raised in the newsprint answers and deciding the order in which to address these issues. (Ten minutes.)

VII. The facilitator leads the team in action planning to deal with as many of the identified issues as possible within the remaining time. During this discussion important points are noted on newsprint. (One hour.)

VIII. If any issues have not yet been addressed at the end of the discussion period, the facilitator suggests deferring them until a follow-up meeting and elicits the members' commitment to a date and time for follow-up. The facilitator asks for a volunteer to reproduce and distribute to all members the newsprint sheets of questions and answers as well as the important points written on newsprint during the previous step. The facilitator encourages each member to read and study the distributed material, to consider reviewing it formally within the group from time to time, and to bring it to the follow-up session if one has been planned. Then the activity is concluded.

Variations

I. After Step V the team members may work together to generate a single representation.

II. The activity may be continued by working any remaining issues (instead of waiting for a follow-up session).

III. The activity may be shortened by waiting until a follow-up session to address all issues. However, the identification of issues should not be postponed until follow-up; also, the facilitator should assure the members that all identified issues will be addressed.

IV. After Step V the team members may share their personal feelings and perceptions about their own team roles.

V. At the conclusion of the activity the members may work together to create a team logo or motto.

VI. After Step VI the members may begin to meet in dyads with those identified in responses to the third question of Step V.

VII. The facilitator may use several decks of the same kind of cards. Using the same kind of cards might make it easier for the team members to compare their representations.

Submitted by Frederick A. Miller, Judith H. Katz, and Ava Albert Schnidman. This activity was initially developed by the late Kaleel Jamison.

Frederick A. Miller is the president of Kaleel Jamison Associates, Inc. (KJA), a management and organization development firm based in Cincinnati, Ohio. He has worked for sixteen years as a consultant in the United States, Europe, and Asia. His specialties include change management, interpersonal communication, and the development of high-performing, culturally diverse organizations. He is a member of the NTL Institute of Applied Behavioral Science and served on its board of directors for four years. He presently serves on the board of directors of the Organization Development Network. He is the author of a number of articles in the fields of human relations and organization development, and he has been quoted in the The Wall Street Journal and in USA Today.

Judith H. Katz, Ed.D., is a vice president of KJA. Her work focuses on team building; race and gender issues; and creating high-performing, culturally diverse organizations. Before joining KJA she held positions as an associate professor of counseling at San Diego State University and at the University of Oklahoma. She has served on the board of directors of the NTL Institute of Applied Behavioral Science and has published two books and over a dozen articles on human resource issues.

Ava Albert Schnidman is an organization development consultant; a vice president of KJA; and a partner in the Deltech Consulting Group, a firm specializing in addressing human issues associated with the introduction of new technology. Her work focuses on team development, sociotechnical design, large-system change, and the valuing of diversity. She is a member of the NTL Institute of Applied Behavioral Science and the Organization Development Network.

IT'S IN THE CARDS
INSTRUCTION SHEET

Your facilitator will provide the group with several decks of cards. During this activity you are to choose cards to represent the individual members of your team, including yourself; the team as a whole; and the total organization. Then you are to arrange these cards in a way that depicts (1) each individual's relationship to the other individual members, (2) each individual's relationship to the team as a whole, and (3) the entire team's relationship to the organization. After you have completed your work, you should be prepared to share your representation with the total group.

Here are some issues to consider as you select cards and arrange them:

1. What it is like to be part of the team;
2. What it is like to do your specific job;
3. What it might be like to do another team member's job;
4. The benefits and drawbacks of your job;
5. The fears, concerns, joys, hopes, opportunities, and risks that you see/ experience;
6. Each individual member's ability/willingness to function as a team player;
7. Relationships among members;
8. The team's environment/culture, attitudes and behaviors with regard to conducting business, and norms and values;
9. The degree to which the team functions in accordance with expressed organizational values and goals; and
10. How the team is perceived in the organization.

457. THE CANDY BAR: USING POWER STRATEGIES

Goals

I. To acquaint the participants with seven bases of power (French & Raven, 1959; Hersey, Blanchard, & Natemeyer, 1979; Raven & Kruglanski, 1975): coercive power, connection power, expert power, information power, legitimate power, referent power, and reward power.

II. To offer the participants an opportunity to experience and compare the effects of strategies associated with the seven bases of power.

Group Size

Seven subgroups of three members each. (The design calls for one member of each subgroup to function as an observer. However, if there are more than twenty-one participants, some subgroups may be assigned more than one observer.)

Time Required

Approximately one and one-half hours.

Materials

I. One copy of each of the seven seller's role sheets (A, B, C, D, E, F, and G).

II. Seven copies of the customer's role sheet.

III. Seven copies of the observer's task sheet for *each* observer.

IV. A pencil and a clipboard or other portable writing surface for each observer.

V. Seven candy bars, all of the same kind.

VI. A newsprint flip chart and a felt-tipped marker.

Physical Setting

A large room in which the subgroups can work without disturbing one another. Movable chairs should be provided.

Process

I. The facilitator introduces the goals of the activity, asks the participants to assemble into seven subgroups, and instructs the subgroups to form a circle around the room. Materials are distributed within each subgroup: one member receives one of the seller's role sheets (a different sheet for each of the seven subgroups) and a candy bar; another receives a copy of the customer's role sheet; a third receives seven copies of the observer's task sheet, a pencil, and a clipboard or other portable writing surface. (If there are more than three members in some subgroups, the extra participants function as observers and are given the appropriate materials.)

II. The participants are told to read their handouts. The facilitator explains that each role play will last three minutes and that the sellers will be moving counterclockwise around the circle from subgroup to subgroup until each seller has played his or her role in every subgroup. After questions have been answered and the participants have spent a couple of minutes thinking about how they will handle their assignments, the facilitator asks the subgroups to begin. (Ten minutes.)

III. The first role play lasts for three minutes. At the end of that time the facilitator instructs the subgroups to stop, asks each seller to move counterclockwise around the circle to the next subgroup, and tells the subgroups to begin the second of the three-minute role plays. This process is followed until each seller has participated in a role play in each of the seven subgroups. (Twenty-five minutes.)

IV. The total group is reconvened. The facilitator leads a discussion of the sellers' roles, treating each of the seven separately. When each new role is considered, the facilitator asks the seller who played that role to announce the letter and the strategy that appear at the top of the role sheet and to read the second paragraph of the role sheet aloud; then the discussion proceeds as follows:

1. The seller describes his or her experiences in playing the role;

2. The customers describe their reactions to the seller;

3. The observers share their observations about that seller's conversation with the customer; and

4. The remaining participants are invited to comment.

During the discussion the facilitator records key words describing each strategy on newsprint. (Thirty minutes.)

V. The facilitator leads a concluding discussion by asking the following questions:

1. Based on what you have experienced and heard about the different power strategies, what is a statement you can make about each (coercive, connection, expert, information, legitimate, referent, reward)?

2. In comparing these statements, what can we conclude about the relative effectiveness of the strategies? Which are more effective and why?

3. Which power strategies do you most frequently experience in your organizational life? Which do you personally use most often in your organizational life? What are the outcomes of those strategies?

4. How might you facilitate a more effective use of power in your organizational life?

Variations

I. The observers may interview customers at the end of each round to determine their reactions to the strategies that were used and the reasons for the decisions that were made about buying.

II. Extra candy bars may be kept on hand so that the sellers can actually "sell" the merchandise. At the end the facilitator would determine who sold the most candy bars (and, therefore, which strategy seemed most effective).

III. An observer may follow each seller as he or she travels from subgroup to subgroup to determine how different customer responses affected the strategy. (This variation would require twenty-eight participants.)

IV. The experience may be concluded by having each participant complete an action plan based on Question 4 in Step V.

References

French, J.R.P., Jr., & Raven, B. (1959). The bases of social power. In D. Cartwright (Ed.), *Studies in social power,* pp. 150-167. Ann Arbor, MI: Institute for Social Research, The University of Michigan.

Raven, B.H., & Kruglanski, W. (1975). Conflict and power. In P.G. Swingle (Ed.), *The structure of conflict,* pp. 177-219. New York: Academic Press.

Hersey, P., Blanchard, K.H., & Natemeyer, W.E. (1979). *Situational leadership, perception, and the impact of power.* Escondido, CA: Leadership Studies.

Submitted by Judy H. Farr and Sandra Hagner Howarth.

Judy H. Farr *is currently working to implement an integrated human resource system at the Indiana National Bank, where she is a personnel officer. She is also an independent trainer and consultant whose interests include group development and MBTI applications to work groups. Ms. Farr previously worked as an internal consultant and trainer for Indiana National Corporation, a bank holding company. She is a graduate of the University Associates intern program.*

Sandra Hagner Howarth *is a private consultant to financial and business industries. She specializes in group work, team building, process consultation, communication, creative thinking, problem solving, and decision making. Ms. Howarth enjoys working with newly formed groups to facilitate the development of mission statements, five-year plans, and goals. She previously served as an assistant vice president of human resource development and organization development for the Indiana National Bank.*

THE CANDY BAR
CUSTOMER'S ROLE SHEET

You are to participate in seven different role plays in which you play the customer and another participant plays the seller. Both of you are employees of the same company. The seller is selling candy bars at work on behalf of his or her daughter, who, in turn, is selling them to make money for her school band.

It is entirely up to you whether you decide to "buy" any candy bars. Respond as you normally would to the different approaches used by the sellers, and assume that whatever situation each seller creates is true.

THE CANDY BAR
SELLER'S ROLE SHEET A

Strategy: Coercive Power

You are selling candy bars on behalf of your daughter, who, in turn, is selling them to make money for her school band. You have decided that taking these candy bars to work with you would be a good idea. During the course of this activity you will be attempting to sell one or more bars to each of seven fellow employees.

Your strategy is to coerce each prospective customer into buying. Your basic attitude is "If you don't buy candy bars from me, I won't cooperate with you the next time you need something from me at work."

Although you should not share the details of your role with anyone before or during the role plays, you should identify the letter of your role sheet (A) for the observer(s) in each subgroup.

THE CANDY BAR
SELLER'S ROLE SHEET B

Strategy: Connection Power

You are selling candy bars on behalf of your daughter, who, in turn, is selling them to make money for her school band. You have decided that taking these candy bars to work with you would be a good idea. During the course of this activity you will be attempting to sell one or more bars to each of seven fellow employees.

Your strategy is to convince each prospective customer to buy because someone important to that customer has already bought candy bars from you. Your basic attitude is something like "You should buy these candy bars because your brother-in-law just bought some from me."

Although you should not share the details of your role with anyone before or during the role plays, you should identify the letter of your role sheet (B) for the observer(s) in each subgroup.

THE CANDY BAR
SELLER'S ROLE SHEET C

Strategy: Expert Power

You are selling candy bars on behalf of your daughter, who, in turn, is selling them to make money for her school band. You have decided that taking these candy bars to work with you would be a good idea. During the course of this activity you will be attempting to sell one or more bars to each of seven fellow employees.

Your strategy is to convince each prospective customer that you are an expert when it comes to candy bars and, therefore, that the customer should have faith in your judgment. Your basic approach is "I know all about candy bars, and this is the best one you can buy."

Although you should not share the details of your role with anyone before or during the role plays, you should identify the letter of your role sheet (C) for the observer(s) in each subgroup.

THE CANDY BAR
SELLER'S ROLE SHEET D

Strategy: Information Power

You are selling candy bars on behalf of your daughter, who, in turn, is selling them to make money for her school band. You have decided that taking these candy bars to work with you would be a good idea. During the course of this activity you will be attempting to sell one or more bars to each of seven fellow employees.

Your approach is to win each prospective customer by promising to share valuable information if that customer buys candy bars from you. An example of this approach is "If you buy candy bars from me, I'll tell you where you can get several other kinds of candy bars at greatly discounted prices."

Although you should not share the details of your role with anyone before or during the role plays, you should identify the letter of your role sheet (D) for the observer(s) in each subgroup.

THE CANDY BAR
SELLER'S ROLE SHEET E

Strategy: Legitimate Power

You are selling candy bars on behalf of your daughter, who, in turn, is selling them to make money for her school band. You have decided that taking these candy bars to work with you would be a good idea. During the course of this activity you will be attempting to sell one or more bars to each of seven fellow employees.

Your approach is based on the fact that you are higher in the organizational hierarchy than each of your prospective customers. Your general attitude is "You should buy these candy bars from me because I have power in this company and I have a right to expect you to do what I want."

Although you should not share the details of your role with anyone before or during the role plays, you should identify the letter of your role sheet (E) for the observer(s) in each subgroup.

THE CANDY BAR
SELLER'S ROLE SHEET F

Strategy: Referent Power

You are selling candy bars on behalf of your daughter, who, in turn, is selling them to make money for her school band. You have decided that taking these candy bars to work with you would be a good idea. During the course of this activity you will be attempting to sell one or more bars to each of seven fellow employees.

Your selling strategy is to convince each prospective customer to buy candy bars from you because of the positive personal qualities that you have and that the customer, by association, would like to be seen as having. An example of your approach is "If you buy these candy bars from me, you will be seen as a person with gourmet taste because that's how I'm seen."

Although you should not share the details of your role with anyone before or during the role plays, you should identify the letter of your role sheet (F) for the observer(s) in each subgroup.

THE CANDY BAR
SELLER'S ROLE SHEET G

Strategy: Reward Power

You are selling candy bars on behalf of your daughter, who, in turn, is selling them to make money for her school band. You have decided that taking these candy bars to work with you would be a good idea. During the course of this activity you will be attempting to sell one or more bars to each of seven fellow employees.

Your approach is to convince prospective customers to buy candy bars from you by promising them rewards. An example of this approach might be "If you agree to buy these candy bars from me, I'll handle some of your work for you next week."

Although you should not share the details of your role with anyone before or during the role plays, you should identify the letter of your role sheet (G) for the observer(s) in each subgroup.

THE CANDY BAR
OBSERVER'S TASK SHEET

In the upcoming activity you are to observe seven different role plays. Each role play consists of a conversation between a seller and a customer who are employees of the same company. The seller will attempt to convince the customer to buy candy bars on behalf of the seller's daughter, who, in turn, is selling them to make money for her school band. The seven sellers will use seven different approaches in their attempts to sell the candy bars.

You are to fill out a separate copy of this sheet during each role play. Before the role play begins, ask the seller which role sheet (A, B, C, D, E, F, or G) he or she has. Record this letter in the blank provided below.

Seller's Role Sheet: _____

Make sure you are seated so that you are slightly separated from the customer and the seller but so that you can see and hear their interchanges. As you watch and listen, jot down answers to the following questions:

1. What kinds of key terms did the seller use? What behaviors accompanied the verbal strategy? How would you describe the strategy?

2. What kinds of responses did the seller elicit from the customer? What is your opinion about how the customer was feeling? On what behaviors did you base that opinion?

3. How would you describe the relationship between the seller and the customer?

4. Did the seller make the sale? How do you account for or explain that result?

5. Would you buy candy bars from this seller? Explain.

458. THE IMPACT WHEEL: AN EMPOWERMENT EXPERIENCE

Goals

I. To help the participants to see ways in which they can empower themselves to affect their work lives.

II. To provide the participants with a useful tool for identifying the effects and ramifications of events in their work lives.

III. To offer the participants an opportunity to use this tool to analyze a particular work-related event.

IV. To enable the participants to experience the variety of perspectives that people can have on the same event and to use those different perspectives productively.

Group Size

All members of an intact work group assembled into subgroups of two to four people each. This activity is intended to help a group prepare for an important, upcoming "central event," such as the implementation of a predetermined course of action. The specific event serves as the focus of the activity.

Time Required

Approximately one hour and forty-five minutes to two hours, depending on the number of subgroups.

Materials

I. A copy of The Impact Wheel Work Sheet for each participant.

II. A newsprint flip chart and several colors of felt-tipped markers for each subgroup.

III. A newsprint flip chart and a felt-tipped marker to be used by the facilitator.

IV. Masking tape for posting newsprint.

Physical Setting

A room large enough so that the subgroups can work without disturbing one another. Movable chairs should be available, and either a table or an easel should be provided for each subgroup.

Process

I. The facilitator distributes copies of The Impact Wheel Work Sheet and asks the participants to read this handout. (Five minutes.)

II. The facilitator leads a discussion of the handout contents, clarifying the process of completing an impact wheel and answering questions. (Ten minutes.)

III. The facilitator announces the specific "central event" that is to serve as the focus of the activity and informs the participants that they will be creating impact wheels to prepare for this event.

IV. The participants are assembled into subgroups of two to four members each, and each subgroup is given a newsprint flip chart and several felt-tipped markers. The facilitator instructs each subgroup to spend forty-five minutes completing the seven steps on the work sheet and to select a spokesperson to explain its completed work to the total group.

V. At the end of the work period, the facilitator asks each subgroup to post its impact wheel as well as its newsprint lists generated during Steps 6 and 7 on the work sheet. Then the participants are instructed to "visit" one subgroup's area at a time and examine its wheel and lists while the spokesperson explains them. The facilitator suggests that the participants note both similarities and differences between other ideas and their own. (Five minutes per spokesperson presentation.)

VI. The facilitator leads a discussion focused on these issues:

1. Similarities and differences among the impact wheels and the lists;

2. Reasons for differences, including such considerations as differences in task approaches, in levels of expertise, and in perspectives; and

3. Strengths and weaknesses of the impact-wheel approach.

(Fifteen minutes.)

VII. The facilitator works with the total group to achieve agreement on the following:

1. What actions the group and individual members agree to take to increase the likelihood of the positive effects (the ones listed on the posted newsprint sheets) and to decrease the likelihood of the negative effects; and

2. Which negative effects are most likely to occur and which proposed actions for transforming them into positive effects would be most likely to succeed.

During this step the facilitator records group decisions on newsprint. (Fifteen minutes.)

VIII. A group representative is asked to keep the newsprint generated during the previous step as well as the individual impact wheels and subgroup lists. The facilitator explains that the group should meet again before the central event occurs to follow up on actions that the group and individual members said they would take to increase the likelihood of the positive effects and to decrease the likelihood of the negative effects. The facilitator also emphasizes that after the central event has occurred, the participants should reconvene, review the newsprint notes and the impact wheels, agree on actual primary and secondary effects and whether they are positive or negative, and plan specific action steps to increase the impact of the positive effects and to turn the negative effects into positive ones. Before adjournment the facilitator elicits a follow-up commitment from the group.

Variations

I. The activity may be used with several different work groups at the same time, all of which are anticipating the same central event. This approach, which can be valuable when an organization is planning a major restructuring, may require extra facilitators.

II. The impact-wheel process may be used with central events from the participants' personal lives.

III. The process may be used in a heterogenous group with a case-study situation as the central event.

IV. In a heterogeneous group, the participants may use the impact-wheel process individually to analyze their own events. Then they may take turns sharing the results with fellow group members and receiving feedback.

Submitted by Bill Searle.

Bill Searle *is the director and president of The Avrion Group, a consulting firm in Enfield, Connecticut, specializing in planning futures and building democratic organizations. Mr. Searle's special interests include the role of power in organizations, team building, managing change, and robotics. He is the co-author of two books on computer programming in BASIC.*

THE IMPACT WHEEL
WORK SHEET

An impact wheel is a simple but powerful tool that can be used to identify the possible effects and ramifications of an event that might or definitely will happen in the future. By identifying possible effects and ramifications in advance, you can plan for them and deal with them more effectively. Although an individual can use an impact wheel to analyze a personal or work-related event, impact wheels are particularly powerful when two or more people collaborate to use them.

Here are the steps involved in creating and using an impact wheel (see Figure 1):

1. *Select a future event.* For example, if you are using the impact wheel with a work-related event, you might concentrate on something like the introduction of a new product that becomes extremely successful or the acquisition of a desktop publishing system. This event is referred to as the ''central event.''

2. *Write this event in abbreviated terms in the middle of a sheet of newsprint.* For example, if you chose to concentrate on one of the events mentioned in Step 1 above, you might write the name of the new product or ''Desktop Publishing.''

3. *Assume that the event has already happened; write the direct consequences close to the central event, each connected to the central event with a single line.* To generate consequences, consider what might happen as a direct result of the event. For example, with the introduction of a successful new product, a direct result might be an influx of orders well beyond what is normally experienced. Direct results like this are referred to as ''primary effects.''

4. *Write the secondary effects—those events that might happen as a result of the primary effects—near their corresponding primary effects, connecting each to its primary effect with a double line.* For example, with the introduction of a successful new product, a secondary effect related to the primary effect of increased numbers of orders might be that the company's phone lines would be tied up to a greater extent.

5. *Designate whether each primary effect and each secondary effect will be positive or negative by writing a + (plus) or – (minus) sign next to it.* For example, an increased influx of orders might be seen as positive, whereas the tying up of phone lines might be perceived as negative.

6. *List what you can do to increase the likelihood of the positive effects and decrease the likelihood of the negative effects.* Make this list on a new sheet of newsprint.

7. *Determine how to turn each negative effect into a positive one.* Think of yourself as empowered to change negative effects in any way that you would like. When you start this process, try not to stifle your thinking with notions of what is or is not possible; instead, be as creative as you can in generating options for changing each negative effect. Once you have come up with a number of different options, you can begin to eliminate some on the basis of practicality or workability; then you can choose and write on a separate sheet of newsprint the best (one or more) of the remaining alternatives. This step requires a great deal of hard thought, but it can make the difference between success and failure of the future event.

For example, the tying up of phone lines might be made positive in that it offers (1) a way to legitimize the purchase of a more sophisticated phone system that would provide better service, (2) an opportunity for employees to share jobs and thereby experience greater variety by donating any extra time to phone work, (3) a chance for employees to start special projects that they have wanted to tackle (while phone lines are busy), or (4) an opportunity to increase mail-order promotions and/or advertising.

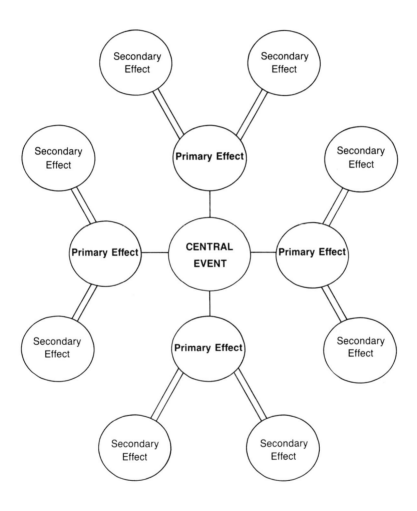

**Figure 1. Illustration of the Structure
of an Impact Wheel**

459. THE ROBOTICS DECISION: SOLVING STRATEGIC PROBLEMS

Goals

I. To introduce the participants to the strategic assumption surfacing and testing (SAST) process as a tool for solving complex strategic problems.

II. To offer the participants an opportunity to use the SAST process in solving a sample problem.

Group Size

Four subgroups of three to seven members each.

Time Required

Approximately three and one-half hours.

Materials

I. A copy of The Robotics Decision Theory Sheet for each participant.

II. A copy of The Robotics Decision Case History Sheet for each participant.

III. A copy of The Robotics Decision Assumption Rating Work Sheet for each participant.

IV. Several sheets of blank paper and a pencil for each participant.

V. A clipboard or other portable writing surface for each participant.

VI. A newsprint flip chart and several felt-tipped markers for each subgroup.

VII. A newsprint flip chart and a felt-tipped marker for the facilitator's use.

VIII. Masking tape for posting newsprint.

Physical Setting

A room large enough so that the individual subgroups can work without disturbing one another. Movable chairs should be provided.

Process

I. The facilitator introduces the goals of the activity, distributes copies of the theory sheet, and instructs the participants to read this sheet. (Ten minutes.)

This structured experience is based on the strategic assumption surfacing and testing (SAST) process developed by R.O. Mason and I.I. Mitroff and described in *Challenging Strategic Planning Assumptions* by R.O. Mason and I.I. Mitroff, 1981, New York: Wiley Inter-Science, copyright 1981 by John Wiley and Sons. The SAST process is incorporated into this design by permission of the publisher and R.O. Mason.

II. The facilitator leads a discussion on the content of the theory sheet, emphasizing the importance of stakeholders and their assumptions and eliciting and answering questions as necessary. (Fifteen minutes.)

III. Each participant is given a copy of the case history sheet and is asked to read this handout. After all participants have read the handout, each is asked to decide individually whether he or she is *for* or *against* the robotics proposal. The facilitator offers these guidelines for deciding on a pro or con position:

1. If you find that you want to focus primarily on issues like profit, competition, and trends within the industry that could affect Elmire Glass and Plastics, choose the *pro* position.

2. If you find that you want to focus primarily on issues like the social consequences of the robotics proposal and the potentially adverse reactions from the employees of Elmire Glass and Plastics, choose the *con* position.

The facilitator stipulates that no participant is allowed to remain undecided; designates one side of the room as the ''pro'' area and the other as the ''con'' area; and asks each participant to go to the area that represents his or her choice, emphasizing that each participant must be willing to complete the next several steps of the activity in support of the pro or con position chosen. After the participants have made their choices, the facilitator asks the members of the pro group to assemble into two subgroups of approximately equal size; the members of the con group are instructed to do the same. Each of the four resulting subgroups is given a newsprint flip chart and several felt-tipped markers; each participant is given blank paper, a pencil, and a clipboard or other portable writing surface. (Fifteen minutes.)

IV. The members of each subgroup are instructed to spend thirty minutes completing Step 3 on their theory sheets by listing the stakeholders in the robotics decision facing Elmire Glass and Plastics as well as *one assumption* about each stakeholder. The facilitator asks each subgroup to select one member to record on newsprint the stakeholders and assumptions that the subgroup ultimately identifies. (Thirty minutes.)

V. The facilitator distributes copies of the assumption rating work sheet, and the members of each subgroup are asked to spend fifteen minutes completing Step 4 on their theory sheets by rating the assumptions generated during the previous step. Each recorder is instructed to complete a newsprint version of the sheet after the subgroup has discussed and debated the issue and determined final ratings. (Fifteen minutes.)

VI. The facilitator instructs the members of each subgroup to spend ten minutes first reviewing Step 5 on their theory sheets and then preparing a short presentation (three to four minutes maximum) on the identified stakeholders, assumptions, and ratings of assumptions. The participants are told that the purpose of the presentation is to express the results of the subgroup work as forcefully as possible, in the form of arguments for the pro or con position that was chosen. They are also told that the newsprint generated during Steps IV and V should be posted during the presentation. (Ten minutes.)

VII. The total group is reassembled. Each participant is given blank paper and is instructed to listen carefully to the other subgroups' presentations and to record those assumptions that are most damaging or threatening to his or her own subgroup's position and assumptions. Then the subgroups are told to take turns making their presentations. The facilitator stipulates that no debate is allowed and that the only permissible comments or questions are those requesting clarification. (Approximately twenty minutes.)

VIII. The facilitator instructs the subgroups to reconvene so that the members can share their notes about other subgroups' assumptions. The subgroups are told to spend ten minutes deciding which one assumption is most damaging and threatening, and each recorder is instructed to record the subgroup's final choice on newsprint. (Ten minutes.)

IX. The total group is reassembled, and the recorders post the newsprint from the previous step. The facilitator reviews the posted assumptions and then assists the participants in discussing and debating each of the four issues. It is not necessary that the participants reach agreement on any of these issues; it is more important to elicit as much information as possible. (Twenty minutes.)

X. Three or four "synthesis" subgroups are formed by combining pro and con members in each. The facilitator announces that the new subgroups are in competition with one another to develop the best action plan for resolving the robotics problem. The facilitator stipulates that each plan should address the conflicting demands of the stakeholders and the four issues discussed during the previous step. Each subgroup is told to select a recorder to make notes about the action plan and to explain it later to the total group in a three- to four-minute presentation. (Twenty minutes.)

XI. The total group is reconvened, and the recorders take turns presenting the action plans. The facilitator makes newsprint notes about the highlights of each plan and posts these notes after each presentation. After all plans have been presented, the facilitator asks the participants to vote for the best plan. The winning subgroup is congratulated. (Fifteen minutes.)

XII. The facilitator explains that if the SAST process were to continue, the total group would extract the most important elements from each of the plans and use them to devise a final action plan. Then the facilitator leads a discussion of the activity by asking these questions:

1. What were your thoughts and feelings as you progressed through the steps of the SAST process?

2. What were your observations of and reactions to the way in which your subgroup went about accomplishing the first five SAST steps? What were your observations and reactions regarding the final step of the process?

3. What can you conclude about the use of SAST in solving complex strategic problems? What might happen if this process were not used? How is this process different from the way in which your organization usually goes about handling strategic issues?

4. What is the most important thing you have learned about SAST? How might you use what you have learned?

Variations

I. With an intact group, the facilitator may substitute a real organizational problem for the Elmire Glass and Plastics case.

II. The activity may be continued by having the total group extract the most important elements from each of the subgroup plans and use them to devise a final action plan to solve the robotics problem.

III. A different approach may be used to create the subgroups in Step III. For example, the facilitator may administer the Personal Values Statement (PVS)[1] and form subgroups on the basis of similar primary value systems. Still another alternative is to have the different subgroups represent the richer stakeholder roles, such as unions, employees, stockholders, and the local community.

IV. If the major focus is on surfacing assumptions, the activity may be stopped after Step V.

Submitted by Charles H. Smith.

Charles H. Smith, Ph.D., *is an assistant professor of management at Hofstra University in Hempstead, New York. His areas of expertise include group dynamics, strategic management of change and innovation, and systems theory. Also a consultant, Dr. Smith works mostly with not-for-profit and service organizations. He has published articles in* Organizational Dynamics, Human Relations, Systems Research, *and* Vision-Action.

---

[1]See "The Personal Value Statement (PVS): An Experiential Learning Instrument" by J.E. Oliver, 1985, in L.D. Goodstein and J.W. Pfeiffer (Eds.), *The 1985 Annual: Developing Human Resources* (pp. 107-116), San Diego, CA: University Associates.

THE ROBOTICS DECISION
THEORY SHEET

Those who attempt to solve strategic problems in an organization find it extremely challenging to try to consider all the issues and constituents involved. People often make the mistake of trying to simplify such situations and avoiding the more complex aspects. The Strategic Assumption Surfacing and Testing (SAST) process (Mason & Mitroff, 1981) offers a systematic way to analyze a strategic problem, particularly one involving ambiguous information, uncertainty, many stakeholders with competing interests, and/or a number of constraints. The following summary describes the basic steps of the process.

Step 1: Understand the Objectives of the SAST Process

Pfeiffer, Goodstein, and Nolan (1986) define "stakeholders" in this way:

> Those who have a stake in an organization's future. Stakeholders typically include the members of the [strategic] planning team; the organization's owners or shareholders; its funding agency if nonprofit or governmental; its employees (including managers); customers; suppliers; unions; government; and members of the community who believe that they have a stake in the organization, regardless of whether or not such a belief is accurate or reasonable. (p. A-139)

It is important to study any strategic problem from the vantage points of all stakeholders and to surface not only the current assumptions of these stakeholders but also how they and their assumptions affect the problem. Either as a result of conscious consideration or by accident, any plan that addresses a strategic problem incorporates many assumptions about stakeholders and how they will react to an organization and its actions. For example, a plan for a health service organization might incorporate a conscious assumption that the number of possible clients in a given geographic area will grow at 5 percent yearly. On the other hand, an organization that is dependent on a supply of electronic components might assume, without conscious consideration, that the presence of many suppliers and large supplies at low prices will continue.

Step 2: Form Subgroups

The optimal number of subgroups needed to complete the SAST process is three or four; two is the minimum, and seven or eight the maximum. Ideally, each subgroup would have three to seven members.

It is crucial to create subgroups that are very different in their perspectives on issues, and there are a variety of ways to form these subgroups. If SAST is being used to evaluate a pro or con position or clearly differing alternatives, opposing subgroups that support the positions may be formed. An alternative method is to engage in an

---

This theory sheet explains the strategic assumption surfacing and testing (SAST) process developed by R.O. Mason and I.I. Mitroff and described in *Challenging Strategic Planning Assumptions* by R.O. Mason and I.I. Mitroff, 1981, New York: Wiley Inter-Science, copyright 1981 by John Wiley and Sons. Adapted by permission of the publisher and R.O. Mason.

activity that surfaces the differing orientations of participants, such as the Nominal Group Technique (Delbecq & Van de Ven, 1971). With this technique each participant writes the ten major issues that he or she perceives as critical to the problem under discussion. Individuals then share their lists and vote on the importance of the issues; those with the most similar voting profiles are placed in subgroups with one another. Still another alternative is to complete a value-clarification instrument such as the Decision Style Inventory (Rowe, Mason, & Dickel, 1986) or a problem-solving style instrument such as a shortened version of the Myers-Briggs Type Indicator (see McKenney & Keen, 1974); subgroups are then formed on the basis of similar styles.

Step 3: Each Subgroup Generates a List of Stakeholders and Their Assumptions

The usual method used to generate a list of stakeholders is to think of the organization in its environment and identify all the key parties that affect or are affected by the problem being addressed. The stakeholders chosen should be ones that are important in relation to the position or perspective that the subgroup represents. The following questions are useful to consider when identifying stakeholders:

1. Who has an interest in the problem and its resolution?
2. Who can affect the adoption, implementation, and execution of any plan to resolve the problem?
3. Because of demographics or other factors, who *ought* to care or *might* care about the problem?

Then the subgroup members identify one or more crucial assumptions about each stakeholder's interests and behavior with regard to the subgroup's position on the problem. For example, if a government agency is identified as an important stakeholder, the impact that this agency is expected to have on the organization should be identified in the form of an assumption. The assumption might be that the government will pressure the organization to meet Environmental Protection Agency guidelines sooner than financially possible.

In generating assumptions the members of the subgroup consider these questions:

1. What effect will our position/perspective have on the stakeholder?
2. How can we assume the stakeholder will react if a course of action reflecting our position/perspective is adopted?

Step 4: Each Subgroup Rates Assumptions

The assumptions generated during the previous step are rated with respect to importance and certainty. The most important of the assumptions are those having the greatest bearing (either supporting or resisting the subgroup's position) on the problem. The most certain of the assumptions are either those that are self-evident or those for which there is a good deal of evidence supporting their validity.

After discussion and debate among the members, each subgroup completes an assumption rating graph representing the results of this step (see Figure 1). Each

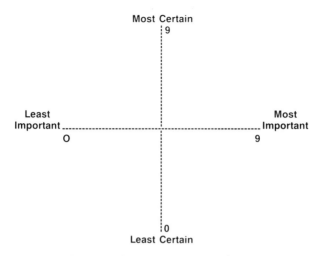

Figure 1. Assumption Rating Graph

assumption is assigned a letter and plotted on the graph to depict its certainty and importance.

Step 5: Subgroups Present Information

Each subgroup presents the total group with its list of key stakeholders and assumptions as well as the importance and certainty of these assumptions as indicated by the completed rating graph. One possible format for the presentation is as follows:

1. A clear statement of the subgroup's position and its four most important assumptions;

2. A list of the key stakeholders and an explanation of why they are important in relation to the subgroup's position; and

3. Display of a newsprint reproduction of the assumption rating graph with the four most important assumptions highlighted and an explanation of why these assumptions are critical to the subgroup's position.

As each subgroup presents, the remaining participants listen carefully and make notes about the assumptions that they believe are most damaging or threatening to those of their own subgroups. At this point the only listener comments permitted are requests for clarification.

After all presentations have been made, the individual subgroups reconvene so that the members can share their notes about damaging and threatening assumptions. Then a summary list of these assumptions is prepared.

Step 6: Subgroups Debate with One Another and Generate Solutions

The final step consists of debate among subgroups based on the summary lists of unresolved issues created during the previous step. After the debate new ''synthesis'' subgroups are created, each of which is composed of individuals representing the conflicting positions. Each of the new subgroups is given the challenge of competing with the others to generate the best integrative plan for solving the problem.

The winning plan should not be considered to be an optimal solution. Instead, after the winner has been announced, the participants should review all the plans presented, extract the important perspectives and recommendations from each, and create an integrated plan to which the total group is willing to commit. If final resolution of the issues is incomplete or impossible, the group can identify all unresolved issues and plan possible ways to move toward resolution.

References

Delbecq, A.L., & Van de Ven, A.H. (1971). A group process model for problem identification and program planning. *Journal of Applied Behavioral Science, 7,* 466-492.

Mason, R.O., & Mitroff, I.I. (1981). *Challenging strategic planning assumptions.* New York: Wiley Inter-Science.

McKenney, J., & Keen, P. (1974, May-June). How managers' minds work. *Harvard Business Review,* pp. 79-90.

Pfeiffer, J.W., Goodstein, L.D., & Nolan, T.M. (1986). *Applied strategic planning: A how to do it guide.* San Diego, CA: University Associates.

Rowe, A., Mason, R.O., & Dickel, K.E. (1986). *Strategic management: A methodological approach.* Reading, MA: Addison-Wesley. (p. 234)

THE ROBOTICS DECISION
CASE HISTORY SHEET

Elmire Glass and Plastics, Inc., is one of the nation's leaders in the production of glass and plastic for industrial use. The company has just received a proposal from United Robotics for the automation of its main production facility in Elmire, Pennsylvania. The change would entail full conversion from human operation to robotic production lines in the Plastic Components Division plant. This plant is the company's principal facility for the production of plastic components, which are used primarily in electronic equipment.

Elmire Glass and Plastics has been an innovator in the plastic components industry, and its components division has consistently yielded a 30-percent pre-tax return on investment. Although the demand for the company's component products appears to be strong, many of its competitors have recently switched to robotic production operations. This shift toward robotics is a source of concern to the company. Some industry analysts believe that robotics will transform the industry and will be a critical success factor in the future. Other analysts warn that robotics is a temporary solution, that it diverts attention from productivity and morale problems, and that the high capital investment required is not warranted because robotic tooling is not flexible enough to adjust to changing plastic product needs.

United Robotics claims that the pessimism of some industry analysts is totally unwarranted and that its products contain built-in design features that will ensure adaptability. The management at United argues that although the risk of obsolescence might naturally be high over a long period—say twenty years—the robotic equipment will have paid for itself five times during that period in terms of labor savings. Financial analysts at Elmire concur with this claim, estimating that the incremental rate of return from the equipment can reasonably be expected to range from 25 percent to 40 percent (pre-tax). This estimate is based on an expected capital investment of $50,000,000 and the generation of yearly savings between $12,500,000 and $20,000,000. The savings computations are based on current labor costs that will be eliminated by the changeover and do not include the cost savings due to increased efficiency. Although efficiency-related savings could be substantial, the components division at Elmire Glass and Plastics is noted to be a highly efficient operation with low defect rates and minimal employee absenteeism and turnover.

In addition to financial considerations, there are numerous other factors involved in the investment decision. This morning local representatives of the union (to which all of the company's manufacturing workers belong), met with top management. They voiced concern, resentment, and their strong opinion that even considering the robotic transition was inconsistent with Elmire's history and reputation as a family organization. They noted that although the transition might bring a substantial return in the short term, it would have an overwhelmingly negative effect on the entire company in the long term. The union leaders pointed out that other Elmire Glass and Plastics divisions, located both in Elmire, Pennsylvania, and in other locations throughout the United States, would not stand for the changeover. They noted that the interdependent divisions that make up the company rely on many unionized skilled craftsmen and technicians and that these workers would be mobilized to strike if the robotic operation were implemented. The union leaders said that the integrity of the entire company was being threatened. Interestingly, middle managers and the secretarial staff were recently overheard in the cafeteria voicing the same concern and questioning the ethics involved in the changeover.

Other pressures are being placed on the company from the local community. The town of Elmire, with a population of 50,000 and located in an already-impoverished anthracite-mining area of northeastern Pennsylvania, has been hurt recently by other plant closings. The prospect of five hundred more layoffs as well as the possibilities of strikes by other workers and layoffs from future robotic implementations are bringing many strong reactions. Several members of the town council and the Chamber of Commerce have phoned Elmire Glass and Plastics to express their concern, as have several congressional representatives and a number of local businesspeople. For the past two days, picketers from Citizens Against Corporate Irresponsibility (CACI) have been in town, organizing demonstrations in front of the components division offices and carrying signs with slogans like "Another Step Toward Greed," "Your Choice: Robots or Food for Elmire's Children," and "Robots or Responsible Management?" Although the CACI is viewed as a moderate group and advocates nonviolent protest, a number of more threatening protesters, believed to be part of an organized radical group that has used sabotage in some upstate New York manufacturing plants, jeered at managers and office employees who were entering and leaving the facility.

Three-year union contract negotiations come up for the components division in one year, just about the time the robotic operation could begin if a contract were signed now. At this point the top managers are divided regarding the best way to proceed. All agree that Elmire Glass and Plastics has survived through its years because of dedicated employees and that it has maintained a commitment to caring for its employees like family members. Layoffs have occurred in the past during difficult economic periods, but none of the magnitude of the one that would ensue with the robotic transition. The industry competition has never been so intense, and there is a fear that missing the opportunity to go with robotics and gain further competitive advantage would be disastrous and an injustice to Elmire's stockholders. A gradual transition to robotics would yield significantly lower returns in at least the next five years; also, replacements of retiring workers by automation would have its own unique set of problems, possibly acting like salt in a wound.

The need for a solution to this dilemma is critical.

THE ROBOTICS DECISION
ASSUMPTION RATING WORK SHEET

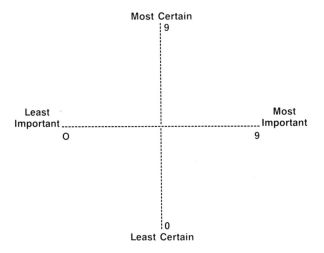

Figure 1. Assumption Rating Graph

460. CITY OF BUFFINGTON: DEVELOPING CONSULTATION SKILLS

Goals

I. To provide the participants with an experience in diagnosing organizational problems.

II. To offer the participants an opportunity to practice interviewing for the purpose of obtaining information for diagnosing organizational problems.

III. To allow the participants to practice giving and receiving feedback on consulting skills used during data-gathering interviews.

Group Size

Eighteen to thirty participants. The activity requires nine participants to play the roles of city employees and nine to play the roles of consultants. However, the design is based on the assumption that the group will probably include more than eighteen participants, with the additional participants functioning as observers.

Time Required

Approximately two hours and fifteen to thirty minutes.

Materials[1]

I. One copy of the City of Buffington Background Sheet for each participant who is to play the role of a city employee.

II. One set of role sheets 1 through 9 for the participants who are to play the roles of city employees (one participant per role).

III. Three copies of the City of Buffington Consultant's Task Sheet for each participant consultant and one copy for each observer.

IV. Three copies of the City of Buffington Feedback Sheet for each participant who plays the role of a city employee and three for each observer.

V. One copy of the City of Buffington Interview Schedule for each participant and several copies posted in various places in the main meeting room before the interviews begin.

VI. One copy of the City of Buffington Diagnosis Guidelines for each participant consultant.

---

[1]The facilitator can save time in distributing the materials by preassembling them into packets. The pattern of distribution is described in Step II of the Process.

VII. A name tag for each participant. Nine tags should be filled out with the titles of the nine city employees. Nine tags should be filled out for the consultants: Consultant A, Consultant B, Consultant C, Consultant D, Consultant E, Consultant F, Consultant G, Consultant H, and Consultant I. Each of the remaining tags should read "Observer."

VIII. A pencil for each participant.

IX. Several sheets of blank paper for each participant consultant.

X. Nine large signs constructed in advance with the titles of the nine city employees.

XI. Masking tape for posting signs and copies of the interview schedule.

Physical Setting

A large, main meeting room in which nine simultaneous interviews can be conducted without disturbing anyone who is participating in or observing these interviews. Movable chairs should be provided; in addition, if movable tables or desks are not available for each city employee's "office" (see Step IV), a portable writing surface should be provided for each participant.

In addition, a separate room should be provided for subgroup work (see Steps III and VIII).

Process

I. The facilitator presents the goals of the activity and then briefly describes the entire process. (Five minutes.)

II. The facilitator assigns the roles of city employees, consultants, and observers. Materials are distributed as follows:

1. Each city employee receives a background sheet, a particular role sheet, three feedback sheets, an interview schedule, a pencil, and the appropriate name tag.

2. Each consultant receives three consultant's task sheets, an interview schedule, a pencil, several sheets of blank paper, and a consultant's name tag.

3. Each observer receives a consultant's task sheet, an interview schedule, three feedback sheets, a pencil, and a name tag reading "Observer."

All participants are instructed to put on their name tags.

III. The city employees are told to spend a few minutes reading their handouts, studying their roles in the context of the situational background, and thinking and making notes about how they might play their roles. They are also cautioned not to discuss their roles with one another. The facilitator leaves the room with the consultants and the observers, assembles the consultants into three subgroups of three (A, B, and C; D, E, and F; and G, H, and I), and assigns observers to individual consultants. Then the facilitator covers the content of the consultant's task sheet, elicits and answers questions, and instructs the subgroups to spend the next twenty minutes discussing how they plan to conduct the upcoming interviews. The observers are instructed to listen carefully while the consultants plan their approaches because later they will be providing their assigned consultants with feedback about their interview performance. (Ten minutes to cover instructions and clarification.)

IV. As soon as the consultants' discussion has begun, the facilitator returns to the main meeting room, elicits and answers questions about the upcoming interviews, and emphasizes the importance of maintaining roles during the role play. Then the facilitator helps each city employee to set up a separate area in the room as an "office" in which interviews can be conducted. The facilitator gives each city employee masking tape and the appropriate sign to post on the wall next to his or her "office." At this time the facilitator also posts several copies of the interview schedule in various places in the room. (Twenty minutes.)

V. At the end of the consultants' twenty-minute planning period, the facilitator invites the consultants and the observers to return to the main meeting room. The facilitator states that during each interview the consultant is to make notes (either on a copy of the consultant's task sheet or on blank paper) and the city employee and each observer are to complete a copy of the feedback sheet. All participants are instructed to remember at the outset of each interview to identify on their sheets which round is about to begin, which consultant is interviewing, and which city employee is being interviewed. Then the facilitator announces Round 1 of the interview cycle.

VI. After ten minutes, the facilitator instructs the consultants and observers to move to the next interview on the schedule and to begin Round 2.

VII. After ten more minutes, the consultants and observers are told to move again and to begin Round 3.

VIII. At the end of the final interview period, the facilitator calls time and gives each consultant a copy of the diagnosis guidelines. The consultants are instructed to retire to the separate room, reassemble into their subgroups, and spend twenty minutes answering the questions on the handout. They are also told to choose spokespersons to share their answers with the total group.

IX. After the consultants have left the main meeting room, the facilitator instructs the city employees to assemble into triads. The observers are told to do the same. (If there are fewer than three observers, each is told to join one of the city-employee triads.) The facilitator explains that when the consultants return, the interview schedule will be followed again, this time so that individual city employees and observers can give individual consultants feedback on how well they conducted the interviews. Then the facilitator briefs the participants on the principles of giving feedback and tells the subgroups to discuss how they can accomplish this process so that it is most helpful to the consultants. If time permits, the city employees and the observers may discuss what problems they believe are facing the city government.

X. At the end of the consultants' twenty-minute diagnosis period, they are instructed to return to the main meeting room. The facilitator covers the contents of the diagnosis guidelines, instructing the consultant spokespersons to share their subgroups' answers to each question. As these answers are presented, the participants are invited to share their reactions and comments. Then the facilitator leads a discussion on the similarities and differences among the subgroup answers. (Twenty minutes.)

XI. The interview schedule is again followed, but this time the city employees and observers give the consultants feedback on their performance during the interviews. (Thirty minutes.)

XII. The facilitator reconvenes the total group and leads a discussion of the experience by asking the following questions:

1. For those of you who served as employees, what were your thoughts and feelings as you played your roles? For those who were consultants, what were your thoughts and feelings? For those who observed, what were your thoughts and feelings?

2. What did you notice about the interaction between the consultant and the employee during the interview? What did you notice about this interaction during the feedback session?

3. What did you notice about the interaction among the consultants in preparing for the interviews? What did you notice about their interaction as they discussed the information from the interviews and diagnosed the problems? How did their interactions affect the answers they provided?

4. What can we conclude about the effect of interviewing method and style on gathering useful information? What can we conclude about the effect of the quality of information on diagnosis of organizational problems?

5. As a result of this experience, how do you assess the method of discovering problems in your own organization? What, if anything, needs to be done to improve that process?

Variations

I. The activity may be continued by having the participants proceed to action planning. In this case the following questions might be covered:

1. What specific actions might be taken by which city employees and over what time spans?

2. What outcomes would you expect from these actions?

3. What procedures would you use to evaluate these outcomes?

4. What is the role of the OD consultant in the action-planning process?

II. The activity may be shortened by eliminating five of the city employees' roles and retaining only those of the city manager, the police chief, the public works director, and the director of parks and recreation.

III. The activity may be preceded by the introduction of a model for organizational diagnosis from which interview questions could be formulated.

IV. The activity may be extended by instructing the consultants and the city employees to switch roles.

Submitted by Willa M. Bruce.

Willa M. Bruce, Ph.D., *is an assistant professor of organizational behavior and organization development in the Master of Public Administration Program at the University of Nebraska at Omaha. She consults with local and state governments in the areas of organizational effectiveness, organization development, and managing the problem employee. In addition, she is presently completing a book on managing the problem employee. She is a member of the national Professional Development Committee of the American Society for Public Administration.*

CITY OF BUFFINGTON
BACKGROUND SHEET

The City of Buffington is a suburb of a large southern city. Its population of about 12,000 has almost doubled in the past ten years. The size of the city government has not. Buffington employs a city manager. The mayor and council members are local businesspeople who take their roles seriously and who are concerned about finances. They have promised their constituents that taxes will not be raised.

The new *city manager,* who recently earned a Master's in Business Administration, came to Buffington about nine months ago and inherited a staff in which all department heads and secretaries, with the exception of three part-time employees, had worked for the city for many years. Before the new city manager's arrival the department heads had been accustomed to operating their units independently; they are all tough-minded people who believe that they, as directors, know the facts and should make the decisions in their own areas. Support staff members pitch in and do what needs to be done as crises occur or as the public demands. Morale in the city government is poor. The city has no plan for managing its phenomenal growth, and the existing descriptions of employee positions are obsolete.

The new city manager firmly believes in a team approach to management and has instituted biweekly staff meetings in the hope of encouraging communication. The department heads attend reluctantly, feeling that meetings are a waste of time and teamwork a fad devised by some management professor in an ivory tower. The meetings usually deteriorate quickly and end with arguments about the fact that the department heads have been making independent decisions without consulting the city manager. The city manager has good relationships with most of the other city employees except the secretary to the city manager, who is the mayor's cousin.

All of the secretarial staff members are housed in offices adjacent to the city manager's. The *secretary to the city manager* gossips a lot and complains of being bored and ill informed about city business. The city manager asks for clerical help from the *secretary to the municipal clerk* when sensitive matters are involved and confidentiality must be maintained. The *municipal clerk,* formerly a member of the secretarial staff and now the supervisor of this staff, feels overwhelmed by the new supervisory duties and hesitant to make requests of subordinates. When an errand needs to be run, the city manager tends to go straight to a member of the secretarial staff without first informing the municipal clerk.

The *receptionist,* who is also responsible for collecting city fees, complains about being interrupted more than five hundred times a week and about not being appreciated. Other clerical staff members resent the receptionist's complaints. The *accounting clerk,* also a member of the secretarial staff, has withdrawn from the group and stays busy at a computer terminal.

The department heads are as follows:

1. The *police chief,* who supervises one secretary and eight police officers. The police chief has the reputation of being the toughest law-enforcement official in the area.

2. The *public works director,* who is responsible for a crew of seventy-two people plus one meter reader and a secretary. The size of the public works staff has not increased in the past ten years, and no new equipment for the staff has been purchased in that time.

3. The *director of parks and recreation,* who operates out of City Hall and wants to build a new community recreation center. In the meantime members of the city secretarial staff do the director's correspondence and collect fees for the use of recreational facilities because the director's assistant works only part-time and must help with program planning and teaching.

The city manager has decided that the problems being experienced within the city government are severe enough that outside help is needed. Consequently, consultants have been contacted to work for the City of Buffington in diagnosing the troubles.

CITY OF BUFFINGTON
ROLE SHEET 1

City Manager

You want to improve your communication with the department heads and develop them into a team. You feel that they are competent but need guidance; in the past they have had entirely too much autonomy, which has resulted in a poorly run city government. If only you could get them to listen to you! You resent their narrow-minded, old-fashioned attitudes and resistance to any kind of change. However, the department heads are not your only problem. You also distrust your secretary, whom you have seen on several occasions at the coffee machine chatting in whispering tones with some of the other secretaries; as soon as you are noticed, the whispered conversation stops. Your secretary is, after all, the mayor's cousin. Who knows what gossip the mayor may be hearing about your problems?

Frankly, you are beginning to fear that this job is too much for you to handle. You need help, and you are hoping that the consultants can provide it.

Do not show this role sheet to anyone.

CITY OF BUFFINGTON
ROLE SHEET 2

Municipal Clerk

You wish that the city manager would observe the chain of command and stop giving work and errand assignments to your subordinates without checking with you first. You have been with the city for over seven years and believe you know more about its operation than the manager does. However, you have never supervised before and feel overwhelmed by your new duties. For example, you are very uncertain about when and how to delegate.

Do not show this role sheet to anyone.

University Associates

CITY OF BUFFINGTON
ROLE SHEET 3

Secretary to City Manager

You feel bewildered about the fact that the city manager gives you less to do than you are accustomed to. You have been with the city for twelve years and feel that you could handle more work; you are continually bored because you do not have enough to keep you busy. Lately you have eased the boredom a bit with frequent trips to the coffee machine to chat with some of the other secretaries. Although you are only engaged in idle conversation with your friends on these occasions, the city manager always looks at you oddly when you are seen doing this.

Do not show this role sheet to anyone.

CITY OF BUFFINGTON
ROLE SHEET 4

Secretary to Municipal Clerk

You sometimes think you are supposed to be all things to all people. Although you like the challenge of the extra work that the city manager gives you, you resent being expected to do more than anyone else. You have been with the city for five years and would like to be promoted to a better-paying job. In fact, since the city manager relies on you so heavily and seems to trust you, you have been thinking about asking if you could be the secretary to the city manager; surely that job would pay more than the one you have now.

Do not show this role sheet to anyone.

CITY OF BUFFINGTON
ROLE SHEET 5

Accounting Clerk

You would just like to be left alone to do your job. You have so many problems at home that you do not want to listen to the complaints of the receptionist or any other co-workers. You have seen the city manager's secretary whispering with friends occasionally at the coffee machine, and this kind of idle gossip annoys you. You believe that if everyone worked as hard as you do, there would be no problems in the city government. You would like to quit, but you need your salary to keep your two sons in college and your daughter in a special school for handicapped children.

Do not show this role sheet to anyone.

———————————————————————————————————

CITY OF BUFFINGTON
ROLE SHEET 6

Receptionist

You have been with the city for three years. You took this job because it was all you could find at the time. Although you have a lot of work to do, you believe that your duties are beneath your skill level; for example, it is ridiculous that you are responsible for collecting city fees, such as those charged for the use of recreational facilities. You are the only member of the secretarial staff who is a certified professional secretary. You also have had a lot of money problems since your spouse left you, and you feel very insecure and depressed much of the time. In addition, you have a feeling that the accounting clerk does not like you; the clerk is so quiet and secretive and never seems to want to sympathize with your problems.

Do not show this role sheet to anyone.

CITY OF BUFFINGTON
ROLE SHEET 7

Police Chief

You have been the police chief for ten years. Ridding the city of crime is your primary objective in life, and you are proud of your record. You do not want to be bothered with the rest of the city operations. You believe that the city manager wastes your time by requiring you to attend staff meetings that usually end in petty power squabbles; you would rather get back to the business of protecting the citizenry. You feel that another city manager would understand the importance of your job and let you get on with it instead of making you attend so many stupid meetings.

Do not show this role sheet to anyone.

CITY OF BUFFINGTON
ROLE SHEET 8

Director of Public Works

You have been in charge of public works for fifteen years; you know what needs doing and when. From what you have seen so far, you believe the city manager to be incompetent. For example, the city manager has not made any moves to increase the size of your staff or to approve the money to purchase the new equipment that you so badly need. Consequently, you have decided to cooperate with the manager as little as possible.

Do not show this role sheet to anyone.

CITY OF BUFFINGTON
ROLE SHEET 9

Director of Parks and Recreation

You have been in charge of parks and recreation for six years. As the city has grown, you have tried to expand your department and get approval to build a new community center; but you are always told that other issues are more important than recreation. You have had to resort to asking for help from members of the city secretarial staff, particularly the receptionist. You are tired of this situation and of all the grumbling at staff meetings. However, because the new city manager seems farsighted—for someone who believes in involving *everyone* in decision making—you have some hope that things will change. If nothing does change and you cannot get the money you need for your department, you have decided that you will quit your job.

Do not show this role sheet to anyone.

CITY OF BUFFINGTON
CONSULTANT'S TASK SHEET

The Situation and the Task

The City of Buffington is a suburb of a large southern city. Its population of about 12,000 has almost doubled in the past ten years. The size of the city government has not. Buffington employs a city manager. The mayor and council members are local businesspeople who take their roles seriously and who are concerned about finances. They have promised their constituents that taxes will not be raised.

The present city manager, who has only held the job for a few months, recently contacted you and two fellow consultants to work for the City of Buffington in diagnosing some serious problems within the city government. You and your colleagues have decided to conduct ten-minute interviews with the city employees:

The new city manager, who hired you

Three department heads supervised by the city manager:
- The police chief
- The public works director
- The director of parks and recreation

Five members of the city's secretarial staff:
- The municipal clerk, who supervises the staff
- The secretary to the municipal clerk
- The secretary to the city manager
- The receptionist
- The accounting clerk

You and your colleagues will each interview three of these employees (see the interview schedule). The data you will use to diagnose the problems in the government of the City of Buffington will be obtained during these interviews. Each interview will be conducted in the office of the city employee being interviewed.

Suggested Steps to Follow in the Interview

You and your colleagues will meet to determine an approach to take while interviewing. When you meet, discuss what you might want to say to cover each of the following steps. Keep in mind that each interview will last only ten minutes; consequently, you need to cover the first eight steps quickly so that the person being interviewed has time to convey information. For some steps you may need to make up some of the information.

The next section of this handout offers some examples of the types of questions you might want to consider asking.

1. Introduce yourself.

2. Define the goals of the interview by explaining why you are involved and what you are doing.

3. Clarify whom you work for.

4. Clarify what information you want from the person being interviewed and why you want it.

5. Explain how you will protect confidentiality.

6. Clarify who will have access to the information provided during the interview.

7. Explain how the person being interviewed will benefit from the process.

8. Emphasize and demonstrate that you can be trusted.

9. Question the person being interviewed.

Sample Interview Questions

1. What would you like this interview to accomplish?
2. What are some of the things that the city government does well?
3. What are some of the problems that the city government is experiencing?
4. If the city government were working perfectly, what would be happening?
5. What helps you perform your job? What hinders you?
6. What has been your proudest moment or your greatest success in your job?
7. What has been your biggest disappointment or your worst failure in your job?

CITY OF BUFFINGTON
FEEDBACK SHEET

Instructions: You will be evaluating one or more consultants on the task of conducting data-gathering interviews. Fill out one of these sheets during each interview that you participate in and/or observe. Use the rating scale beneath each item (from 1= not effective to 10= extremely effective) to assess the consultant's effectiveness in the particular area described in the statement above the scale; circle the number that represents your rating. Then jot down any comments you have about the consultant's performance in that area.

After you have completed all eight ratings, use the spaces provided to write your evaluation of the consultant's interviewing strengths and areas for improvement.

1. The consultant introduced himself or herself.

1	2	3	4	5	6	7	8	9	10

Not
Effective

Extremely
Effective

Comments:

2. The consultant acknowledged the employee being interviewed.

1	2	3	4	5	6	7	8	9	10

Not
Effective

Extremely
Effective

Comments:

3. The consultant established a positive climate for the interview.

1	2	3	4	5	6	7	8	9	10

Not
Effective

Extremely
Effective

Comments:

4. The consultant structured the interview by explaining:

- Goals
- Consultant involvement
- Consultant's employer
- The information wanted
- Who gets the information
- Confidentiality
- Benefits to the employee

1	2	3	4	5	6	7	8	9	10

Not   Extremely
Effective   Effective

Comments:

5. The consultant asked open-ended questions.

1	2	3	4	5	6	7	8	9	10

Not   Extremely
Effective   Effective

Comments:

6. The consultant asked follow-up questions to elicit details.

1	2	3	4	5	6	7	8	9	10

Not   Extremely
Effective   Effective

Comments:

7. The consultant summarized and checked understanding of employee responses.

1	2	3	4	5	6	7	8	9	10

Not
Effective

Extremely
Effective

Comments:

8. The consultant thanked the employee.

1	2	3	4	5	6	7	8	9	10

Not
Effective

Extremely
Effective

Comments:

THE CONSULTANT'S STRENGTHS:

THE CONSULTANT'S AREAS FOR IMPROVEMENT:

CITY OF BUFFINGTON
INTERVIEW SCHEDULE

Subgroup	Consultant	Round 1	Round 2	Round 3
I	A	City Manager	Secretary to City Manager	Director of Public Works
	B	Police Chief	Municipal Clerk	Receptionist
	C	Director of Parks and Recreation	Secretary to Municipal Clerk	Accounting Clerk
II	D	Director of Public Works	City Manager	Secretary to City Manager
	E	Receptionist	Police Chief	Municipal Clerk
	F	Accounting Clerk	Director of Parks and Recreation	Secretary to Municipal Clerk
III	G	Secretary to City Manager	Director of Public Works	City Manager
	H	Municipal Clerk	Receptionist	Police Chief
	I	Secretary to Municipal Clerk	Accounting Clerk	Director of Parks and Recreation

CITY OF BUFFINGTON
DIAGNOSIS GUIDELINES

1. What specific organizational problems have you identified?

2. What systems or subsystems are affected by these problems? How are they affected?

3. What variables seem to be contributing to these problems?

4. What causes can be cited for these problems?

5. If all the problems you identified were solved, what would be the situation in the city government? How would the people involved be acting?

INTRODUCTION TO THE INSTRUMENTATION SECTION

The instruments in this section are provided for training and developmental purposes. They are *not* intended for in-depth personal growth, psychodiagnostic, or therapeutic work. They *are* intended for use in training groups; for demonstration purposes; to generate data for training or organization development sessions; and for other group applications in which the trainer, consultant, or facilitator helps the group to use the data generated by the instrument to move the work of the group along.

One of the dilemmas of most people is that they lack an adequate vocabulary with which to describe other people in nonpejorative ways, especially if the behavior of others has had an adverse effect on them. One of the principal benefits of using instrumentation in human resource development is that instruments typically provide participants with new, relatively neutral words to use in describing others. With such a new vocabulary, one can begin to describe another person's behavior as ''stemming from a strong need for inclusion'' or ''representing a weak economic value commitment'' rather than in more subjective and emotionally laden terms that interfere with, rather than enhance, communication (especially communication with the person being described).

In addition to helping participants to identify behavior, the comparison of scores from an instrument provides group members with a convenient and comparatively safe way to exchange interpersonal feedback. The involvement with their own scores helps participants to better understand the theory on which the instrument is based—a typical reason for using an instrument in training. Thus, there are strong, positive reasons for using instruments in training and development work.

The important caveat here is that the trainer, consultant, or facilitator must recognize that the scores obtained by individuals on any instrument are the result of their answers to a series of verbal questions at one point in time and that such scores should not be treated with any undue reverence. Such responses typically change over time, for a variety of reasons. The individual's interpretation of the question the next time may affect his or her answer, a variety of experiences may change the person's self-perception, and so on. Professionals in human resource development are encouraged to use instruments simply as one additional means of obtaining data about individuals, with all the risks and potential payoffs that any other data source would yield.

There are three instruments in this *Annual*. The first, ''The Cognitive-Style Inventory,'' helps respondents to identify and characterize their approaches to the cognitive behaviors of thinking, learning, problem solving, and decision making. Five individual cognitive styles are identified: systematic, intuitive, integrated, undifferentiated, and split. The results of the instrument can be especially useful in raising people's awareness of cognitive styles and their significance; helping people to develop the skills, attitudes, and behaviors associated with styles that they do not typically use; training people to be facilitators in group problem-solving processes; examining interaction strengths and weaknesses in team-building sessions; forming task forces whose members are specialists in specific cognitive styles; and determining whether an organization, as a whole, practices or prefers a particular cognitive style.

The second instrument, "The Organizational-Health Survey," examines organizational approaches to seven dimensions of organizational "health": strategic position, purpose, alignment, stretching versus coasting, control versus responsiveness, growth versus profit, and the individual versus the organization. There are two versions of the instrument, a short form and a long form. The short form is used primarily as a discussion starter and agenda builder for management groups. The long form can be administered to all employees and functions more as a typical survey. The purposes of the two instruments are to provide a means for assessing an organization's health and its potential for success, to provide data for action planning, to encourage the use of a broad range of data in evaluating organizational health, to motivate key organizational members to engage in constructive change, and to define efforts for developing individual employees as well as the organization as a whole.

The last instrument, "Motivational Analysis of Organizations—Climate (MAO-C)," links six motives with twelve dimensions of organizational climate. The six motives are achievement, affiliation, expert influence, control, extension, and dependency. The twelve dimensions are orientation, interpersonal relationships, supervision, problem management, management of mistakes, conflict management, communication, decision making, trust, management of rewards, risk taking, and innovation and change. Respondents complete the instrument to assess the motivation of their unit, department, branch, division, or organization. The results place the unit being assessed into one of thirty categories based on combinations of the unit's highest or dominant score and its second-highest or backup score. These categories are described in the article accompanying the instrument in terms that yield basic organizational characterizations. The characterizations can then be used to diagnose organizational climate from the standpoint of motivation.

Readers of earlier *Annuals* will note that the theory necessary for understanding, presenting, and using each instrument now is included with the instrument itself. This eliminates the necessity of referring to several sections of the *Annual* in order to develop a program based on any of the instruments. All scales or inventory forms, scoring sheets, and interpretive sheets for each instrument also are provided.

THE COGNITIVE-STYLE INVENTORY

Lorna P. Martin

INTRODUCTION

In organizations the quantity and quality of cognitive behaviors—those associated with the activities of thinking, learning, problem solving, and decision making—produce a dramatic impact on productivity, performance, and potential for growth. The Cognitive-Style Model and its accompanying instrument, The Cognitive-Style Inventory, provide a basis for identifying the patterns of behavior that typify people's approaches to these critical activities. The instrument identifies cognitive styles that imply preferred and consistent patterns of responses that are both habitual and unconscious as well as deliberate.

By introducing individuals, groups, and organizations to both the model and the instrument, the HRD practitioner can accomplish the following:

- Help people to identify their own cognitive styles and to understand the benefits as well as the drawbacks of all cognitive styles;

- Teach people how to predict their own behaviors as well as those of others with regard to thinking, learning, and problem solving;

- Prescribe developmental strategies that people can use to enhance their own cognitive styles and/or to build strength in styles that they do not generally use;

- Increase people's skill and flexibility in various problem-solving situations; and

- Facilitate the interactions between individuals and groups.

BACKGROUND AND DEVELOPMENT OF THE COGNITIVE-STYLE MODEL

Theories about cognitive style were developed as a result of early studies conducted by Witkin, Lewis, Hertzman, Machover, Meissner, and Wapner (1954); Witkin, Dyk, Patterson, Goodenough, and Karp (1962); and Bruner (1966). These and other studies resulted in theories that generally assumed a single dimension of cognitive style, with an individual's style falling somewhere on a continuum between the extremes of this dimension. Many of the theories assigned a positive value to one of the extremes and a negative value to the other. The two extremes are described in general terms by Keen (1973), McKenney and Keen (1974), and Botkin (1974): the *systematic* style (generally viewed as "good" when a value is assigned) is associated with logical, rational behavior that uses a step-by-step, sequential approach to thinking, learning, problem solving, and decision making; in contrast, the *intuitive* style (generally viewed as "bad" when a value is assigned) is associated with a spontaneous, holistic, and visual approach. Subsequently, many studies, books, and journal and magazine articles on the subject of cognitive styles have appeared, for example, Sargent (1981), Martin (1983), Buzan (1983), Wonder and Donovan (1984), and Latting (1985). Each addresses the same basic elements identified earlier as the systematic and intuitive styles.

These theories can be linked with those of left-brain/right-brain thinking, which follow the same bipolarity pattern. Brain research in the late 1960s and early 1970s resulted in the discovery that the two sides of the brain are responsible for different mental functions (Buzan, 1983). Taking brain theory one step further and linking it to the concept of cognitive style, Wonder and Donovan (1984, p. 3) state, "Because of our specific genetic inheritance, our family life, and our early training, most of us prefer to use one side of the brain more than the other." The types of behaviors associated with the two sides are as follows (Wonder & Donovan, 1984):

1. *Left brain:* analytical, linear, sequential, concrete, rational, and goal oriented; and

2. *Right brain:* intuitive, spontaneous, holistic, symbolic, emotional, and visual.

A review of the material on both cognitive style and left-brain/right-brain theory resulted in the following generalizations about cognitive styles:

1. There are distinct, observable, and measurable differences among people's cognitive styles.

2. Cognitive style can easily be detected through language and nonverbal behavior patterns. Dialog between individuals can reveal differences and can highlight the need for awareness and understanding of these differences.

3. Styles are frequently associated with career choices; therefore, there are connections between behavioral styles and certain functions or divisions within an organization. In fact, style can dominate an organization's culture.

4. Styles take on connotations of "good" or "bad," with one style generally considered to be "better" or "best" depending on the individual interpreter or system evaluator.

5. There is a need to understand, recognize, and develop each area of cognitive specialty.

6. Creativity and effectiveness can be increased when the bipolar dimensions are fused.

In addition, most of the recent studies regarding brain functioning and cognitive style assert the need to use each of the bipolar elements of the systematic and intuitive styles (either by combining or alternating between them) in order to generate greater performance, productivity, and creativity.

EXPLANATION OF THE COGNITIVE-STYLE MODEL

Although the systematic and intuitive styles provided the foundation for The Cognitive-Style Model, these two styles had not previously been shown to reflect the entire spectrum of people's behavior with regard to thinking, learning, and especially problem solving and decision making. Therefore, a multidimensional model intended to reflect the entire spectrum was created (Martin, 1983). This model consisted of two continua: (1) high systematic to low systematic and (2) high intuitive to low intuitive. Ongoing observational studies, along with efforts to develop measurement devices for assessing cognitive behavior, have resulted in an expanded version of that original model. As a result, the most current thinking is reflected and best illustrated by the grid presented in Figure 1.

The five styles displayed on the grid in Figure 1 are described in the following paragraphs. (The descriptions of the systematic and intuitive styles are based on Keen, 1973; McKenney & Keen, 1974; and Botkin, 1974.)

1. *Systematic style.* An individual identified as having a systematic style is one who rates high on the systematic scale and low on the intuitive scale. According to findings in the Harvard studies, an individual who typically operates with a systematic style uses a well-defined, step-by-step approach when solving a problem; looks for an overall method or programmatic approach; and then makes an overall plan for solving the problem.

2. *Intuitive style.* An individual who rates low on the systematic scale and high on the intuitive scale is described as having an intuitive style. Someone whose style is intuitive uses an unpredictable ordering of analytical steps when solving a problem, relies on experience patterns characterized by unverbalized cues or hunches, and explores and abandons alternatives quickly.

3. *Integrated style.* A person with an integrated style rates high on both scales and is able to change styles quickly and easily. Such style changes seem to be unconscious and take place in a matter of seconds. A result of this ''rapid-fire'' ability is that it appears to generate an energy and a proactive approach to problem solving. In fact, integrated people are often referred to as ''problem seekers'' because they consistently attempt to identify potential problems as well as opportunities in order to find better ways of doing things.

4. *Undifferentiated style.* An individual rating low on both the systematic and the intuitive scale is described as having undifferentiated cognitive behavior. Such a person appears not to distinguish or differentiate between the two style extremes and,

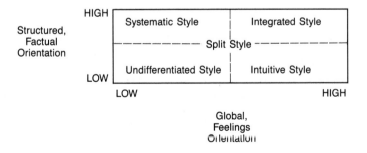

Figure 1. Illustration of The Cognitive-Style Model

therefore, appears not to display a style. In fact, in a problem-solving or learning situation, he or she may exhibit a receptivity to instructions or guidelines from outside sources. Undifferentiated individuals tend to be withdrawn, passive, and reflective and often look to others for problem-solving strategies.

5. *Split style.* An individual rating in the middle range on both the systematic and the intuitive scale is considered to have a split style involving fairly equal (average) degrees of systematic and intuitive specialization. At first glance the split style appears to differ from the integrated style only in the degree of specialization. However, people with a split style do not possess an integrated behavioral response; instead, they exhibit each separate dimension in completely different settings, using only one style at a time based on the nature of their tasks or their work groups. In other words, they consciously respond to problem solving and learning situations by selecting the most appropriate style.

Due to the fact that an assessment score identifying a split style generally indicates an equal degree of both dimensions, it might be assumed that both dimensions would be equally exhibited. However, actual observational findings have not produced this result. As a rule, in stressful situations, one dimension appears to dominate, generally as a result of habit. It has been significant that many individuals exhibiting this particular cognitive style have indicated that they were in the process of a cognitive transition; they were moving into a new area of cognitive specialization and were "trying out new behaviors and skills."

Figure 2 presents a more detailed overview of findings about the five styles from formal as well as informal studies and data collections.

EFFECTS OF COGNITIVE SPECIALIZATION

There are indications that the result of extreme cognitive specialization in one dimension can dramatically impact overall effectiveness in personal and professional situations. Extreme specialization may limit an individual's or a group's ability to think, learn, solve problems, and interact with others.

Effects on the Individual

Cognitive-style specialization—particularly in systematic, intuitive, and undifferentiated styles—appears to limit one's ability to fully function in learning and problem-solving situations. In many cases individuals whose styles are specialized are highly successful in most endeavors but have a blind spot in the ways in which they take in information, sort the data, and ultimately respond.

The same blind spots appear in conversations and interactions between individuals or groups that specialize in different cognitive styles. The dialog frequently becomes stilted and often breaks down. Barriers and misunderstandings between individuals occur due to the differences in methodologies and language or nonverbal communication patterns. Differences in cognitive specialization also can lead to poor performance reviews, conflict situations, and a lack of "job fit" or match between an individual

	Descriptors of Style	Language Patterns	Nonverbal Patterns	Projected Career Positions
SYSTEMATIC STYLE	Convergent thinker	"Let's examine the facts."	Creates an endless list	Engineer
	Concrete	"The data indicate. . . ."	Establishes a chrono-logical ordering of steps to be taken	Systems analyst
	Highly structured	"The specific objectives must be measurable."		Computer programmer
	Logical		Spends a great deal of time on detail	Production manager
	Rational	"Here are my points: A, B, C, . . . ,"		Accountant
	Ordered	"What's your rationale?"	Often belabors a point or step of the process before proceeding to the next step	Purchasing agent
	Linear	"Where's the logic in that?"		Personnel specialist
	Step-by-step approach	"Do the following: 1, 2, 3, ..."		Public administrator
	Concentrates on facts, figures, and data	"I have to figure this out carefully before I can come to a conclusion."		
	Reduces problems to workable segments			
	Product focused			
	Deductive			
	Very conscious of approach			
	Uses a well-defined method or plan for solving a problem			
	Uses a highly sequential process			
	Handles a problem by breaking it down into a series of smaller (often hierarchical) and man-ageable components			

Figure 2. Overview of Cognitive Styles

This overview was inspired by Keen, 1973; McKenney and Keen (1974); and Botkin, 1974.

	Descriptors of Style	Language Patterns	Nonverbal Patterns	Projected Career Positions
INTUITIVE STYLE	Divergent thinker	"Somehow my gut tells me..."	Very visual in approach	Advertising agent
	Global	"I have a sense that..."	"Plays" with (pores over) data	Marketing manager
	Abstract	"Let's look at the whole picture."	Can appear to be disorganized	Graphic artist
	Visual	"You're not looking at the big picture."	Thinks with eyes, has to see the problem, very frequently draws or graphically displays the problem or alternative solutions	Counselor
	Spontaneous	"The solution is simple."		Therapist
	Concentrates on ideas and feelings	"Common sense dictates..."		
	Emotion based	"I see the answer, but I don't know how I got it."		
	Process focused			
	Inductive			
	Not consciously aware of approach, but does use a method that is generally driven by experience			
	Keeps the overall problem in mind continually			
	Frequently redefines the problem			
	Looks at the "the big picture" or the entirety of the problem			

Figure 2 (continued). Overview of Cognitive Styles

	Descriptors of Style	Language Patterns	Nonverbal Patterns	Projected Career Positions
INTEGRATED STYLE	Has highly developed, dual cognitive specialties Is highly flexible and adaptable; alternates easily and quickly from one style specialty to another. Exhibits high degrees of internal locus of control. Looks for opportunities to solve problems Creative, innovative Proactive	"I'm just as concerned about the process as I am about the product." "Before we establish measurable objectives, we should develop a philosophy, a vision of the future. Our objectives should be consistent with that philosophy." "I have the answer, but I need to determine how I arrived at it."	Active Alert High participation and involvement Frequently acts as facilitator or interpreter of language in groups Appears to be comfortable with "disorganized organization"	Entrepreneur Consultant Researcher
UNDIFFERENTIATED STYLE	Receptive Is not a problem-solving specialist; does not exhibit a specific specialty Passive, reflective Relies heavily on rules, procedures, instructions, suggestions, or guidelines Reacts to the problem stimulus and does not impose a process on the problem. Exhibits high degrees of external locus of control. Has difficulty making decisions Procrastinates; delays action	"I don't need to know the whys, whens, and wherefores....Just tell me what you want me to do." "I don't ask questions; I just do what I'm told." "Tell me exactly what you want to have done."	Passive, mostly nonverbal Reflective Low involvement Confluent Waits patiently for specific directions	Bookkeeper Administrative assistant Clerical worker

Figure 2 (continued). Overview of Cognitive Styles

	Descriptors of Style	Language Patterns	Nonverbal Patterns	Projected Career Positions
SPLIT STYLE	Has approximately equal degrees of systematic and intuitive style that are average/medium in terms of degrees of intensity. Styles are used as completely separate entities. Styles are not at all integrated and are consciously selected for each specific situation. Out of habit, one style is used more often than the others.	Pattern changes according to the style being used at the time of observation. Generally an individual with a split style is in the process of a cognitive transition involving building new strengths and skills in the dimension that is perceived to be the weaker of the two (systematic or intuitive).	Pattern changes according to the style being used at the time of observation. Generally an individual with a split style is in the process of a cognitive transition involving building new strengths and skills in the dimension that is perceived to be the weaker of the two (systematic or intuitive).	All careers

Figure 2 (continued). Overview of Cognitive Styles

and an organization. Indeed, the success of the "fit" between an individual and a group or an organization can be predicted by the degree to which the cognitive styles match. Once a group or an organization becomes characterized by a particular style, it may begin to reward that style exclusively; for example, managers might insist that subordinates use the same processes or approaches that they use. In such a situation people whose styles are different from the organization's may be labeled "resistant," "stubborn," "weird," or even "incompetent"; consequently, they may find it difficult or even impossible to succeed in the organization.

When such a bias occurs within an organization, often it is in favor of the systematic style, which is generally associated with the left side of the brain. Wonder and Donovan (1984) describe this phenomenon as follows:

> Researchers refer to the left brain as the dominant hemisphere and the right as the nondominant one, because the skills of the left brain are dominant in our society. Money, technology, efficiency and power are thought to be the rewards of left-brain planning. (p. 14)

In an industrial and highly technological society, systematic ability is critical; therefore, the systematic style has become favored. Yet innovation is fostered by the intuitive style.

Effects on the Work Group

Differences in style among members of a work group can also create difficulties in achieving goals. Cognitive-specialization differences in groups frequently result in process and communication problems. If severe enough, the problems can cause communication breakdowns, which, in turn, can lead to spending a great deal of time on the process of problem solving rather than on accomplishing the task with the greatest effectiveness. In a few isolated cases when the degree of cognitive difference is extreme, the group members sometimes experience a mental "log jam." The group becomes immobilized and gets stuck, actually unable to proceed. If the problem of differences is severe enough and the group has the option to do so (as may be the case with a task force), it may choose to terminate its efforts.

However, when differences and similarities among cognitive styles in a group are recognized and taken into consideration, a type of synergy can be created. This synergy results when the group honors the efforts of each of its members to use his or her particular cognitive expertise in those stages of the problem-solving process where it is most appropriate. For example, systematics and intuitives might work together on the first phase of the problem-solving process (problem identification). Then the intuitives might use a divergent approach by expanding all of the problem possibilities in order to identify all potential problems. Subsequently, the systematics might employ a convergent approach, using the intuitives' list to identify realistic problems. Ultimately, the focus of the group's problem-solving activity would become more and more narrow and specific until a problem statement could be generated.

Another type of synergy is created when a group's members all share the same cognitive style and begin to work on a task that requires a methodology characteristic of that style. In this case members easily understand one another's language and readily pick up on nonverbal cues. As a result they communicate and work well together. However, it is important to understand that the opposite result also could occur when the members share one style. For example, the group might find it necessary to complete an assignment that requires behaviors characteristic of an opposite style.

Effects on the Organization

Organizational systems can sometimes experience the difficulties brought about by cognitive-style specialization of entire divisions. For example, one young, newly appointed vice president of a well-known publishing company explained that she was having a great deal of difficulty managing her work unit. She reported behaviors of resistance, sabotage, and raging battles that she described as an ongoing war. She was in charge of coordinating the activities of the Production Division (a function characterized by a systematic style) and the Marketing and Advertising Division (a function characterized by an intuitive style). Her performance evaluation and position were dependent on her ability to instill and maintain peace and harmony between the two divisions. What she did not know and was surprised to discover was the notion that these two groups essentially spoke different languages and thought and acted in distinctly different ways. As a result, each division perceived the other as "misfits." Once she understood the implications of their cognitive-style differences, she could address the problem.

THE INSTRUMENT

The Cognitive-Style Inventory consists of forty statements, half of which pertain to the systematic style and half to the intuitive style. Respondents evaluate each statement according to the degree to which they agree with it. Subsequently, the respondents transfer their responses to the scoring sheet, which yields a systematic score and an intuitive score. These scores are then transferred to the interpretation sheet, which allows them to determine to what degree they specialize in systematic and intuitive styles. Finally, they locate their scores on the scales provided in the interpretation sheet to identify their own specific styles.

Validity and Reliability

The Cognitive-Style Inventory has face validity. Because it is used primarily as a basis for discussion of the effects of cognitive style on individual, group, and organizational functioning, no attempt has been made to establish validity and reliability beyond this point.

Administration

The instrument, the scoring sheet, and the interpretation sheet can be completed by most respondents in approximately twenty to thirty minutes. It is advisable to follow scoring and interpretation with a lecturette and discussion on cognitive styles. If the HRD practitioner prefers, respondents may be instructed to complete the instrument, listen to the lecturette and participate in the discussion, and then predict what their styles will be before they complete the scoring and interpretation sheets. If the practitioner wants the respondents to practice identifying styles, he or she may distribute copies of Figure 2 from this paper; cover the contents with the respondents; and then show a videotape of a group problem-solving session, asking the respondents to monitor verbal and nonverbal patterns and to identify individual styles.

Uses of the Instrument and the Model

The HRD practitioner can play an important role in helping an organization to understand, appreciate, and expand the range of cognitive behaviors used by its members. To fulfill this role, the practitioner can administer The Cognitive-Style Inventory and explain the model to organizational members for the following purposes:

1. *Raise people's awareness of the significance of cognitive styles in general and of their own in particular.* Organizational members need to learn the benefits and liabilities associated with each specific style, particularly as it interacts with other styles. Botkin's (1974) study suggests that an individual's awareness of his or her own cognitive style can improve that person's ability to communicate and interact with others.

2. *Help people to develop the skills, attitudes, and behaviors associated with styles that they do not typically use.* According to Buzan (1983), research has shown that a synergistic effect takes place in all mental performance when an individual develops one mental area (either the systematic or the intuitive style) that was previously considered to be weak. The HRD specialist can provide training and development activities to enhance people's present styles and/or to build each person's underutilized or weaker style. For instance, a seminar on creativity that focuses on lateral thinking and creative problem-solving techniques such as brainstorming and visualization would greatly benefit people with a systematic style while supporting those with an intuitive style.

3. *Train people to be facilitators and/or advisors in the problem-solving process of a work group or a task force.* These individuals would become familiar with both The Cognitive-Style Model and the inventory and would act as interpreters or even negotiators in groups as needed in order to bridge the gap of cognitive differences. This strategy would be particularly useful in helping groups to deal with conflict. In addition, these people could be trained in team-building strategies so that they could assist groups in developing better intragroup relationships.

4. *Use individual style similarities and differences in team-building sessions to examine interaction "pinch points" and "synergy points" in order to establish group guidelines.* The HRD specialist, through process observation, could identify when and how cognitive barriers occur in the problem-solving process and could then offer preventive and prescriptive measures.

5. *Form task forces or product-innovation groups whose members are identified as specialists in specific cognitive styles.* This approach would "champion" creative designs from the inception phase to introduction in the marketplace. The HRD practitioner could help to create such groups throughout an organization (much like "quality circles") in an attempt to foster a cultural change geared toward innovative responses. Training

and development activities could build and integrate systematic and intuitive skills, both of which are needed for creative growth.

6. *Determine whether the organization, as a whole, practices a cognitive-style specialization.* The HRD specialist could provide management-development programs to address the issue and build the skill base that is needed. A single style throughout an organization imposes limitations; consequently, the practitioner could conduct interventions designed to alter the culture to foster change.

REFERENCES

Botkin, J.W. (1974). *An intuitive computer system: A cognitive approach to the management learning process.* Unpublished doctoral dissertation, Harvard University, Cambridge, MA.

Bruner, J.S. (1966). *Toward a theory of instruction.* Cambridge, MA: Belknap Press.

Buzan, T. (1983). *Use both sides of your brain.* New York: E.P. Dutton.

Keen, P.G.W. (1973). *The implications of cognitive style for individual decision-making.* Unpublished doctoral dissertation, Harvard University, Cambridge, MA.

Latting, J.E. (1985). A creative problem-solving technique. In L.D. Goodstein & J.W. Pfeiffer (Eds.), *The 1985 annual: Developing human resources* (pp. 163-168). San Diego, CA: University Associates.

Martin, L.P. (1983). *Examination of the relationship of multidimensional analytic cognitive behaviors and multidimensional sex-role behaviors.* Unpublished doctoral dissertation, The Pennsylvania State University, University Park, Pennsylvania.

McKenney, J.L., & Keen, P.G.W. (1974, May-June). How managers' minds work. *Harvard Business Review,* pp. 79-88.

Sargent, A. (1981). *The androgynous manager.* New York: AMACOM.

Witkin, H.A., Dyk, R.B., Patterson, H.F., Goodenough, D.R., & Karp, S.A. (1962). *Psychological differentiation.* New York: John Wiley.

Witkin, H.A., Lewis, H.B., Hertzman, M., Machover, K., Meissner, P.B., & Wapner, S. (1954). *Personality through perception: An experimental and clinical study.* New York: Harper & Row.

Wonder, J., & Donovan, P. (1984). *Whole-brain thinking.* New York: William Morrow.

Lorna P. Martin, Ed.D.*, is an independent human resource development consultant who has conducted programs for corporations, health professionals, schools, and government personnel. She is also a faculty member at Stockton State College, Pomona, New Jersey, where she teaches management and organizational behavior. Her specialty is training and intervention design as it pertains to management and organization development. She has conducted extensive research in the areas of problem-solving styles and creativity.*

THE COGNITIVE-STYLE INVENTORY

Lorna P. Martin

Instructions: For each of the statements in this inventory, refer to the following scale and decide which number corresponds to your level of agreement with the statement; then write that number in the blank to the left of the statement.

1	2	3	4	5
Strongly Disagree	Disagree	Undecided	Agree	Strongly Agree

_____ A. I get a "feel" for a problem or try to "see" it before I attempt a solution.

_____ B. I analyze a problem or situation to determine whether or not the facts add up.

_____ C. I create pictorial diagrams/visual images while problem solving.

_____ D. I have a classification system ("pigeon holes") where I store information as I solve a problem.

_____ E. I catch myself talking out loud as I work on problems.

_____ F. I solve a problem by first "spotlighting" or focusing on the critical issues.

_____ G. I solve a problem by first "floodlighting" or broadening the scope of the problem.

_____ H. I attack a problem in a step-by-step, sequential, and orderly fashion.

_____ I. I attack a problem by examining it in its entirety before I look at its parts.

_____ J. The most efficient and effective way to deal with a problem is logically and rationally.

_____ K. The most efficient and effective way to deal with a problem is to follow one's "gut" instinct.

_____ L. I carefully solve a problem by ordering, combining, or building its parts in order to generate a solution for the whole problem.

_____ M. I carefully solve a problem by examining it in its entirety, in relationship to its parts, before I proceed.

1	2	3	4	5
Strongly Disagree	Disagree	Undecided	Agree	Strongly Agree

_____ N. All problems have predetermined, "best or right" answers in a given set of circumstances.

_____ O. All problems are open ended by nature, allowing for many possible answers or solutions.

_____ P. I store volumes of data in my memory, much like a computer, by compartmentalizing each entry for easy recall.

_____ Q. I store a lot of data in my memory by adding to the image that is already there and then determining how the information "fits" (like the relationship between a jigsaw puzzle and its individual pieces).

_____ R. Before solving a problem, I tend to look for a plan or method of solving it.

_____ S. I generally rely on "hunches," gut feelings, and other nonverbal cues to help me in the problem-solving process.

_____ T. I generally rely on facts and data when problem solving.

_____ U. I create and discard alternatives quickly.

_____ V. I generally conduct an ordered search for additional information and carefully select the sources of data.

_____ W. I consider a number of alternatives and options simultaneously.

_____ X. I tend to define the specific constraints of a problem early in the problem-solving process.

_____ Y. When analyzing a problem, I seem to jump from one step to another and back again.

_____ Z. When analyzing a problem, I seem to progress from one step to another in a sequential way.

_____ AA. I generally examine many sources of data, letting my eyes "play" over the information while searching for guiding clues.

_____ BB. When I work on a problem involving a complex situation, I break it into a series of smaller, more manageable blocks.

_____ CC. I seem to return to the same source of data several times, deriving different insights each time.

1	2	3	4	5
Strongly Disagree	Disagree	Undecided	Agree	Strongly Agree

_____ DD. I gather data methodically, at a chosen level of detail, and in a logical sequence.

_____ EE. I generally sense the size and scope of a problem to produce the "whole picture."

_____ FF. When I solve a problem, my approach is detailed and organized; as a result, arriving at a solution is generally a time-consuming process.

_____ GG. I am able to solve a problem quickly and effectively; I do not spend a great deal of time on the problem-solving process.

_____ HH. I have an excellent memory and a good aptitude for mathematics.

_____ II. I am comfortable with uncertainty and ambiguity.

_____ JJ. I would describe myself—and so would others—as predictable and reliable.

_____ KK. I have an abundance of ideas and an inquisitive nature.

_____ LL. It is my nature to avoid "making waves" with change.

_____ MM. I would describe myself—as would others—as a risk taker.

_____ NN. I am comfortable with the status quo; "new ways" are not always better ways.

THE COGNITIVE-STYLE INVENTORY
SCORING SHEET

Instructions: Transfer your inventory responses to the appropriate blanks below. Add the numbers in each column, and record the totals in the blanks provided.

_____ A		_____ B
_____ C		_____ D
_____ E		_____ F
_____ G		_____ H
_____ I		_____ J
_____ K		_____ L
_____ M		_____ N
_____ O		_____ P
_____ Q		_____ R
_____ S		_____ T
_____ U		_____ V
_____ W		_____ X
_____ Y		_____ Z
_____ AA		_____ BB
_____ CC		_____ DD
_____ EE		_____ FF
_____ GG		_____ HH
_____ II		_____ JJ
_____ KK		_____ LL
_____ MM		_____ NN

_____   _____

Total Intuitive   **Total Systematic**
Score   **Score**

THE COGNITIVE-STYLE INVENTORY
INTERPRETATION SHEET

Place an "X" in the appropriate block to indicate your degree of cognitive specialization.

**Your
Systematic
Score**

High > 81	
Medium High 71-80	
Medium Low 61-70	
Low < 60	

**Your
Intuitive
Score**

High > 81	
Medium High 71-80	
Medium Low 61-70	
Low < 60	

Instructions: Scan the numbers listed below, one style at a time, until you find a style that lists your degree of systematic specialization *as well as* your degree of intuitive specialization. The style that lists *both* is your own cognitive style.

	Systematic Score	Intuitive Score
Systematic Style	High > 81	Low < 60
	High > 81	Medium Low 61-70
	Medium High 71-80	Low < 60
Intuitive Style	Low < 60	High > 81
	Medium Low 61-70	High > 81
	Low < 60	Medium High 71-80
Integrated Style	High > 81	High > 81
	High > 81	Medium High 71-80
	Medium High 71-80	High > 81
Undifferentiated Style	Low < 60	Low < 60
	Medium Low 61-70	Low < 60
	Low < 60	Medium Low 61-70
Split Style	Medium High 71-80	Medium High 71-80
	Medium High 71-80	Medium Low 61-70
	Medium Low 61-70	Medium High 71-80
	Medium Low 61-70	Medium Low 61-70

For each style, the more extreme degrees of that style are listed at the top.

THE ORGANIZATIONAL-HEALTH SURVEY

Will Phillips

DIMENSIONS OF ORGANIZATIONAL HEALTH

In examining organizational health, certain key questions should be addressed in seven dimensions:

1. *Strategic Position.* Strategic position is a measure of how well the organization is situated in relation to its external world. A well-positioned organization supplies a growing market; high barriers prevent competitors from entering the market; supplies are plentiful; and there are no threats of changes in legislation, economy, technology, or social climate. How well has the organization designed itself to respond to its market in the current external environment? Is the external environment helping or hindering?

2. *Purpose.* A well-defined purpose directs all of the organization's resources and energy toward achieving a goal. Purpose focuses on meeting the needs of five entities: the customers, the business (cash, profit, and growth), the owners, the employees, and the community. A healthy organizational purpose is clear, and everyone in the organization agrees to it. The most successful purposes add meaning to each individual's work by integrating the organization's purpose with the individual's purpose. How well is the organization focused on its direction, and how well do the key people and employees understand and adhere to the direction and priorities?

3. *Alignment.* A well-aligned organization is very powerful and efficient. It does not waste human energy. The organization's purpose is used to align, evaluate, and refocus every other organizational decision. How well do the organization's strategic support factors (such as culture, plans, structure, systems, and incentives) actually support the purpose of the organization?

4. *Stretching versus coasting.* People stretch when four conditions exist: they are challenged; they feel that they can make a difference in the outcome; they are rewarded rather than punished for stretching; and they are trusted. Is the organization challenging itself and its people? Is there too much challenge (causing strain), too little challenge (resulting in coasting), or just the right amount for maximum productivity?

5. *Control versus responsiveness.* An organization that is overcontrolled will not allow for flexibility, change, and creativity. What is the balance between control and responsiveness in the organization? A well-controlled organization is rarely surprised. A responsive organization is able to innovate and adapt to changes quickly.

6. *Growth versus profit.* When an organization is in a fast-growth mode, there is a high likelihood that growth may become its downfall. On the other hand, an organization that is spinning off very high amounts of cash and is not growing will also undermine itself. What is the balance between these two goals? Is there enough profit to sustain growth? Is there enough growth to challenge people and to provide opportunities for individual growth?

7. *Individual versus organization.* Every successful organization must find an appropriate balance between serving the needs of the individuals and the needs of the organization. One measure of an organization's focus on individual needs is its ability to attract, develop, and keep talented people. When organizations do not respond to individual needs for challenge, promotion, and increased income, those individuals move or transfer, and the organization loses. What is the balance needed for the organization to meet its own goals and needs along with the goals and needs of individuals in the organization?

THE INSTRUMENTS

The Organizational-Health Survey (Short Form) and The Organizational-Health Survey (Long Form) both measure an organization's health along these seven dimensions. The short form consists of seven scales along which participants are asked to position the organization. Although this placement is highly individual, strong agreement exists within the same level in an organization. Scoring of the instrument is done subjectively by the participants.

The long form consists of forty-five questions, each with a five-point scale ranging from "strongly agree" to "strongly disagree." Questions are asked relating to each of the seven dimensions of organizational health. Scoring is objective; participants can score their own instruments, or the facilitator can do all the scoring.

The short form of the instrument saves time in administration and scoring. However, a lecturette on the seven dimensions must be presented before using the instrument. The short form is especially useful in companies with a history of open and honest communication. Perhaps the best use of the short form is as a discussion starter and agenda builder for management groups.

The long form does not require a lecturette on the seven dimensions. In fact, if a lecturette is given, it should follow the administration of the instrument in order to avoid biased responses. Long forms can be administered individually in advance and scored before a group meeting.

Although no controlled research compares the two forms, experience shows the short form will yield a diagnosis that essentially matches that of the long form. The latter does hold certain advantages, including (1) more depth, (2) more specific input for use in action planning, and (3) more power for eliciting results that motivate organizations to change constructively.

Purpose of the Instruments

These instruments address the following purposes:

1. To provide a structure through which an organization can broadly assess its current health and its potential for future success;

2. To provide diagnostic output that can be used to build an action plan for organizational improvement;

3. To encourage consultants and managers to use a broader range of data in understanding and evaluating an organization's health;

4. To provide a tool to motivate and energize key organization members to engage in constructive change; and

5. To define more clearly the goal of organizational and individual development efforts in an organization.

Validity and Reliability

The instruments and the seven dimensions of organizational health have been presented to approximately three hundred company presidents in one-half- to one-day sessions. They have also been used for in-depth workshops with the top-management teams of approximately two dozen organizations. In each case the dimensions and the results of the instruments found a high degree of acceptance.

Agreement on ratings among members of an organization is quite uniform (less than 10-percent variation) when the organization is characterized as having open and honest communication. When this is not the norm, variation may go up to 30 percent on some items. Most variations occur between levels in an organization; that is, the president usually scores the organization as healthier on all dimensions than the next level of managers. Lowest-level scores come from the lowest hierarchical level. The more unhealthy the organization, the more dramatic the differences between levels.

Whom to Survey

Regardless of how well the executive director, president, or CEO knows an organization, that person has a strong tendency to see the organization as he or she wants it to be rather than as it is. Additional opinions should be sought from others, such as members of the management team, employees, customers, board members, and vendors.

One of the more effective and efficient ways of getting valuable opinions on the health of the organization is to administer the instruments with members of some or all of these groups plus the CEO in a single meeting. Interaction between the members will lead to more depth, more learning and eventually more commitment and energy for making improvements and changes in the organization's health.

Certain dangers must be considered before bringing a group of people together to do this, including the following:

- The process will not work if the norm in the organization is not to speak openly and frankly.

- Without adequate structure and appropriate control, the process can degenerate into a gripe session, which is nonproductive.
- It is possible to generate too much data and to be locked into a state of paralysis by overanalysis.

When the survey is used in an organization with a closed culture where communication is guarded and criticism is not accepted well, a good deal of time must be devoted to discussing results. The benefits of team diagnosing can be gained and dangers avoided if a competent outside facilitator with experience in diagnosis conducts the session. The facilitator must have established clear expectations with the CEO, Division Manager, Owner, and others about how the closed culture will be opened before leading a team discussion on the results.

INTERPRETATION OF SCORES

In interpreting scores, it is important to realize that all of the dimensions share a dynamic relationship with one another. Increasing one often decreases another. The skill is to balance them correctly. A discussion of the results should not get stalled on the instruments and their accuracy. The best use of the instruments is to open discussions among key people and launch an improvement process.

The following statements offer an overview of how scores on the instruments can be interpreted.

- High strategic position scores are a cause for celebration. However, medium and low scores need quick attention; if not corrected, they will make little difference in how well the organization is managed internally, but future failure is likely. Strategic planning and management are the recommended treatments, in an effort to unfreeze and reorient the organization's focus.

- High purpose scores reflect a very proactive organization. When purpose scores are medium or low, inefficiency and frustration begin to build. Strategic planning and strategic management are the key treatments to improving the organization's purpose. Thorough communication of the purpose throughout the organization then must follow.

- Once the purpose is clear, focused, and agreed on, the rest of the organization can be aligned. Long-term improvements in culture, structure, systems, or incentives depend on a clear purpose to provide healthy guidelines for design.

- When purpose and alignment scores are high, the organization will naturally be stretched. In addition, stretch can be facilitated by a management team skilled in delegation, listening, performance appraisal, and holding people accountable.

- Low control scores are often a precursor to going out of control, particularly in cash management, hiring, acquisitions, or legal suits. Immediate short-term controls should be instituted to provide time to build effective control systems. These systems should also be aligned with the organization's desired purpose, culture, structure, and systems.

- High control and low flexibility scores indicate great barriers to making any significant changes in the organization. The key treatment in this case is in-depth unfreezing of the organization so that a new culture can be designed and commitment to changes can be made with integrity. A long-term follow-up system will be needed to ensure results. Well-led strategic planning can be the vehicle for this unfreezing, but it requires significant participation by key people in a cathartic diagnosis and planning activity.

- Lack of balance in growth and profit may lead to immediate problems. This is especially true when growth exceeds the organization's ability to generate cash, train qualified people, and make good decisions. Rapid growth often creates a sense of invincibility, which is a sure precursor to problems. Treatment consists of recognizing the dangers of growth; having the humility to accept the need to change; and taking specific actions to increase control and build good foundations for growth in the areas of strategy, money, and people. Revitalization of growth must be initiated by a commitment from the top plus in-depth strategic planning.

- High-profit/low-growth organizations have severe problems, but the impact is long term. An organization with low growth will not attract and keep high performers because they see little future for personal growth. Such an organization tends to be managed by good stewards at best and bureaucrats at worst.

- In most cases, organizations pay more attention to organizational needs than to those of individuals. Low ratings on the organizational area are best treated by a clear and agreed-on purpose with an increase in the control areas. Low individual scores may be superficially treated with an increase in personnel or human resource management activities. More significant changes usually require an accompanying change in the culture.

SUMMARY

These two instruments are the result of extensive work with company presidents and their executive teams. They were developed to help executives and managers to understand better the purpose of organizational and individual development efforts. The instruments are based on a model of organization health which centers around seven essential dimensions. These dimensions seek to maximize strategic position, purpose, and alignment, while balancing stretching and coasting; control and responsiveness; growth and profit; and needs of the individual and the organization.

Either of the instruments may be used any time management is willing to spend a half a day or more to gain better insight about the organization, its current health, and its potential for future success. The impact of either instrument is significantly enhanced if the top management team is also fully involved.

Although the instruments should not be overused with the same people, they are very useful on an annual basis for comparisons and as measures of progress. One practical and effective use of the instruments is as structure for all or part of an organizational retreat. In most cases, a two-day retreat is spent first learning about the dimensions and rating them and then assessing what should be done about changing them in the organization. The output of the session is an agreed-on action plan detailing who will do what by when over the next year to make changes in the seven dimensions.

THE SHORT FORM

Administration

The following steps are suggested for administering the short form:

1. Deliver a lecturette on the seven dimensions of organizational health, using the questions posed earlier in this article as guides.
2. Have participants rate the organization on the seven dimensions using a scale of one to ten, indicating the organization's present position on each continuum with an ''X''.
3. Have participants draw arrows to indicate any trends of movement to the right or left along the continua.
4. Have participants draw circles to indicate where they believe the organization should be on the continua in order to be healthy.

Using the Data from the Short Form

Information obtained from more than one person can be summarized on a blank form. A simple mathematical average can hide valuable information; therefore, it is more useful to plot each X, circle, and arrow on a master short form. A different color for each person may add clarity. As an alternative presentation, the short form can be drawn on a flipchart or overhead transparency; each participant then publicly expresses his or her data. Each type of information (X's, circles, and arrows) can be discussed separately. The facilitator might follow this procedure:

1. Decide whether or not the master score summary accurately represents the organization. If not, discuss and agree on changes to the summary.
2. Select the two or three dimensions that would be most beneficial to improve.
4. Identify specifics of these dimensions. Avoid involved discussions of what is or is not true, or what is and is not improvable.
5. Design tasks to address improvement in these dimensions.
6. Assign people and deadlines.
7. Decide how to monitor progress.

THE LONG FORM

Administration

Suggestions for administering the long form include the following:

1. Select participants as outlined in "Whom to Survey."
2. Schedule a meeting of one-half to one and one-half days so that the participants can interpret the data and build an action plan.
3. Have the participants complete the long form.
4. Decide if the facilitator will score the instruments or if the participants will score their own.
5. Combine the individual score summaries before the meeting and prepare a master score summary.

Using the Data from the Long Form

Begin the meeting with the lecturette or an expanded presentation based on the material in this article. Lead a discussion which focuses on the following:

1. Decide whether or not the master score summary accurately represents the organization. If not, discuss and agree on changes to the summary.
2. Select the two or three dimensions that would be most beneficial to improve.
4. Identify specifics of these dimensions. Avoid involved discussions of what is or is not true, or what is and is not improvable.
5. Design tasks to address these areas.
6. Assign people and deadlines.
7. Decide how to monitor progress.

Will Phillips is the founder of The Small Business Advantage, a management consulting firm in San Diego, California, which specializes in small businesses. His work has focused heavily on developing organizational diagnostic instruments and procedures which are used to launch significant change programs. Over the past twenty years, he has worked with clients in more than a dozen countries. He designed the firm's Problem Solving and Teamwork Workshop, which is used with most of their clients. Currently, Phillips is working in partnership with the San Diego Chamber of Commerce to design and lead a series of Chief Executive Round Tables.

THE ORGANIZATIONAL-HEALTH SURVEY (SHORT FORM)

Will Phillips

Name _____

Instructions: The following items were chosen to assess seven major dimensions of organizational functioning. Taken together they will give an overall indication of the state of health of the organization. Respond to each question to the best of your experience even though you may not have complete background knowledge.

Rate the organization on each of the following seven dimensions using a scale of one to ten, indicating the organization's position on each continuum with an "X". Next, draw arrows to indicate any trends of movement to the right or to the left along the continua. Finally, draw circles to indicate where you believe the organization should be in order to be healthy.

1. Strong Strategic Position   Weak

   10 - - 9 - - 8 - - 7 - - 6 - - 5 - - 4 - - 3 - - 2 - - 1

2. Purposeful   Unfocused

   10 - - 9 - - 8 - - 7 - - 6 - - 5 - - 4 - - 3 - - 2 - - 1

3. Aligned   Unaligned

   10 - - 9 - - 8 - - 7 - - 6 - - 5 - - 5 - - 3 - - 2 - - 1

4. Strained   Stretched   Coasting

   10 - - 9 - - 8 - - 7 - - 6 - - 5 - - 4 - - 3 - - 2 - - 1

5. Control   Flexibility
   Continuity   Change
   Stability   Creativity

   10 - - 9 - - 8 - - 7 - - 6 - - 5 - - 4 - - 3 - - 2 - - 1

6. Profit   Growth

   10 - - 9 - - 8 - - 7 - - 6 - - 5 - - 4 - - 3 - - 2 - - 1

7. Individual   Organization
   Needs Met   Needs Met

   10 - - 9 - - 8 - - 7 - - 6 - - 5 - - 4 - - 3 - - 2 - - 1

THE ORGANIZATIONAL-HEALTH SURVEY (LONG FORM)

Will Phillips

Name _____

Instructions: The items starting on the next page were chosen to assess the major dimensions of organizational functioning (represented in the instrument by sections SP, P, A, S, C, F, PR, G, I, and O). Taken together they will give an overall indication of the state of health of the organization. Respond to each question to the best of your experience even though you may not have complete background knowledge.

    Circle the response following each question that corresponds to one of the following:

> SA = Strongly Agree
> A = Inclined to Agree
> U = Unsure
> D = Disagree
> SD = Strongly Disagree

Respond to all forty-five items first; then go back through the instrument and complete the scoring for each section.

SECTION SP

1. Our market is growing.   SA   A   U   D   SD

2. There is a steady demand for our products/services.   SA   A   U   D   SD

3. In the eyes of our customers, we are clearly distinguished from our competitors.   SA   A   U   D   SD

4. It is very difficult and/or costly to enter our line of business.   SA   A   U   D   SD

5. We are not overly dependent on suppliers of materials, information, or labor.   SA   A   U   D   SD

6. We are not overly dependent on a small number of customers.   SA   A   U   D   SD

7. There are no products or services that are likely to replace ours in the near future.   SA   A   U   D   SD

8. There are few threats to our organization from changes in technology, laws, demography, the economy, or social attitudes.   SA   A   U   D   SD

SP SCORING

	SA	A	U	D	SD
Number of circles in each column:	—	—	—	—	—
Multiply column total by the weighting factor shown:	x10	x8	x0	x-10	x-20
Compute the total: =	—	+ —	+ —	+ —	+ —

=

SP Total

SECTION P

9. I clearly understand the direction
   in which our organization is heading.   SA   A   U   D   SD

10. We listen to our customers.   SA   A   U   D   SD

11. I know how my work contributes to
    the overall organization.   SA   A   U   D   SD

12. I am proud of our company.   SA   A   U   D   SD

13. We have clear priorities.   SA   A   U   D   SD

P SCORING

	SA	A	U	D	SD
Number of circles in each column:	—	—	—	—	—
Multiply column total by the weighting factor shown:	x16	x13	x0	x-15	x-30
Compute the total: =	—	+ —	+ —	+ —	+ —

$$= \boxed{}$$

P Total

SECTION A

14. We have a strong sense of teamwork
    and cooperation.   SA   A   U   D   SD

15. The people who work here trust and
    respect one another.   SA   A   U   D   SD

16. The way our jobs are divided is clear
    and makes sense.   SA   A   U   D   SD

17. I get accurate and timely information
    that helps me do my job.   SA   A   U   D   SD

18. Our resources (people, money, time,
    equipment, and so on) are focused to
    produce the best results.   SA   A   U   D   SD

19. There are incentives to encourage
    us to do what is important.   SA   A   U   D   SD

A SCORING

	SA	A	U	D	SD
Number of circles in each column:	—	—	—	—	—
Multiply column total by the weighting factor shown:	x13	x12	x0	x-10	x-20
Compute the total: =	— +	— +	— +	— +	—

A Total

SECTION S

20. The work I do is very challenging.   SA   A   U   D   SD

21. The people I work with try to do
    their best.   SA   A   U   D   SD

22. We are not overworked or overstressed.   SA   A   U   D   SD

23. We are not spread too thin.   SA   A   U   D   SD

S SCORING

	SA	A	U	D	SD
Number of circles in each column:	—	—	—	—	—
Multiply column total by the weighting factor shown:	x20	x15	x0	x-15	x-20
Compute the total: =	— +	— +	— +	— +	—

$$= \boxed{}$$

S Total

SECTION C

24. Our actual sales, cost, or profit
    figures rarely surprise us.   SA   A   U   D   SD

25. We are in compliance with all laws
    and with agreements we have made.   SA   A   U   D   SD

26. We have accurate, useful, and timely
    reports on key performance areas.   SA   A   U   D   SD

27. We regularly measure customer
    satisfaction.   SA   A   U   D   SD

28. We regularly measure employee
    satisfaction.   SA   A   U   D   SD

C SCORING

	SA	A	U	D	SD
Number of circles in each column:	—	—	—	—	—
Multiply column total by the weighting factor shown:	x16	x13	x0	x-15	x-30
Compute the total: =	— +	— +	— +	— +	—

=

C Total

SECTION F

29. We respond to changes in the outside
world that may affect our organization.   SA   A   U   D   SD

30. We regularly seek and use ideas and
comments from our customers.   SA   A   U   D   SD

31. Everyone is encouraged to think of ways
of doing things better.   SA   A   U   D   SD

32. We regularly fine tune or make
improvements in how we do things in
all departments.   SA   A   U   D   SD

33. We have a high readiness to make
changes if needed.   SA   A   U   D   SD

F SCORING

	SA	A	U	D	SD
Number of circles in each column:	—	—	—	—	—
Multiply column total by the weighting factor shown:	x16	x13	x0	x-15	x-30
Compute the total: =	—	+ —	+ —	+ —	+ —

= ☐

F Total

SECTION PR

34. We produce enough profit to regularly invest it in people, our facility, or improving our products and services. SA A U D SD

35. We have an ample gross margin that does not erode during production or delivery. SA A U D SD

36. We have ample cash available. SA A U D SD

PR SCORING

	SA	A	U	D	SD
Number of circles in each column:	—	—	—	—	—
Multiply column total by the weighting factor shown:	x27	x22	x0	x-30	x-50

Compute the total: = __ + __ + __ + __ + __

= [___]

SECTION G

PR Total

37. Our market share is growing significantly. SA A U D SD

38. Our sales are increasing at over 25 percent per year. SA A U D SD

39. We are not growing too fast. SA A U D SD

G SCORING

	SA	A	U	D	SD
Number of circles in each column:	—	—	—	—	—
Multiply column total by the weighting factor shown:	x27	x22	x0	x-30	x-50

Compute the total: = __ + __ + __ + __ + __

= [___]

G Total

University Associates

SECTION I

40. There is a real opportunity for
    employees to grow and develop here. SA   A   U   D   SD

41. We have little undesired turnover. SA   A   U   D   SD

42. The organization cares for its employees. SA   A   U   D   SD

I SCORING

	SA	A	U	D	SD
Number of circles in each column:	—	—	—	—	—
Multiply column total by the weighting factor shown:	x27	x22	x0	x-30	x-50
Compute the total: =	— +	— +	— +	— +	—

$$= \boxed{}$$

I Total

SECTION O

43. People are held accountable for their
    performance. SA   A   U   D   SD

44. People will give a lot to help our
    organization. SA   A   U   D   SD

45. Our organization demands a lot
    from everyone. SA   A   U   D   SD

O SCORING

	SA	A	U	D	SD
Number of circles in each column:	—	—	—	—	—
Multiply column total by the weighting factor shown:	x27	x22	x0	x-30	x-50
Compute the total: =	— +	— +	— +	— +	—

$$= \boxed{}$$

O Total

THE ORGANIZATIONAL-HEALTH SURVEY
SCORING AND INTERPRETATION SHEET

INSTRUCTIONS

1. Transfer the score from each section on the long form to this score summary.

    1. SP = Strategic Position Score   _____

    2. P = Purpose Score   _____

    3. A = Alignment Score   _____

    4. S = Stretch Score   _____

    5. C = Control Score   _____

       F = Flexibility Score   _____

    6. PR = Profit Score   _____

       G = Growth Score   _____

    7. I = Individual Score   _____

       O = Organization Score   _____

2. Transfer the scores to the following graph by indicating the score on the vertical line. For dimension 5, plot the control score on the left of line 5, and plot the flexibility score on the right-hand side. Plot the scores for 6 and 7 in the same manner.

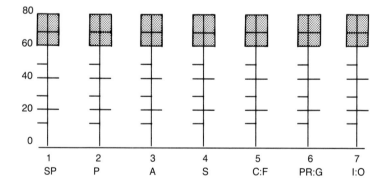

INTERPRETATION

Scores that fall in the shaded area (60-80) indicate health. Other scores indicate "not sick" if it feels good or "sick" if it feels bad. In many organizations, the employees will score less than 60 yet not feel as if anything is wrong with the organization. This is exactly what "not sick" feels like. Weightings for the scores are quite harsh. "Disagree" and "Strongly Disagree" responses will drop scores significantly. This is intentional in order to surface areas that "feel good" now but can lead to disaster in the future (for example the well-performing organization that depends 100 percent on a single customer). If the stretch score is below 60, individual questions should be examined to determine if there is too much or too little tension.

MOTIVATIONAL ANALYSIS
OF ORGANIZATIONS—CLIMATE (MAO-C)

Udai Pareek

Most organizations have a structure (division of work into units and establishment of linkages among units) and systems (specific ways of managing the major functions of the organization, such as finance, production, marketing, personnel, information, and the relationship with the external environment). Most also have norms (accepted patterns of behavior), values, and traditions; and these three elements constitute the organizational culture. The main actors in the organization are its top leaders; they and the other employees have their own individual needs in addition to those of the organization. All of these organizational components—structure, systems, culture, leader behavior, and psychological needs of employees—interact with one another and create what can be called organizational climate.

Organizational climate can only be discussed in terms of how it is perceived or felt by organizational members. Consequently, a climate may be perceived as hostile or supportive, as conducive to achievement or stifling, and so on. Hellriegel and Slocum (1974, p. 225)—adapting the concepts suggested by Beer (1971); Campbell, Dunnette, Lawler, and Weick (1970); Dachler (1973); and Schneider (1973)—defined organizational climate as "a set of attributes which can be perceived about a particular organization and/or its subsystems, and that may be induced from the way that organization and/or its subsystems deal with their members and environment."

While most authors have used organizational climate as a descriptive concept, some have used it for classifying organizations into categories. For example, Burns and Stalker (1961) describe organic versus mechanical climates, whereas Likert (1967) proposes four types of climates: exploitive, benevolent, consultative, and participative. Such frameworks generally use described categories. Only one framework, proposed by Litwin and Stringer (1968), emphasizes the effect of organizational climate on the motivation of its members. In a rigorous study Litwin and Stringer simulated three different climates (each fostering, respectively, achievement, affiliation, and power motives) and monitored the effects of these climates on productivity. Because climate affects people's motivation (for example, Likert, 1967), a framework based on motivation seems to be quite relevant in studying organizational climate.

SIX MOTIVES CONNECTED
WITH ORGANIZATIONAL CLIMATE

Six motives are particularly appropriate in developing a framework that facilitates analysis of the connection between organizational climate and motivation:[1]

1. *Achievement.* This motive is characterized by concern for excellence, competition in terms of the standards set by others or by oneself, the setting of challenging goals for oneself, awareness of the obstacles that might be encountered in attempting to achieve these goals, and persistence in trying alternative paths to one's goals.

2. *Affiliation.* Affiliation is characterized by a concern for establishing and maintaining close, personal relationships; an emphasis on friendship; and a tendency to express one's emotions.

3. *Expert influence.* This motive is characterized by a concern for making an impact on others, a desire to make people do what one thinks is right, and an urge to change situations and to develop people.

4. *Control.* Control is characterized by a concern for orderliness, a desire to be and stay informed, an urge to monitor events and to take corrective action when needed, and a need to display personal power.

5. *Extension.* Extension is characterized by concern for others; interest in superordinate goals; and an urge to be relevant and useful to large groups, including society.

6. *Dependency.* This motive is characterized by a desire for the assistance of others in developing oneself; a need to check with significant others (those who are more knowledgeable or have higher status, experts, close associates, and so on), a tendency to submit ideas or proposals for approval, and an urge to maintain a relationship based on the other person's approval.

TWELVE DIMENSIONS OF ORGANIZATIONAL CLIMATE

Likert (1967) proposed six dimensions of organizational climate (leadership, motivation, communication, decisions, goals, and control), while Litwin and Stringer (1968) proposed seven dimensions (conformity, responsibility, standards, rewards, organizational clarity, warmth and support, and leadership). A review of their studies and those of others indicates that twelve processes or dimensions of organizational climate relate specifically to motivation:

1. *Orientation.* The dominant orientation of an organization is the main concern of its members, and this dimension is an important determinant of climate. If the dominant orientation or concern is to adhere to established rules, the climate will be characterized by control; on the other hand, if the orientation is to excel, the climate will be characterized by achievement.

---

[1]These six motives are also discussed in "Motivational Analysis of Organizations—Behavior (MAO-B)" by U. Pareek, 1986, in J.W. Pfeiffer & L.D. Goodstein (Eds.), *The 1986 Annual: Developing Human Resources* (pp. 121-133), San Diego, CA: University Associates.

2. *Interpersonal relationships.* An organization's interpersonal-relations processes are reflected in the way in which informal groups are formed, and these processes affect climate. For example, if groups are formed for the purpose of protecting their own interests, cliques may develop and a climate of control may result; similarly, if people tend to develop informal relationships with their supervisors, a climate of dependency may result.

3. *Supervision.* Supervisory practices contribute significantly to climate. If supervisors focus on helping their subordinates to improve personal skills and chances of advancement, a climate characterized by the extension motive may result; if supervisors are more concerned with maintaining good relations with their subordinates, a climate characterized by the affiliation motive may result.

4. *Problem management.* Problems can be seen as challenges or as irritants. They can be solved by the supervisor or jointly by the supervisor and the subordinate(s) concerned, or they can be referred to a higher level. These different perspectives and ways of handling problems contribute to the creation of an organization's climate.

5. *Management of mistakes.* Supervisors' attitudes toward subordinate mistakes develop the organizational orientation, which is generally one of annoyance or concern or tolerance. An organization's approach to mistakes influences the climate.

6. *Conflict management.* Conflicts may be seen as embarrassing annoyances to be covered up or as problems to be solved. The process of dealing with conflicts has as significant an effect on climate as that of handling problems or mistakes.

7. *Communication.* Communication, another important determinant of climate, is concerned with the flow of information: its direction (top-down, bottom-up, horizontal), its dispersement (selectively or to everyone concerned), its mode (formal or informal), and its type (instructions or feedback on the state of affairs).

8. *Decision making.* An organization's approach to decision making can be focused on maintaining good relations or on achieving results. In addition, the issue of who makes decisions is important: people high in the hierarchy, experts, or those involved in the matters about which decisions are made. These elements of decision making are relevant to the establishment of a particular climate.

9. *Trust.* The degree of trust or its absence among various members and groups in the organization affects climate. The issue of who is trusted by management and to what degree is also relevant.

10. *Management of rewards.* Rewards reinforce specific behaviors, thereby arousing and sustaining specific motives. Consequently, what is rewarded in an organization influences the motivational climate.

11. *Risk taking.* How people respond to risks and whose help is sought in situations involving risk are important determinants of climate.

12. *Innovation and change.* Who initiates change, how change and innovation are perceived, and how change is implemented are all critical in establishing climate.

The way in which these twelve dimensions of climate operate in an organization indicates the underlying motive of top management and the principal motive that is likely to be generated and sustained within the organization's population. When the twelve dimensions are combined with the six motives discussed previously, a matrix is formed that can be useful in diagnosing the motivational climate of an organization.

THE INSTRUMENT

The Motivational Analysis of Organizations—Climate (MAO-C) instrument was developed to study organizational climate, specifically with regard to motivation. The instrument employs the twelve dimensions of organizational climate and the six motives previously described. It consists of twelve categories, each of which includes six statements; each of the twelve categories corresponds to one of the twelve climatic dimensions, and each of the six statements represents one of the six motives. Respondents work individually to rank order the six statements within each separate category according to their perceptions of how much each statement is like the situation in their organization (or unit, branch, division, or department within the organization).

Scoring and Interpretation

Usually organizational-climate instruments require respondents to rate organizational processes, and respondents tend to assign ratings in the middle of the scale provided for this purpose. The MAO-C, in contrast, is based on rankings so that the respondent cannot escape in the "golden middle."

After completing the instrument, the respondent refers to the scoring key to discover which motives are indicated by his or her responses and then transfers rankings of motives to the matrix. Then the respondent adds the numbers in each vertical column of the matrix and writes the totals in the appropriate blanks; each of these totals is the score for the related motive or motivational climate. These scores can range from 12 to 72. Next the respondent refers to the conversion table, locates the total for each motive, and writes the corresponding MAO-C index number in the blank provided. The indexes can range from 0 to 100. The following formula was used to arrive at the index for each motive:

$$\text{Index} = \frac{(S - 12) \times 100}{60}$$

For each horizontal row on the matrix representing a dimension of organizational climate, the dominant motive (the one with the highest number in the row) and the backup motive (the one with the next-highest number) are noted in the blanks provided (see the two vertical columns on the extreme right of the matrix). The dominant and backup columns are helpful in diagnosing and in planning action to improve the motivational climate of the organization or unit involved. Finally, the respondent determines which motives appear most often in the dominant and backup columns and writes these motives in the blanks provided for *overall dominant motive* and *overall backup motive.*

An organization may total all respondents' index numbers for each motive and then average the numbers for an overall organizational index of each; or the total of the numbers in each vertical column of the individual respondents' matrices can be added and averaged and the index number written, using the conversion table. The advantage of the index is to show the relative strength of the climate with regard to the motives; the cutoff point is 50. If the index number for a particular dimension is greater than 50, the climate is relatively strong in that dimension; if the index number is less than 50, the climate is relatively weak in that dimension. The index also helps in comparing organizations or units within an organization.

Reliability

Retest reliability of the MAO-C has been reported by Sen (1982) and by Surti (1982).

Validity

Validity studies have not been done for the MAO-C. However, indirect evidence of the instrument's validity has been provided as a result of other research on organizational climate. Research on organizational climate as an independent measure and measures of organizational effectiveness share enough in common to warrant some generalizations. Hellriegel and Slocum (1974) have summarized these generalizations as a significant relationship between climate and both job satisfaction and performance.

Deci (1980) suggested three different kinds of environments as being associated with three different attributional patterns. A "responsive and informational" environment (in the terms of the MAO-C, one that is characterized by achievement and expert influence) has been linked with internality; a "controlling and demanding" environment (one characterized by control and dependency) has been linked with externality; and a "nonresponsive and capricious" environment has been linked with "impersonality."

Organizational environments and climate seem to influence the development of internality. Baumgartel, Rajan, and Newman (1985), using four indices of organization environment (freedom-growth, human relations, performance pressure, and personal benefit) found clear evidence of the influence of organizational environments on locus of control. They concluded that internality could be developed by creating educational and work environments characterized by freedom to set personal performance goals, opportunity for personal growth, and opportunity to influence important events or conditions.

A regression analysis of data from 320 professional women, using role efficacy as a variable, showed that of the fourteen variables that finally emerged in the regression, organizational climate alone explained about 34 percent of the variance, thereby exhibiting a great effect on role efficacy (Surti, 1982).

Theoretically (see, for example, Litwin and Stringer, 1968), one might predict a negative relationship between organizational effectiveness and climates characterized by affiliation, dependence, and control. Litwin and Stringer (1968) found that an authoritarian climate (referred to in the MAO-C as a "control" climate) produced low job satisfaction and low performance. A climate characterized by achievement, extension, and expert influence might be assumed to be related to higher job satisfaction and performance. Cawsey (reported in Hellriegel and Slocum, 1974), using Litwin and Stringer's instrument, found higher job satisfaction among insurance personnel who perceived the motivational climate as one of achievement.

One study reported on the administration of the MAO-C to 392 executives of a manufacturing firm (Khanna, 1986). Each executive was instructed to complete the MAO-C by evaluating the climate or culture of his or her specific unit or department (as opposed to that of the entire organization). Correlations were noted between the six perceived motives or motivational climates and measures of organizational effectiveness (consisting of consensus, legitimization, the need for independence, self-control, job involvement, innovation, organizational commitment, organizational attachment, and job satisfaction). The climates were also correlated with total satisfaction, that is, satisfaction with work and with the organization as a whole. No significant correlation was found between the climates and the need for independence, self-control, and innovation. With regard to job involvement, the only positive correlation significant at the .05 level was with an achievement climate.

In the same study there were positive correlations (significant at the .01 level) between five other aspects of organizational effectiveness (organizational commitment, organizational attachment, job satisfaction, total satisfaction, and total effectiveness) and an achievement climate, and there was a negative correlation between these five aspects and a control climate. An extension climate correlated positively with organizational commitment at the .05 level and with job satisfaction, total satisfaction, and total effectiveness at the .01 level. A dependence climate showed no relationship with any measure. An affiliation climate had a negative correlation with job satisfaction at the .05 level and with total satisfaction and total effectiveness at the .01 level. A climate perceived as characterized by expert influence had only one positive correlation (at the .05 level) with organizational attachment. All correlations were in the predicted direction, although more correlations were expected with climates characterized by dependence and expert influence.

Negative correlations might be predicted between role stress and climates perceived as characterized by achievement, extension, and expert influence; and positive correlations might be predicted between role stress and climates characterized by affiliation, dependence, and control. Khanna (1986) correlated climate scores with ten aspects of role stress and total role stress (as reported in Pareek, 1983). Specific correlations between role stress and the various climates were as follows:

- No significant correlation with a climate characterized by expert influence;

- Two positive correlations with an affiliation climate (role erosion at the .01 level and personal inadequacy at the .05 level);

- One positive correlation with a dependency climate (role stagnation at the .01 level);

- Six negative correlations with an extension climate (at the .05 level for inter-role distance, role overload, and role isolation, and at the .01 level for role-expectation conflict, self-role distance, resource inadequacy, and total role stress);

- Negative correlations with an achievement climate at the .01 level for all aspects of role stress except interrole distance and personal inadequacy; and

- Positive correlations with a control climate at the .01 level for all aspects of role stress except personal inadequacy.

Similar results were reported by Sen (1982) and Surti (1982). All of these results were in the predicted directions.

In summary, organizational climate has an enormous influence on organizational effectiveness, role efficacy, and role stress. An achievement climate seems to contribute to effectiveness, satisfaction, and a sense of internality; a climate characterized by expert influence seems to contribute to organizational attachment; and a climate characterized by extension seems to contribute to organizational commitment. All of these climates foster relatively low levels of role stress. A control climate seems to lower role efficacy, job satisfaction, organizational commitment, organizational attachment, and total effectiveness and to foster relatively high levels of role stress. An affiliation climate tends to lower both satisfaction and effectiveness and increase role erosion and feelings of personal inadequacy.

Effectiveness Profiles

The completed matrix provides scores for all six motives tested by the MAO-C. The highest of these scores represents the perceived dominant motive within an organization. The general connections between dominant motives and particular types of organizations are shown in Figure 1.

A combination of an organization's highest or "dominant" score and its second-highest or "backup" score results in a basic characterization of that organization's climate. When the six motives are combined in patterns of dominant and secondary or backup styles, thirty organizational profiles are possible. Brief descriptions of these thirty profiles are provided below. In each description the first motive noted represents the organization's dominant motive, and the second represents its secondary or backup motive. Some of these profiles are based on studies that have been made; others need

Motive	Type of Organization
Achievement	Industrial and business organizations
Expert influence	University departments and scientific organizations
Control	Bureaucracies such as governmental departments and agencies
Dependency	Traditional or autocratic organizations
Extension	Community-service organizations
Affiliation	Clubs

Figure 1. Connections Between Dominant Motives and Types of Organizations

to be studied to validate the concept. In general, climates dominated by achievement, expert power, and extension are conducive to the achievement of results, whereas climates dominated by control, dependency, and affiliation retard the achievement of results.

1. *Achievement-Expert influence.* Employees are involved in and highly stimulated by challenging tasks, and the specialists within the organization dominate in determining these tasks. The organization rewards specialization.

2. *Achievement-Control.* Most employees are involved in challenging tasks, but they face a lot of constraints attributable to rigid procedures and an inflexible hierarchy.

3. *Achievement-Dependency.* In spite of an emphasis on high achievement that is shared by most employees, there is a tendency to postpone critical decisions for the approval of a higher authority. The organization discourages making such decisions without approval from a higher level, resulting in a sense of frustration.

4. *Achievement-Extension.* Employees work on challenging tasks and devote equal attention to the social relevance of these tasks. The organization has a highly developed sense of social responsibility as well as a strong sense of its responsibility to fulfill employee needs.

5. *Achievement-Affiliation.* While employees work on challenging goals, they also form strong groups based on common interests or other factors. The organization pays a lot of attention to maintaining good relations among these cliques.

6. *Expert influence-Achievement.* The organization places a high value on specialization. The specialists influence most decisions, and they emphasize high work quality and unique contributions.

7. *Expert influence-Control.* The organization is controlled by experts who employ cumbersome procedures. The result is generally a lack of job satisfaction and low to moderate (rather than high) output.

8. *Expert influence-Dependency.* The organization has a rigid hierarchy dominated by experts. Decisions are made only at the upper levels of the hierarchy, and bright employees are highly dissatisfied.

9. *Expert influence-Extension.* Specialists play the major roles in the organization, working in a planned way on socially relevant matters. The organization pays attention to the employees' needs and welfare.

10. *Expert influence-Affiliation.* Although the organization is dominated by experts, strong groups are formed on the basis of common interests or other factors. Because primary attention is placed on maintaining a friendly climate, results usually suffer.

11. *Control-Achievement.* The organization is bureaucratic, is run in accordance with detailed procedures, and has a clear hierarchy. Quality of work is emphasized, but most employees with an achievement orientation feel frustrated. This climate is sometimes found in public-sector organizations.

12. *Control-Expert influence.* The organization is a bureaucracy in which specialists' opinions are valued but rules are treated as more important.

13. *Control-Dependency.* A bureaucracy and a rigid hierarchy dominate the organization. Because actions are generally referred to levels above for approval, decisions are usually delayed. It is more important to follow rules and regulations than to achieve results. The senior employees protect those subordinates who do not make any procedural mistakes. Most government offices function in this way.

14. *Control-Extension.* Although the organization is hierarchical, it emphasizes social concern and attends to the needs and welfare of its employees.

15. *Control-Affiliation.* The organization is hierarchical but places more emphasis on good relations among employees than on results. Informal groups based on relationships are seen as important. Some voluntary organizations are of this type.

16. *Dependency-Achievement.* Respect for those in positions of power is emphasized, and so is achievement. Freedom is granted to employees, with the exception that key decisions are controlled by those in power. Many family-owned organizations have such a climate.

17. *Dependency-Expert influence.* The organization has a hierarchy, with decisions made by those at higher levels. Experts play an important role in the various aspects of organizational life.

18. *Dependency-Control.* The organization has clear-cut channels of communication and is controlled by a few people who ultimately make all decisions.

19. *Dependency-Extension.* A few people dominate and control the organization and demand respect from all other members. However, they take care of the members' needs; and the organization works in socially relevant areas.

20. *Dependency-Affiliation.* The top managers control the organization and employ their own "in-group" members, who are extremely loyal to these managers.

21. *Extension-Achievement.* The organization strives to be relevant to society and emphasizes the achievement of results. People are selected for their competence and are given freedom in doing their work.

22. *Extension-Expert influence.* Social consciousness is emphasized by the organization, and experts influence all major decisions.

23. *Extension-Control.* The organization's goals have to do with serving a larger cause; but the structure is bureaucratic, with rules and regulations that are to be followed strictly.

24. *Extension-Dependency.* The business of the organization is community service (for example, education, health, or development). Emphasis is placed on conformity to the policies laid down by the top person or team, to whom all final decisions are referred.

25. *Extension-Affiliation.* The organization's business is community service, and members with similar backgrounds (ideology, specialization, and so on) form strong linkages with one another.

26. *Affiliation-Achievement.* The organization places great importance on relationships and draws people with similar backgrounds. Although the organization values

achievement of results and excellence in performance, rewards are given mainly on the basis of an employee's relationship with the person or persons who are in a position to give such rewards.

27. *Affiliation-Expert influence.* The organization consists mainly of experts, emphasizes good relations, and either employs people of similar backgrounds or has cliques based on common links.

28. *Affiliation-Control.* Although the organization is concerned with maintaining good relations among members, its form is bureaucratic. (For example, a club with strict rules and procedures might be in this category.)

29. *Affiliation-Dependency.* The organization values the maintenance of friendly relations among members, and one or two people make most decisions. Employees are rewarded on the basis of their closeness to the top person(s).

30. *Affiliation-Extension.* The organization's main goal is to maintain good relations among members, and its work involves socially relevant issues. (The Lions Club and similar organizations might be in this category.)

Use of the Instrument

The MAO-C can be used to diagnose organizational climate from the standpoint of motivation. The focus of the instrument can be perceptions of the overall organizational climate or of individual units, divisions, branches, or departments within the organization. After the instrument has been administered, the respondents may individually use a rating scale to evaluate the operating effectiveness of the climate that has been analyzed. Then the administrator may lead a discussion on the basic characteristics of the different effectiveness profiles represented in the group (see the previous section). Subsequently, the respondents may discuss their individual scores and ratings and then arrive at a consensus regarding the diagnosis and evaluation of the climate, which of the twelve dimensions of organizational climate need improvement, why particular dimensions are weak, and what steps may need to be taken in response. Another approach is to discuss individual rankings and to develop a consensus regarding the desired rankings of motives and what might be done to affect the perceived climate accordingly. Any specific action ideas that are developed may be presented to top management for discussion, approval, and commitment. Then the agreed-on action steps may be carried out and followed up with monthly reviews to determine the success of implementation.

REFERENCES

Baumgartel, H.J., Rajan, P.S.S., & Newman, J. (1985). Eucational environments and attributions of causality: Some exploratory research findings. *Quality of Work Life, 2*(5-6), 309-328.

Beer, M. (1971, September). *Organizational climate: A viewpoint from the change agent.* Paper presented at the American Psychological Association Convention, Washington, DC.

Burns, T., & Stalker, G. (1961). *The management of innovation.* London: Tavistock.

Campbell, J.P., Dunnette, M.D., Lawler, E.E., III, & Weick, K.E., Jr. (1970). *Managerial behavior, performance, and effectiveness.* New York: McGraw-Hill.

Dachler, H.P. (1973). *Work motivation and the concept of organizational climate.* Paper presented at the 10th Annual Eastern Academy of Management Meeting, Philadelphia, PA.

Deci, E.L. (1980). *The psychology of self-determination.* Lexington, MA: Lexington Books.

Hellriegel, D., & Slocum, J.W. (1974). Organizational climate: Measures, research and contingencies. *Academy of Management Journal, 17*(2), 255-280.

Khanna, B.B. (1986). *Relationship between organizational climate and organizational role stress and their impact upon organizational effectiveness: A case study.* Unpublished doctoral dissertation, Banaras Hindu University, Varanasi, India.

Likert, R. (1967). *The human organization.* New York: McGraw-Hill.

Litwin, G., & Stringer, R. (1968). *Motivation and organizational climate.* Cambridge, MA: Harvard University Press.

Pareek, U. (1983). Organizational role stress. In L.D. Goodstein & J.W. Pfeiffer (Eds.), *The 1983 annual for facilitators, trainers, and consultants* (pp. 115-123). San Diego, CA: University Associates.

Pareek, U. (1986). Motivational analysis of organizations—behavior (MAO-B). In J.W. Pfeiffer & L.D. Goodstein (Eds.), *The 1986 annual: Developing human resources* (pp. 121-133). San Diego, CA: University Associates.

Schneider, B. (1973). *The perceived environment: Organizational climate.* Paper presented at the meeting of the Midwest Psychological Association.

Sen, P.C. (1982). *Personal and organizational correlates of role stress and coping strategies in some public sector banks.* Unpublished doctoral dissertation, University of Gujarat, Ahmedabad, India.

Surti, K. (1982). *Some psychological correlates of role stress and coping styles in working women.* Unpublished doctoral dissertation, University of Gujarat, Ahmedabad, India.

Udai Pareek, Ph.D., is a freelance writer, researcher, and consultant. Most recently he was an organization development advisor (US-AID) to the Ministry of Health of the Republic of Indonesia. For a number of years he was Larsen & Toubro Professor of Organizational Behavior at the Indian Institute of Management in Ahmedabad. He has been the president of the Indian Society of Applied Behavioural Science and a fellow of the National Training Laboratories. His fields of interest are organization development, human resource development, and action research.

MOTIVATIONAL ANALYSIS
OF ORGANIZATIONS—CLIMATE (MAO-C)

Udai Pareek

Date _____

Name _____ Title _____

Instructions: Completing this inventory will allow you to evaluate the climate or culture of your organization (or your unit or department, if the administrator of this inventory instructs you to interpret the inventory in this way). Below are twelve categories representing twelve dimensions of organizational climate, and within each category are six statements. You are to rank the statements in each category from 6 (*most* like the situation in your organization or unit) to 1 (*least* like the situation in your organization or unit). *Do not give the same rank to more than one statement.*

Rank   **1. Orientation**

_____ a. People here are mainly concerned with following established rules and procedures.

_____ b. The main concern of people here is to help one another develop greater skills and thereby advance in the organization.

_____ c. Achieving or surpassing specific goals seems to be people's main concern here.

_____ d. Consolidating one's own personal position and influence seems to be the main concern here.

_____ e. The dominant concern here is to maintain friendly relations with others.

_____ f. The main concern here is to develop people's competence and expertise.

Rank   **2. Interpersonal Relationships**

_____ a. In this organization most informal groups are formed around experts.

_____ b. The atmosphere here is very friendly, and people spend enough time in informal social relations.

_____ c. In this organization strong cliques protect their own interests.

_____ d. Businesslike relationships prevail here; people are warm, but they get together primarily to ensure excellence in performance.

_____ e. People here have strong associations mostly with their supervisors and look to them for suggestions and guidance.

_____ f. People here have a high concern for one another and tend to help one another spontaneously when such help is needed.

Rank   **3. Supervision**

_____   a. The purpose of supervision here is usually to check for mistakes and to "catch" the person making the mistake.

_____   b. Supervisors here strongly prefer that their subordinates ask them for instructions and suggestions.

_____   c. Supervisors here take pains to see that their subordinates improve personal skills and chances of advancement.

_____   d. Supervisors here reward outstanding achievement.

_____   e. In influencing their subordinates, supervisors here try to use their expertise and competence rather than their formal authority.

_____   f. Supervisors here are more concerned with maintaining good relations with their subordinates than with emphasizing duties and performance.

Rank   **4. Problem Management**

_____   a. People here take problems as challenges and try to find better solutions than anyone else.

_____   b. When problems are faced here, experts are consulted and play an important role in solving these problems.

_____   c. In dealing with problems, people here mostly consult their friends.

_____   d. When working on solutions to problems, people here keep in mind the needs of organizational members as well as society at large.

_____   e. People here usually refer problems to their superiors and look to their superiors for solutions.

_____   f. Problems here are usually solved by supervisors; subordinates are not involved.

Rank   **5. Management of Mistakes**

_____   a. When people here make mistakes, they are not rejected; instead, their friends show them much understanding and warmth.

_____   b. Here the philosophy is that the supervisor can make no mistake and the subordinate dare not make one.

_____   c. Usually people here are able to acknowledge and analyze their mistakes because they can expect to receive help and support from others.

_____   d. When a subordinate makes a mistake here, the supervisor treats it as a learning experience that can prevent failure and improve performance in the future.

_____   e. Subordinates here expect guidance from their supervisors in correcting or preventing mistakes.

_____   f. Here people seek the help of experts in analyzing and preventing mistakes.

Rank   **6. Conflict Management**

_____   a. Most interpersonal and interdepartmental conflicts here arise as a result of striving for higher performance; and in analyzing and resolving these conflicts, the overriding consideration is high productivity.

_____   b. Here conflicts are usually avoided or smoothed over to maintain the friendly atmosphere.

_____   c. Arbitration or third-party intervention (usually performed by experienced or senior people) is sought and used here.

_____   d. In a conflict situation here, those who are stronger force their points of view.

_____   e. In resolving conflicts here, appeal is made to principles, organizational ideals, and the larger good of the organization.

_____   f. Experts are consulted and their advice used in resolving conflicts here.

Rank   **7. Communication**

_____   a. After due consideration those in authority here issue instructions and expect them to be carried out.

_____   b. Most communication here is informal and friendly and arises from and contributes to warm relations.

_____   c. People here ask for information from those who are experts on the subject.

_____   d. Relevant information is made available to all who need it and can use it for the purpose of achieving high performance here.

_____   e. People here communicate information, suggestions, and even criticism to others out of concern for them.

_____   f. Communication is often selective here; people usually give or hold back crucial information as a form of control.

Rank   **8. Decision Making**

_____   a. While making decisions, people here make special attempts to maintain cordial relations with all concerned.

_____   b. Decisions are made at the top and communicated downward, and people here generally prefer this.

_____   c. People who have demonstrated high achievement have a big say in the decisions made here.

_____   d. Decisions here are generally made without involving subordinates.

_____   e. Decisions here are made and influenced by specialists and other knowledgeable people.

_____   f. Decisions are made here by keeping in mind the good of the employees and of society.

Rank   **9. Trust**

_____ a. Only a few people here are trusted by management, and they are quite influential.

_____ b. Trusting and friendly relations are highly valued here.

_____ c. Here high value is placed on trust between supervisor and subordinate.

_____ d. The specialists and the experts are highly trusted here.

_____ e. A general attitude of helping generates mutual trust here.

_____ f. Those who can achieve results are highly trusted here.

Rank   **10. Management of Rewards**

_____ a. Here the main things that are rewarded are excellence in performance and the accomplishment of tasks.

_____ b. Knowledge and expertise are recognized and rewarded here.

_____ c. Loyalty is rewarded more than anything else here.

_____ d. The people who are rewarded here are those who help their junior colleagues to achieve and develop.

_____ e. The ability to control subordinates and maintain discipline is afforded the greatest importance in rewarding supervisors here.

_____ f. The ability to get along well with others is highly rated and rewarded here.

Rank   **11. Risk Taking**

_____   a. When confronted by risky situations, supervisors here seek the guidance and support of friends.

_____   b. In risky situations supervisors here strongly emphasize discipline and obedience to orders.

_____   c. In risky situations supervisors here have a strong tendency to rely on expert specialists for their advice.

_____   d. Supervisors here generally go to their superiors for instructions in risky situations.

_____   e. In responding to risky situations, supervisors here show great concern for the people working in the organization.

_____   f. In responding to risky situations, supervisors here take calculated risks and strive above all to be more efficient or productive.

Rank   **12. Innovation and Change**

_____   a. Innovation or change here is initiated and implemented primarily by experts and specialists.

_____   b. Here innovation or change is primarily ordered by top management.

_____   c. Before initiating innovation or change, supervisors here generally go to their superiors for sanction and guidance.

_____   d. Those who initiate innovation or change here demonstrate a great concern for any possible adverse effects on others (in the organization or outside) and try to minimize these effects.

_____   e. Innovation or change here is mainly initiated and implemented through highly results-oriented individuals.

_____   f. Supervisors here seldom undertake innovations that disturb their existing friendships in the organization or earn the enmity of organizational members.

MOTIVATIONAL ANALYSIS
OF ORGANIZATIONS—CLIMATE (MAO-C)
MATRIX SHEET

Instructions: Organizations (and units, branches, divisions, or departments within organizations) tend to be perceived as driven by one or more of six specific motives. The *scoring key* will show you which motives are indicated by your responses on the MAO-C and, therefore, which motives you perceive as driving your organization or unit; then completing this *matrix sheet* will help you arrive at a profile of the general motivational climate of your organization or unit as you perceive it. For example, for the first category or dimension of organizational climate, *Orientation*, if you ranked item *a* as 4, you would look at the scoring key and learn that *a* indicates the *dependency* motive; then you would refer to this matrix sheet and find the horizontal row that corresponds to Orientation, locate the heading "Dependency," and write the number 4 under that heading in the Orientation row. Follow this process until you have transferred all six of your rankings for each of the twelve categories covered in the MAO-C.

Add the numbers in each vertical column of this matrix and write the totals in the blanks provided; each of these totals is your score for that particular motive. Then refer to the *conversion table*, locate your total for each motive, and write the corresponding MAO-C index number in the blank provided on this matrix sheet.

Next, for each horizontal row on the matrix, which represents a dimension of organizational climate, write the dominant motive (the one with the highest number in the row) and the backup motive (the one with the next-highest number) in the blanks provided (see the two vertical columns on the extreme right of the matrix). The dominant and backup columns are helpful in diagnosing and in planning action to improve the motivational climate of the organization or unit. Finally, determine which motives appear most often in the dominant and backup columns and write these motives in the blanks provided for *overall dominant motive* and *overall backup motive*.

| Dimensions of Organizational Climate | Motives | | | | | | | |
	Achievement	Expert Influence	Extension	Control	Dependency	Affiliation	Dominant (Abbreviate as necessary)	Backup (Abbreviate as necessary)
1. Orientation								
2. Interpersonal relationships								
3. Supervision								
4. Problem management								
5. Management of mistakes								
6. Conflict management								
7. Communication								
8. Decision making								
9. Trust								
10. Management of rewards								
11. Risk taking								
12. Innovation and change								
Total Scores							Overall Dominant Motive	Overall Backup Motive
MAO-C Index								

MOTIVATIONAL ANALYSIS
OF ORGANIZATIONS—CLIMATE (MAO-C)
SCORING KEY

Dimensions of Organizational Climate	Achievement	Expert Influence	Extension	Control	Dependency	Affiliation
1. Orientation	c	f	b	d	a	e
2. Interpersonal relationships	d	a	f	c	e	b
3. Supervision	d	e	c	a	b	f
4. Problem management	a	b	d	f	e	c
5. Management of mistakes	d	f	c	b	e	a
6. Conflict management	a	f	e	d	c	b
7. Communication	d	c	e	f	a	b
8. Decision making	c	e	f	d	b	a
9. Trust	f	d	e	a	c	b
10. Management of rewards	a	b	d	e	c	f
11. Risk taking	f	c	e	b	d	a
12. Innovation and change	e	a	d	b	c	f

Conversion Table

Score	Index	Score	Index	Score	Index	Score	Index	Score	Index
12	0	25	21	37	41	49	61	61	81
13	2	26	23	38	43	50	63	62	83
14	3	27	25	39	45	51	65	63	85
15	5	28	26	40	46	52	66	64	86
16	7	29	28	41	48	53	68	65	88
17	8	30	30	42	50	54	70	66	90
18	10	31	31	43	51	55	71	67	91
19	12	32	33	44	53	56	73	68	93
20	13	33	35	45	55	57	75	69	95
21	15	34	36	46	56	58	76	70	96
22	17	35	38	47	58	59	78	71	98
23	18	36	40	48	60	60	80	72	100
24	19								

INTRODUCTION TO THE
PROFESSIONAL DEVELOPMENT SECTION

This is the sixth year of the *Annual's* Professional Development section. In the 1984 *Annual* we inaugurated this section to bring together a variety of materials that would be useful to human resource development (HRD) practitioners in their personal and professional development. These materials, written by professionals for professionals, provide information about the trends that are at the cutting edge of the rapidly developing, ever-changing field of human resource development: the directions in which the field is heading; new technologies (and new uses of old technologies); the dilemmas experienced by HRD professionals in their daily work; new areas for application; new processes, perspectives, outlooks, and theoretical developments; and attempts to integrate specific content areas.

This section includes articles that HRD professionals can bring to the attention of management or use in a training session. Such articles often are useful in documenting or supporting a position or in explaining a complex or subtle point. These articles also can be used to help HRD professionals to ''sell'' a broader understanding of the HRD function to line managers who need distance, time, and documentation in order to modify their views or to support their emerging understanding.

The Professional Development section includes the contents that previously were found in the Lecturette, Theory and Practice, and Resources sections of the first twelve *Annuals*. This year's section consists of eight articles. The section begins with ''New Age Training Technologies: The Best and the Safest,'' which presents a comprehensive analysis of New Age training and its impact as well as a thorough discussion of the most effective ways to use the safest technologies available. The next article, ''Creative Risk Taking,'' emphasizes the need for situationally specific risk taking, describes various styles of risk taking, and presents profiles of creative versus addicted risk takers.

''Evaluation: Issues First, Methodology Second'' tackles a difficult issue being faced by trainers: the requirement to evaluate training in bottom-line terms. This article presents a way to respond to this requirement with integrity, and it offers a model for guiding the planning of an evaluation project.

''Leadership Is in the Eye of the Follower'' presents the results of surveys of more than ten thousand managers, who were asked what they look for in leaders. The article describes the qualities cited—honesty, competence, being forward-looking, inspiration, and credibility—as well as leadership practices that help leaders to manifest these qualities. The next article, ''Fostering Intrapreneurship in Organizations,'' deals with another kind of leader, the ''intrapreneur'' who creates innovation within an organization. This piece suggests ways in which an organization can encourage innovation and empower intrapreneurs as well as ways in which an HRD practitioner can help in this process.

Three articles offer models. "A Model for the Executive Management of Transformational Change" defines transformational change in an organization, presents the prerequisites of such change, offers a model for accomplishing transformational change, and illustrates the use of the model in case studies. "Model A: A Design, Assessment, and Facilitation Template in the Pursuit of Excellence" presents a model that can be used in an organization to design, assess, or facilitate the functioning of the entire company or a unit within the company. The last article, "A Causal Model of Organizational Performance," answers the need for a model of organizational performance that predicts behavior and performance consequences—a model that deals with cause (organizational conditions) and effect (resultant performance).

As usual, the range of topics covered in this section is broad; not every article will appeal to every reader. Nevertheless, the range and scope of what we offer should encourage a good deal of thought-provoking, serious discussion about where the field of HRD is now and where it is going.

NEW AGE TRAINING TECHNOLOGIES: THE BEST AND THE SAFEST

Beverly Byrum

The *New Age* is influencing many different arenas (Friedrich, 1987; Trachtenberg, 1987; Zemke, 1987):

1. *New Age books are finding a place of their own.* Bantam Books reports that its New Age titles have increased tenfold in the past decade and that the number of New Age book stores has doubled in the past five years, bringing the total to about 2,500. Publishers estimate total sales to be at least $100 million. Bantam, Simon & Schuster, and Random House all produce New Age books in cassette form.

2. *New Age periodicals are being born. New Age Journal* counts 150,000 readers, and *WholeLife* counts 60,000 readers. Other magazines, such as *Brain/Mind Bulletin, East/West Journal,* and *Body Mind Spirit,* contribute to the proliferation of New Age ideas.

3. *New Age music is making a name for itself.* The Grammy Awards now have a special category for New Age music, and the number of radio stations playing New Age music is increasing. Windham Hill Productions, a New Age record company, estimates that it will sell $50 million of its own label this year.

4. *New Age healing is gaining hold.* The American Medical Association reports that 10,000 doctors practice holistic medicine. Nurses are taught therapeutic touch to help patients to deal with pain and illness. In his book *Love, Medicine and Miracles,* surgeon Bernie Siegel discusses alternative methods of healing (Siegel, 1987). Sales of crystals used for healing account for $100 million a year.

5. *New Age is infiltrating the corporation.* Stockbrokers use astrology, millionaires use psychics, and investment bankers talk about past-life experiences. The United States Army has commissioned a West Coast firm to explore not only the military potential of meditation and extrasensory perception but also the feasibility of conducting non-traditional training programs based on these New Age techniques. Werner Erhard sells his Transformational Technologies programs to managers in the Soviet Union and NASA. A firm called Innovation Associates runs $15,000 seminars to strengthen top management's commitment to a common purpose. Training consultants enter corporations to do everything from stress-management seminars to organizational transformation.

News about New Age is not all treated seriously. *Newsweek* (Miller, 1987) reports on "Corporate Mind Control," a description of the California Public Utilities Commission's investigation of complaints of mind control in Pacific Bell's mandatory Krone training program.[1] In other companies, employees who have refused to participate in New Age training have been fired and have taken legal action based on violation of their right to religious freedom. For example, a car dealer has filed suit against his former employer, maintaining that he was terminated for refusing to participate in a mandated New Age training program. Similarly, a human resources manager with Firestone Tire was fired for refusing to conduct a New Age training program; he filed suit and subsequently reached an out-of-court settlement with his employer.

Incidents like these bring into question the legality of mandating training that some say is against their beliefs; this casts another critical eye on New Age training. Two of the most widely read periodicals in the field of human resource development, *Training: The Magazine of Human Resources Development* and *Training and Development Journal*, recently printed major articles and letters to the editor about New Age training. Their overtones range from cautious at best to ominous at worst. Any trainer or consultant would certainly pause before using the psychotechnologies listed in an article entitled "New Age training in the workplace: Intrusive at best and malevolent at worst?" (Zemke, 1987).

New Age training was censured in human resource development (HRD) periodicals long before it attracted such heavy publicity in the mass-communication media. Gordon (1985) called New Age training "weirdness at large," claiming that it scored a 10 on "the woo-woo factor." New Age also bore the major brunt of the Training Zone Awards, given for dubious achievement in HRD, for the past three years. In fact, in 1988 New Age had its own categories of awards: "New Age Event of the Year" and "New Age Threat of the Year" (The Training Zone Awards, 1986, 1987, 1988).

However, not all of the commentary in HRD periodicals is negative. New Age is here, whatever it is, and it is something with which HRD practitioners need to contend. This article offers a definition of New Age, an identification of the issues involved, a description of New Age training technologies, an analysis of the best and safest of these technologies, and a discussion of how they might best be delivered and what results and benefits to expect.

A DEFINITION OF NEW AGE

Friedrich (1987) states most concisely the problem involved in defining New Age: "There is no unanimity of New Age belief in anything." However, *The Guide to New Age Living,* published by *New Age Journal,* a widely read publication of New Age material, attempts a collective definition of New Age thinking. The author quotes a variety of New Age thinkers and then summarizes their definitions: "New age thinking can be characterized as a form of utopianism, the desire to create a better society, a 'new age' in which humanity lives in harmony with itself, nature, and the cosmos" (Adolph, 1988, p. 6).

---

[1]Charles Krone is a management consultant; Krone training is based on the teachings of George Gurdjieff, Armenian philosopher and mystic. Pacific Bell employees objected to the training, which was billed as "Leadership Development" and complained to the Utilities Commission that the exercises were mind-control sessions.

Some view New Age as a resurrection of the Human Potential Movement (Zemke, 1987). Others who are not aligned with the New Age movement define it in various ways. For example, Burrows (1986, p. 22) defines it negatively and abstractly with, "...ways that glorify the self, deny the reality of human depravity, and hold out pure, contentless experience as ultimate truth and the final arbiter of meaning and value." Ferguson, on the other hand, is more positive and concrete: "[New Age] sees us as stewards of all our resources, inner and outer. It says we are *not* victims, not pawns, not limited by conditions or conditioning" (cited in Adolph, 1988).

A recent survey gleaned notions of New Age from American Society for Training and Development chapter members who had neither studied New Age, promoted it, nor carried on a crusade against it. Fifty-nine percent were intuitively close in their responses when asked "What does the term New Age Training Technology suggest to you?" Their responses included the following:

- Self-improvement;
- Taking self-responsibility;
- Self-expanding;
- Holistic attitude toward training;
- Opens a person up to full abilities;
- Using both sides of the brain; and
- Nontraditional, new methods.

The last statement summarizes the beliefs held in common about the New Age training technologies born of New Age thinking. New Age thinking is a willingness to explore nontraditional lifestyle alternatives; as Carlson (1987) maintains, New Age training technologies are those that depart "from traditional systems of both teaching and learning...to empower employees to maximize both their potential and their inner resources" (p. 18).

New Age training technologies create *New Age Learning*, which is based on different assumptions than traditional learning, as outlined in Figure 1 (Meier, 1985). The disparity of definitions and feelings about New Age training reflect the controversy it stimulates among proponents and opponents alike. *Training and Development Journal* reported, "As the general level of human consciousness continues to evolve in our culture, training in the use of the 'higher self' for improving job performance and satisfaction will become more commonplace" (Trends in Training, 1986, p. 6). What began as an innocent report ended in "sounding the alarm" and vicious attacks on New Age training in general.

ISSUES AFFECTING ACCEPTANCE OF NEW AGE TRAINING TECHNOLOGIES

Three major issues plague the acceptance of New Age training technologies. First and most significant is the religious issue. Though *New Age Journal* contends that "the New Age Movement is not a religion" (Adolph, 1988, p. 10), some Christians believe

Dimension	Traditional Learning	New Age Learning
Training Concern	External behavior	Whole person
Mind focus	Rational	All mind states
Aim	Fill mind with information	Stimulate mind to release full powers
Effectiveness judged by	Standardized program	Individualized program
Knowledge viewed as	Fixed	Changing
Learning seen as	Work	Joyful

Figure 1. Traditional Learning Versus New Age Learning

that New Age thinking and, therefore, training associated with it are ''demonic'' (Burrows, 1986); are universally anti-Christian (Burrows, 1986); teach ''a false religion'' (Deo, 1987); and promote a world view of ''monism'' and ''spiritism...involving occult correspondence'' (Watring, 1987). Because New Age training is said to create religious conflict in employees forced to participate, the religious issue becomes a legal one.

The second major issue is the charge of *brainwashing* or *mind control*, as in the Pacific Bell/Krone case. Participants may be asked to suspend critical judgment (Zemke, 1987) or to enter a trancelike state in which they are subject to suggestion (Watring, 1987), which, Carlson (1987) maintains, can cause emotional distress. On the lighter side, New Age training claims are seen as humorously irrational, objects of intellectual derision that are mocked in the periodical *Training* by issuing awards for silliness rather than taking them seriously. Some people are alarmed rather than amused and allege that New Age training causes thousands of instances of debilitating effects which ''hurtle [trainees] into flights of uncontrollable fantasy or throw them into the depths of despair...[as]...the fragile balance between intellect, sensory response, judgment, and action does not always survive a New Age Training'' (Garvey, 1987).

A third issue is distrust of the profit being made by New Age gurus. Reports about Shirley MacLaine, who is funding a spiritual center in Colorado with the proceeds from her seminars (Friedrich, 1987; Zemke, 1987), J.Z. Knight, who channels a $400-a-session spirit (Friedrich, 1987; Hackett, 1986), or other New Age proponents who make money from their offerings meet with much skepticism. Viewed as ''new money-making adventures'' (Showers, 1987), New Age training technologies are distrusted because psychic sensitivity is being sold, according to Utne (Zemke, 1987), or because it is seen as promoting ''childish self-indulgence'' as opposed to anything seriously concerned with human development (Ornstein, 1986).

These issues are serious concerns for those in human resource development; methods for dealing appropriately with them will be explored in this article after New Age training technologies are identified.

AN OVERVIEW OF NEW AGE TRAINING TECHNOLOGIES

The term *New Age training technology* needs to be distinguished from more personal or spiritual New Age explorations (such as lucid dreaming, therapeutic prayer, channeling, crystal healing, past-life regression, or occult sciences like astrology, tarot, or numerology). These training technologies, or "psychotechnologies" (Zemke, 1987), include such diverse methods as affirmations, meditation, biofeedback, and self-hypnosis. The following sections explain New Age training technologies in accordance with the major proponents of each technology.

Affirmations

An affirmation is "a positive thought consciously chosen to be immersed in consciousness to produce a certain desired result" (Ray, 1981, p. 34). An affirmation is spoken or written as if the result is already present (Gawain, 1982); it directs one's mind, behavior, and, therefore, life (Leonard & Laut, 1983). Usually phrased in the first person present tense with a positive active verb, an affirmation describes that which is desired as already accomplished (for example, "I am calm and cool when my boss yells at me.") Affirmations are also called positive thinking, positive self-talk statements, positive programing, or thought selection (Helmstetter, 1986; Spice & Kopperl, 1984).

Affirmations work as follows: Beliefs present in one's mind create emotions, which influence actions, which in turn determine the results or effects on one's life. If the thoughts or beliefs are negative, results will be negative; if positive, the results will be positive. The intensity of results will be proportional to the depth of the belief and the intensity of the feeling (Helmstetter, 1986; Robbins, 1986). Changing negative beliefs to positive beliefs will change the circumstances of one's life. In training situations, a positive affirmation such as "I am now learning this new procedure easily and effortlessly" replaces a negative "I'll never get this right," in order to change the speed and ease of learning.

Biofeedback

The term *biofeedback* originated in experimental psychology. It refers to a continuous aural or visual report of changes in bodily reactions brought about by changes in thoughts and emotions (Marcer, 1986; Shealy, 1977; Smith, 1975). A feedback machine is electronically calibrated to communicate minute changes in brain waves, muscle contractions, temperature, or galvanic skin response. As Olson reports, a person can bring previously autonomic functions under conscious (if not rational or verbal) control (cited in Schwartz, 1987).

Biofeedback works by providing information about a bodily state frequently enough that the person can learn to recognize the link between thoughts and feelings and physical reactions. People can be taught to control their bodies, thereby producing relaxed and pleasant sensations instead of tense and painful ones. For example, an EEG indicates when a person is in the relaxed (alpha) brain-wave state as opposed to the normal daily activity (beta) brain-wave state. After exposure to EEG feedback and practice with it over a period of weeks under the guidance of a biofeedback professional, Olson reports that a person's subjective awareness of his body increases to the point that he no longer needs the artificial device and can consciously rely on internal psychophysical cues to exert control over his physical reactions (cited in Schwartz, 1987).

Although this technique is not likely to be used in group training, a project team manager consistently under the pressure of deadlines could use biofeedback to learn to keep himself relaxed and calm in the midst of constant rush and change.

Centering

Centering creates a sense of inner balance (mental, emotional, physical, spiritual) through mechanisms that focus the person on a single point. Using these techniques pulls the mind and body away from external stimuli, detaching and stabilizing them. Centering is a path to meditation rather than a substitute for it. Centering devices, such as focusing on a word, phrase, or object, prepare one for a deep state of spiritual communion; when a practitioner is advanced enough, the centering technique can be discarded and meditation can be entered directly. Westerners consider centering to be practical meditation, or meditation used for purposes other than spiritual enlightenment (Carrington, 1977). For example, participants in a training session could be asked to close their eyes, ''go inside,'' and pay attention to their breathing, allowing all parts of themselves to achieve harmonious balance before beginning a difficult task.

Dianetics

Dianetics, the foundation of Scientology, is ''a science of mind'' following the ''natural laws of thought'' (Hubbard, 1978). Negative past events *(engrams)* are stored as cellular traces in the body structure and can trigger irrational actions (Hubbard, 1978). Dianetics works by *clearing*, eliminating negative past events by *auditing*, or *pastoral counseling*. A specially trained auditor listens, asks questions, recognizes psychological reactions by using an *E-meter* (a device that records electrical resistance in the hands), and probes reactions to help the client find the answers that will lead him to clear (Henderson, 1975).

Clearing might be used in a counseling session with an employee who reacts to a question about his work environment, and when probed more deeply, finds the feeling related to a childhood experience. He then is guided to re-experience the childhood situation and emotion; as he resolves it, he simultaneously resolves his feelings about the work situation. Practitioners believe that with this particular form of self-actualization, every aspect of the person improves, including posture, health, and vision (Henderson, 1975).

Guided Imagery

Guided imagery gives external direction to the way a person represents objects and experiences to his mind. These images might be visual, auditory, or kinesthetic (Zilbergeld & Lazarus, 1987). In guided imagery, a facilitator either suggests the outline of an experience and the person imaging completes it with personal information, or the facilitator suggests an exact sequence, such as is used in relaxing each muscle of the body in turn (Carrington, 1977).

Guided imagery works by allowing a person to release the analytical part of his mind to a guide who leads him to receive information from the intuitive part of the mind, which will then be helpful in problem solving. This information may provide answers, emotions, or experiences that were formerly subconscious or blocked. For example, a common unstructured guided imagery is the *expert within*. In this experience, a person is given the framework of speaking to a wise person, asking a question and receiving an answer. With these minimal instructions, each person creates his own image of a wise person, his own question, and his own answer. This imagery is said to carry great power for influencing thoughts and behavior (Meier, 1984). Sometimes, for relaxation, a facilitator may conduct a guided imagery that is more detailed and structured, such as describing a beach, the sun, a gentle breeze, and the sound of waves; the participant is asked to see and hear these things and then is guided through a relaxation sequence.

Meditation

Meditation is a method of attaining spiritual development through disciplines of concentration (practices that involve thinking about meaning) and/or contemplation (practices that control thought by focusing on one object, internal or external to the meditator) (Bloomfield, Cain, Jaffe, & Kory, 1975). Meditational practices also can be categorized by the aspect of human experience addressed:

1. *Intellectual,* or a deep mental understanding of reality;
2. *Emotional,* or an expansion of positive emotions like love;
3. *Bodily,* or complete absorption in movement; and
4. *Action,* or the practice of a particular kind of skill useful to others (LeShan, 1974).

In addition to helping a person to attain spiritual development, meditation also is used practically, for the purpose of bettering one's experience of life. Many of the techniques are the same ones used for spiritual development; however, the goals are more limited (Carrington, 1977). As in guided imagery, meditations may be structured (those that define precisely what internal experience one is seeking) or unstructured (those that allow one to experience a subject, such as compassion, and concomitant thoughts and feelings) (LeShan, 1974).

Meditation works by providing a nondistracting, focusing experience, a disengagement from the continuous impressions of normal living (Bloomfield et al., 1975) This disengagement allows relaxation by altering the rhythm of the brain waves, either by changing them or by evening them out so that they pulsate together, thus slowing bodily functions (Carrington, 1977). Relaxing and focusing reduces stress and tension and may provide side benefits, such as more positive emotions and outlook. Researchers believe that the ability to use focused attention disconnects thinking and emotional systems from each other, thus allowing a state of continued relaxed alertness (Smith, 1975). Permissive and unstructured meditation might be used in training before a strategic planning session.

Transcendental Meditation (TM) is one of the most commonly described methods of meditation. Its key element is a mantra, assigned by a trained TM teacher. Use of the mantra moves one's attention from the active, fully developed thought level of the mind toward the depth of less elaborated, more basic, and simple thought (Bloomfield et al., 1975). Whereas other types of meditation use contemplation or concentration, TM uses the nonfocused, nonconcentrative repetition of the mantra to release the natural propensity of the mind to quiet itself; thus TM's results are considered to be spontaneous and to involve no forced learning (Bloomfield et al., 1975).

Neurolinguistic Programming (NLP)

Neurolinguistic programming originated as a therapeutic practice; it uses a detailed model of human experience and communication to make fast, deep, and lasting changes in human behavior (Bandler & Grinder, 1979).

This technique begins by determining the client's *representation system* from his language and eye movements. The three representation systems are categorized as follows:

1. *Visual:* "It's clear to me"—eyes up;

2. *Auditory:* "That sounds good"—eyes center or down left; and

3. *Kinesthetic:* "I don't like the feel of that proposal"—eyes down right.

A therapist matches or mirrors this representation system *(pacing)* to achieve rapport. Once rapport is established, the therapist or trainer can then change his or her own behavior *(leading)* to cause changes in the client (Bandler & Grinder, 1979; Robbins, 1986). For example, if a client who is auditory becomes anxious when his or her supervisor yells, the facilitator can teach the client to switch to a visual mode when the supervisor is present. The yelling then will not cause the same reaction. Or, a trainer can lead a visual participant to reduce anxiety about learning a new procedure by replacing a picture of failure with one of success.

Anchoring is a verbal response or physical movement that solidifies the client's desired feeling or behavior change. For example, when the client says something positive about his own abilities, the facilitator can anchor that feeling with a smile or a touch on the arm. Because it is important for the client to be able to use these skills on his own, *bridging,* or making an anchor out of the context itself, gives the client the power to change. The client might be asked to think about situations in which he or she would like to feel competent. As the client creates those situations, the facilitator touches the client's arm and says, "When you are in these situations, you will feel this touch''; this anchor will remind the client to feel competent (Bandler & Grinder, 1979). Anchors ground the client in re-experiencing a success; an anchor is developed, such as touching the thumb and middle finger together, and the client can use that anchor whenever he needs to feel powerful and resourceful (Robbins, 1986).

Reframing is another technique used to ensure that other behaviors or motives do not obstruct change. Reframing works to generate options, other than the present behavior, to satisfy the client's goals. For example, if a client receives negative feedback about his or her behavior, the consultant asks the client what the behavior was intended to achieve, then helps the client discover alternative behaviors (Bandler & Grinder, 1979). Reframing works by changing the content (for example, ''I'm not failing, I'm just discovering what won't work'') or by changing the context (such as, ''My spouse may think I'm too aggressive at home, but it's a terrific quality to have at work'') (Robbins, 1986).

Metaphor, a symbolic representation of ideas, is another NLP technique. Metaphors work by linking the unfamiliar to the familiar; for example, in dealing with computer anxiety, fears might be compared to first learning to ride a bicycle or to write in cursive (Ludwig & Menendez, 1985).

Neurolinguistic programming is used in therapy for remedial, functional change and for generative, creative change (Bandler & Grinder, 1979). This technique also is taught to managers and trainers to improve interpersonal and persuasive skills (Ludwig & Menendez, 1985; Robbins, 1986).

Relaxation

Relaxation is the absence of muscular tension and the accompanying mental calm. Relaxation works by slowing breathing and metabolic rates (Carrington, 1977), reducing oxygen consumption, eliminating carbon dioxide from the system, and minimizing the frequency of visual and auditory imagery and stimuli. As a consequence, both thought and emotional processes diminish (Shealy, 1977). Relaxation techniques may be used in training in the same ways as suggested meditation or as preparation for another technique, such as affirmation.

One of the most well-known methods for achieving relaxation is the *relaxation response*. This technique calls for four steps to be followed:

1. *Select a quiet environment* with few distractions;
2. *Use a constant, repetitive stimulus* as a mental device to help minimize externally focused, distracting thoughts (a word, phrase, or gazing at an object while paying attention to breathing);
3. *Maintain a passive attitude* by not being concerned about the concentration level, allowing thoughts to appear if they will and then returning to the mental device, without worrying about performance; and
4. *Relax muscles* by sitting (not lying) in a comfortable position and avoid falling asleep (Benson, 1975).

Another common technique is *progressive relaxation*. In this technique, participants are instructed to tighten muscles in each muscle group and then to relax them, thus learning to identify the difference (Jacobson, 1938). Typically, the client is taught to go through progressive tensing and relaxing (Marcer, 1986) and eventually learns to relax without tensing the muscles first (Jacobson, 1938).

Self-Hypnosis

Self-hypnosis is sometimes called autogenic (meaning self-created) training (Smith, 1975). It involves focused attention on suggestions one gives oneself in a self-induced trance (Henderson, 1975; Shealy, 1977).

Self-hypnosis works ". . . [by] playing a game with yourself. Your conscious and subconscious make a contract that after certain rituals and signals your subconscious will accept as true some untruths your conscious may suggest" (Henderson, 1975, p. 14).

A light, goal-oriented trance state is the result; attention narrows to one or two thoughts, thereby reducing awareness of external surroundings and usual ways of perceiving and thinking (Carrington,. 1977). Suggestions first target muscular and breathing outcomes, such as "My arms are heavy, my heartbeat is calm" and later cognitive or action outcomes, such as "I am now working effortlessly on this article" (Marcer, 1986; Shealy, 1977). Suggestions also can vary by being directed to a present state (such as, "I am now relaxed") or a future state, sometimes called post-hypnotic suggestion (Zilbergeld & Lazarus, 1987) (for example, "When I proceed to write my proposal, ideas will come easily to me"). Suggestions can be given at the moment in a state of relaxation or they can be tape-recorded to reduce the amount of thinking necessary and to increase receptivity (Zilbergeld & Lazarus, 1987). Because the subconscious takes what it is given, affirmations are useful for positive results (Murphy, 1963).

Self-hypnosis is used in mental training (Zilbergeld & Lazarus, 1987), for tension release leading to better sleep, in management of stress and increased efficiency (Carrington, 1977), and under the term self-suggestion to treat neurotic, compulsive, and depressive disorders as well as numerous physiological maladies (Romen, 1981). Autogenic training can go beyond healing to achieve a state of optimum health (Pelletier, 1980).

Silva Mind Control

Silva Mind Control is a process of changing one's awareness from everyday consciousness (beta) to a lower frequency consciousness (alpha) for better problem solving and increased memory, efficiency, and creativity. This method "uses the mind to mind itself" by first physical and mental relaxation, then affirmation, visualization, and anchoring (Silva & Stone, 1983, pp. 93-94).

The suggested relaxation method consists of turning the eyes upward and counting back from one hundred to one (with practice, a count from five to one will suffice). The suggested anchor is to put three fingers together. The suggested vision process is to see the situation first as it is; then to see the situation in the process of positive change, viewing the second image on the left to activate the right brain; and finally, to see the situation resolved (Silva & Stone, 1983). This combination can be used to accomplish personal goals, to increase group commitment, or to maintain energy and enthusiasm. Those who continue the training improve their extrasensory perception; some even engage in psychic healing.

Suggestology

Suggestology is the science of the art of freeing and stimulating the personality, both under guidance and alone. *Suggestopedy* is its application in instruction (Lozanov, 1978). The goal of suggestopedy is to help people to use both the body and the mind at peak efficiency to develop supermemory and superlearning capacities (Ostrander & Schroeder, 1979).

Suggestopedy operates on the principles of joy and relaxation in learning, integration of conscious and paraconscious brain activity, and maximum use of reserve capacities (Lozanov, 1978). The American method works by first training the participants in relaxation, visualization, breathing, and positive affirmations. Next, the material to be learned is presented dramatically with readings, plays, and games. The last or memory-reinforcement session requires the participants to relax and to breathe deeply and rhythmically in time to Baroque music, while the instructor recites or chants in time to the music, using three different intonations (Ostrander & Schroeder, 1979).

Suggestopedy is used in education to enhance foreign language learning and to increase memory. During the learning process, it also has beneficial psychological and physical side effects (Lozanov, 1978). Additionally it has been used to heal and control pain and to develop extrasensory abilities (Ostrander & Schroeder, 1979).

Visualization

Visualization uses the imagination to create experience in one or more sensory modes. Visualization can be either receptive, relaxing and allowing images and impressions to surface as they will; or active, consciously choosing or creating what is desired to be felt or experienced (Gawain, 1982). Active visualization "is not the same as wishful thinking. . . it is enlisting the powerful resources of human imagination in systematic and proven ways to achieve certain ends" (Zilbergeld & Lazarus, 1987, p. 130).

Receptive visualization works by reducing the analytical activity of the brain, allowing subconscious thoughts, emotions, ideas, or insights to emerge. A common example of this type of visualization is having a solution to a researched problem emerge in a state of quiet. Active visualization works by giving form to thought; if a thought is held in attention, eventually its material form is created (Gawain, 1982). The most powerful visualizations, those most likely to result in tangible effects are specific, clear, controlled, positive, active, simple, repeated, and self-rewarding. Repeated visualization works to change one's view of self, which is a means of changing identity; the new identity makes it more feasible to become and to do what is being visualized (Simonton, Matthews-Simonton, & Creighton, 1978; Zilbergeld & Lazarus, 1987). An example of active visualization is creating an image of a new job or a successful training program.

Yoga

Yoga is a Hindu practice that takes four forms:

1. *Raja yoga,* meditation through contemplation and concentration on universal truths;

2. *Jnana yoga,* meditation on the various natures of one's self;

3. *Karma yoga,* active meditation or the path of service to others; and

4. *Bhaki yoga,* meditation using prayer and chanting for the purpose of praising others and divinity.

Hatha yoga, which is a preparation for any of these four forms, follows the principle that a healthy body means a healthy mind. Hatha yoga uses breathing exercises and postures in a set of systematic movements designed to keep the body in a constant balance state (Oki, 1970). Its postures *(asanas)* give the body strength and stimulation, while the breathing exercises *(pranayama)* increase energy and relaxation. Both work to cleanse the internal body (Henderson, 1975). Additionally, the deep calm acquired through the consistent practice of yoga helps the mind to function fully and exceptionally (Oki, 1970).

Yoga is used as a means of spiritual enlightenment, which was its original purpose (Henderson, 1975). However, in the Western world, hatha yoga is more often used as a form of exercise to promote good health, to alleviate stress and its related illnesses (Brena, 1972; Udupa, 1978), to increase attractiveness and sexuality (Phelan & Volin, 1963), and to energize and to relax the body and mind.

Summary of New Age Training Technologies

Many of the techniques described in this section involve inducing a state of relaxation and/or imagining. In some techniques, this state is used to minimize a dysfunctional condition; in others, the technique is used to connect with a higher self or a higher power for self-actualization or spiritual enlightenment. The next section will demonstrate how the best and safest of these techniques can be used in human resource development to maximize performance.

THE BEST AND THE SAFEST OF NEW AGE TRAINING TECHNOLOGIES

Relaxation, affirmation, and visualization emerge as the best and safest of the New Age training technologies for the following reasons:

1. They combine both the analytical and the intuitive functions of the brain (Meier, 1984), especially if the experience is adequately explained and processed; therefore, suspension of critical judgment is less of a problem than with other techniques.

2. They are "readily available, easy to learn, and simple to use. . .[they] harness natural abilities" (Zilbergeld & Lazarus, 1987, p. 12).

3. They empower the participants to control the process (choosing whether or not to relax and how, determining their own affirmations, and creating their own visualizations) because the trainer gives process instructions rather than content instructions.

4. They have a proven success record in the learning field (Ostrander & Schroeder, 1979) and the human resource development field (Chalofsky, 1987; Gentilman & Nelson, 1983; Robinson, 1984; Spice & Kopperl, 1984; Wilson, 1987).

Trainers who successfully use these New Age training technologies:

- Know the purposes and effects of the techniques;
- Have been trained in the processes themselves;
- Experience positive personal results with the techniques;
- Use the techniques voluntarily; and
- Frame the training in familiar concepts to participants and in terms of its dollar value to management.

In order for the techniques to be safe (both legally and psychologically) as well as workable, participants must be in control of choosing and using the techniques (Anderson, 1987; Fitzgerald, 1987a; Robinson, 1985). To put participants in control, or to *empower* them, trainers should follow six key steps:

1. *Meet in advance* with a cross-section team of employees to plan the program and adapt it to local needs; when the program is devoted solely to teaching the techniques, run a pilot program. Stress that employee use of the techniques must not be tied to retention, evaluation, or promotion.

2. *Present the techniques as voluntary learning aids* in a program, giving an alternative technique to achieve the same result wherever possible; although the techniques should not be tied to a particular value system, the trainer should be willing to discuss his own value system if the question arises. Participants must be allowed to stop at any time in the process. If teaching the techniques constitutes the program, the entire program should be voluntary.

3. *Explain the techniques thoroughly,* reviewing the assumptions governing the technique, documenting the technique statistically whenever possible, and explaining what is going to happen, the expected results, and step-by-step instructions in the process. Present the techniques in language familiar and acceptable to the participants first, then give them their formal names so that the participants will not feel duped. If the techniques constitute the program, the techniques to be covered should be publicized thoroughly so that participants will be operating from informed consent. Present the techniques in increments, one or two at a time. Present unfamiliar techniques as experiments that can be tried and discarded if they do not suit an individual's style.

4. *Process the outcomes thoroughly* during the training session; trainees should be encouraged to discuss and to analyze any experiences they had while using the techniques.

5. *Support practice outside the session* by including handouts of blank work sheets (if required by the technique) and the instructions used during the session. Suggest that a journal be kept of the experiences and their short- and long-term consequences.

6. *Encourage completion of an action plan* for both the participants and the trainer; schedule follow-up sessions if at all possible as well as sessions with the participants' supervisors for the purpose of common understanding and environmental support.

How To Present Relaxation, Affirmation, and Visualization Techniques

Successful presentation of the New Age training techniques of relaxation, affirmation, and visualization requires careful planning on the part of the trainer. Ten components will be described, each of which is critical to the participants' understanding and acceptance of the techniques.

1. State the Purpose of the Technique

One purpose of the technique can be a means to a specific training goal; for example, "To ensure success with the sales skills learned last week, this technique can help you to retain what you've learned, to use it with your customers, and to pattern yourselves for success." A second purpose could be stated as a learning goal itself: "The purpose of this technique is to provide you with more control over the use of your mind, so that you are more likely to achieve success in whatever you desire."

2. Introduce the Technique in Familiar Language

The following are examples of introductions in familiar terms: "All of these techniques are called 'accelerated learning techniques' and can be considered as stress-free, fast-learning methods to develop memory and to improve performance."

Relaxation. "This technique quite simply is called relaxation; it relaxes you and helps you to reduce the tension that builds up in your body."

Affirmation. "This technique is called 'positive talk' or 'positive statement' or 'self-fulfilling prophecy'; some know it as 'affirmation.' It helps you create what you desire by focusing on the realization of your goal through positive thinking."

Visualization. "This technique is called 'imaging' or 'visioning' or 'envisioning'; some know it as 'visualization.' It helps you experience what you want to happen by seeing, by hearing, or by feeling. By using your senses, you will bring more force to materializing your goal."

3. Support the Use of the Technique

The following types of statements could be given to support the use of the techniques: "According to Sheila Ostrander and Lynn Schroeder, who have researched alternative learning systems for over fifteen years and published their methods in *Super-Learning* (Ostrander & Schroeder, 1979), these techniques contribute to supermemory, superperformance, and super-rapport. Weston Agor, after discovering that top managers scored higher than middle or lower managers in underlying intuitive ability, began using these techniques to teach managers how to develop *intuitive management* (Agor, 1984a, 1984b). If you are interested in further documentation or evidence that these techniques work, I will provide a bibliography at the end of the session."

Relaxation. "According to Herbert Benson, M.D., relaxation has been used to reduce common stress-related problems such as headaches and tension and even more serious illnesses, such as heart disease and cancer (Benson, 1975; Benson, 1984). *The Hardy Executive* (Maddi & Kobasa, 1984) demonstrated from an eight-year study of 259 managers in a stressful environment that those who reach the top and manage not to suffer from the climb are skilled at *focusing,* a method that begins with relaxation. In *Corporate Pathfinders* Leavitt (1986) found from a historical study of visionary people that relaxation and meditation heighten creativity."

Affirmation. "According to *What to Say When You Talk to Yourself* (Helmstetter, 1986), positive self-talk has been used successfully to change habits, to solve problems, and to accomplish goals. A study of over five hundred *peak performers* (Garfield, 1986) indicated that one of the aptitudes which helped them to perform was the ability to use positive thoughts, eliminating preconceived limitations. After an eight-year study of 259 managers in stressful environments, Maddi and Kobasa (1984) found that the *hardy executive* engaged in 'transformational coping' or thinking positively about events. Additionally, Bennis and Nanus (1985) studied ninety leaders and discovered that they had incredible self-confidence fueled by using words other than failure. Deborah Bright (1985) also found a high level of self-confidence in the 2,000 high-tech managers she studied for *Gearing Up for the Fast Lane*:

> High tech managers see themselves as better managers. . . . Such a self-image tends to function as a self-fulfilling prophecy. A manager who sincerely believes himself or herself to be more capable, more creative, more able to overcome myriad obstacles and achieve substantial goals is likely to become so. These managers who see themselves as different and better right off the mark set higher expectations for themselves and their work groups. They find exceptional energy and drive for performance at a higher than routine level. (pp. 2-3)"

Visualization. "According to two noted behavioral therapists, Zilbergeld and Lazarus (1987), they and their clients have experienced success in using visualization to deal with stressful situations and to accomplish goals. Great athletes, such as Mary Lou Retton, Greg Louganis, Bill Russell, and Jack Nicklaus, also use this technique. Successful corporate leaders also use 'vision' to mentally rehearse for events, to imagine alternative futures, to synthesize facts, and to keep themselves flexible (Bennis & Nanus, 1985; Brown & Weiner, 1984; Garfield, 1986; Leavitt, 1986). Probably the most powerful evidence of the power of visualization comes from cancer studies. As early as 1978, *Getting Well Again* reported that of patients considered medically incurable, 68.4 percent of those who visualized themselves getting well later showed no evidence of cancer (22.2 percent), showed remission (19.1 percent), or stability (27.1 percent) (Simonton et al., 1978)."

4. Relate It to the Participants' Experience

Each of these techniques can be described as situations and events common to everyday life, minimizing any fears participants may feel about trying the technique. The following examples describe the techniques in this way.

Relaxation. "You've probably helped yourself relax by taking a coffee break, by talking to a friend, or by watching TV. Closer to this method, you might have told yourself to relax and take a deep breath when in a pressured situation."

Affirmation. "Perhaps you've had experience with negative self-talk; you told yourself that you would have a terrible day and you did! You also might have had positive experiences because you rehearsed the way you wanted an event to turn out. Perhaps you believed that the day would be *your* day and you received that praise or raise."

Visualization. "You've probably pictured yourself in a situation many times or maybe you've actually seen in your mind the house or car you've always wanted or the sign on your office door that says you've arrived."

5. Indicate How the Technique Has Worked for You

Personal examples (such as the following) of ways in which relaxation, affirmation, and visualization work for the trainer help participants to feel more comfortable with the techniques.

Relaxation. "I use relaxation exercises before I have meetings with my boss about disagreements we share."

Affirmation. "I use positive self-talk to get training proposals accepted."

Visualization. "I use imagining to see myself giving successful presentations."

6. Indicate That the Technique Is Voluntary

Teaching the technique should be preceded by the following type of statement: "This technique is voluntary, so you don't have to do it if you feel uncomfortable with it.

It is simply one method of achieving results. Probably what will be new is learning conscious control of the technique and setting aside a special time to use it, so you may want to experiment with it today. If there are any techniques with which you feel uncomfortable, use this time to review your notes or take a break." (If several people are not willing, they could work on a group task that would target the same outcome for which the technique is designed.)

7. Give an Overview of What Will Happen

In each case, let the participants know briefly what they can expect to happen during the entire exercise—as indicated in the following examples.

Relaxation. "We'll first get into a comfortable position, then pay attention to our breathing, then begin to relax various muscle groups throughout the body until the entire body is relaxed."

Affirmation. "We'll first think of some goals you want to achieve, than narrow to one focus goal. Then we'll make some positive statements about that goal and work with it to see what may prevent it from occurring and how to counteract those obstacles."

Visualization. "We'll start by closing our eyes, if that is comfortable for you, then we'll experience what you want by whatever sense is easiest for you: sight, hearing, or feeling. After the visualization, we'll review ways to strengthen the experience."

8. Take Participants Through the Process

Go through the process step by step, reminding the participants why they are doing each step and what they are trying to accomplish. Below are some examples.

Relaxation. "You may find it easier to do this exercise if you get comfortable in your chair. Some people find it best to put both feet on the floor, to have their backs fully supported by the chair, and to put their arms on the sides of the chair or their hands in their laps. You may want to try that now or any other position that is most comfortable for you. Some also find that closing their eyes helps them to focus and to avoid distractions; however, you can allow your eyes to focus wherever you wish. In the position that is comfortable for you, begin to focus on your breathing. You don't have to change it or control it; you will probably find it slowing down as you pay attention to it. Continue that focus for a moment. Remember you can change position any time you wish to reach a greater level of relaxation and comfort.

"Now, imagine a pleasant feeling of warmth in your feet that relaxes them and releases tension. Allow any tension to leave and be replaced by a comfortable, warm, relaxed feeling. Now proceed to your ankles with that feeling of pleasant warmth and relaxation and release the tension. When you are comfortable, take that feeling to your calves and relax them, letting the tension go, then your thighs, up to your torso, to your chest, now your back, imagining comfortable warmth spreading and tension leaving. Now your shoulders are pleasantly warm and relaxed; now all the tiny muscles in your face are relaxing, the tension leaving. Finally the top of your head, pleasantly warm and completely relaxed. Your entire body is relaxed, relaxed and warm and comfortable. Stay with that pleasant, totally relaxed feeling as long as you wish; when you feel ready, open your eyes and redirect your focus slowly and gently to something in the room. Then you may want to take a few moments to make some notes to yourself about that experience and its meaning for you.''

Affirmation. "Write down all the things you want to accomplish; they can be future-oriented or short-term or a mix of both. Then choose one goal to use in practicing this technique.

"State that goal in as many different ways as possible. Write your statements in the first person as things already accomplished or on their way to being accomplished; they need to be positive and active. This simple and direct method is the most effective way to make the statements work. We are more likely to make things happen if we involve ourselves by using 'I' in some positive action.

"Now choose one statement and write it at the top of a piece of paper. You will write it ten times in this session. Repetition reinforces; it also allows you to pay attention to any other thoughts, even negative ones, that come to mind. When these thoughts come to you, record them next to the positive statement.''

Negative thoughts interfere with achieving goals; therefore, participants should be instructed to counteract them in the following ways:

- Continue writing the positive thought until no more negative thoughts occur;
- Write that it will be all right if the negative occurs ("I'm okay if I don't own a Porsche");
- Look at what positive might lie underneath the negative ("If I don't make $25,000 in commissions, my boss won't have such high expectations of me");
- Dispute the negative, especially if it comes from the past ("I can do it. I've done harder things before"); or
- Create a new positive thought more basic and powerful than the original ("I can achieve anything I set my mind to do").

Additional instructions may include the following: "These methods take the power out of negative statements so that you do not spend time and energy programing yourself with the negative; instead you concentrate on the positive and strengthen yourself.

"Write your final positive statement again on a three-by-five card. Underline it, add exclamation points, anything you want. Then put it in your wallet and look at it often. You might make other copies and put them in various places as reminders. You also could write these thoughts several times daily or tape record them with other positive statements and listen to them often. These forms of repetition are recommended for the positive self-talk to work effectively.''

Visualization. "Think of some goal you'd like to achieve; just let anything come to mind. If it changes in the course of this process, that's okay. We're going to imagine that you are achieving or have achieved this goal. If you would like to try and 'see' or visualize yourself arriving at your goal or already there, it may be helpful to close your eyes. If you want to hear or feel the results, you can do it either way.

"As you begin to relax, feeling pleasantly warm and comfortable all over, you find that your breathing is regular and calm as your entire body relaxes. Your mind becomes quiet so that you can move inside to your mind's eye. Imagine that you are watching a movie screen; you are going to see, hear, or feel your goal being realized or already realized on that screen. Allow yourself, if possible, to see the picture you have created or hear the results or feel the experience. Imagine specifically what you are doing, what you are saying, what you are hearing, and how you are feeling. As you do this, fully experience the success you have created for yourself. When you are ready to leave that image, experience it once more—perhaps the happiness and success of it—and remember that you can capture that image again any time that you wish. It is in your power to do so. Come gently and slowly to focus on something in the room.

"If you'd now like to switch to a more analytical mode, take a few minutes to interpret what you experienced and jot down some notes about the implications and potential solutions. If you decide to use this technique, you may find it useful to keep a journal of your experiences. If any visualization produces significant or powerful images for you, you may want to represent those images in some way and display them where you can see them often."

9. Process the Experience

The purpose of this step is to ensure that participants understand thoroughly the technique they experienced and that they have the opportunity to express any questions or concerns. Examples are given below for helping participants to process the experience.

Relaxation. "I'd like to give you the opportunity to talk about how you reacted to that technique. Who would like to tell what he or she experienced? Did anyone else feel that way? Who felt something different? Who isn't sure? What are some themes we need to discuss? What do those themes seem to suggest about the relaxation technique? How do you think you might be able to adapt this technique for use on the job?"

Affirmation. "What were some of the positive statements you chose? What kind of thoughts came up in response to your writing? What did that tell you about your positive statement? What did you do to counteract any negative thoughts that surfaced? How did that work? What are you thinking or feeling about your positive statements right now? What's a theme about positive self-talk in this group right now? What do you think we can say that might be true about positive self-talk? What might that mean for you in your job?"

Visualization. "How did you react to imaging your goal realized? What was that experience like? How did it feel? What seems to be some common experience in the group? What does that seem to say about the technique of visualization? How might you use visualization to give you better experiences in your job? What other job-related applications might imaging have?"

For all (after the processing). "Is there anything left that someone would like to say? Are there any questions about the use of this technique? I will be available at the break to discuss this technique further with you."

10. Provide for Action and Follow-Up

A statement like the following is appropriate before the participants depart: "To get you started on transferring this technique to your job, fill out an action plan for how you will use the technique, for what purpose and when. We'll have a chance to see how this worked for you at our next session. Feel free to work with another person if you like. You will also notice that handouts are available that will allow you to walk through this process on your own whenever you wish. You may also wish to keep some kind of journal to record your experiences and their results."

Difficulties That May Be Encountered

If the preceding guidelines are followed carefully, most difficulties will be circumvented or their impact lessened. Any difficulties that do arise will probably take one of two forms: (1) resistance to the methods themselves or (2) a negative occurrence while using the technique.

Resistance to the Methods Themselves

After the techniques are explained and documented in the participants' own language and made voluntary, the remaining resistance most likely will be a product of one of the major issues mentioned at the beginning of this article. Some may argue that New Age training is against religious beliefs, as in the Pacific Bell case. In addition to reaffirming that use of the technique is voluntary, the trainer may wish to explain that even those who dispute these techniques from a religious point of view do not condemn them entirely. As Richard Watring, an evangelical Christian, explains, "I am not against all training technology more advanced than the lecture. In fact, the only so-called New Age techniques I greatly object to are those that depend on trainees' loss or suspension of [critical judgment]" (cited in Zemke, 1987, p. 30). Even *Christianity Today,* a conservative Christian publication states that some of the techniques "may seem neutral, even desirable...[and] have a legitimate function. What is objected to is placing them within a religious 'interpretive framework' or using them for 'devotional purposes'" (Burrows, 1986, p. 23). Again, if they are presented as a means to achieving some training goal, they should not be seen within a religious framework.

On the other hand, it seems inaccurate to state that these techniques are value free. If the techniques are used to solidify sales skills, then sales success is a value; if they are used to create corporate policy, then quality or service or profit or community may be values; if they are used in management development, then compassion and empathy or better performance management may be values. It has been asserted that great companies are "value-driven" (Peters & Waterman, 1980), often because their great leaders attend to values (Bennis & Nanus, 1985; Leavitt, 1986).

A second argument may stem from the *brainwashing* or "suspension of critical judgment" issue. Two responses can be made to this argument:

1. "Irrational" actions are different from "nonrational" or "arational" actions (Ornstein, 1986, p. 182).
2. When people choose to suspend critical judgment for the purposes of creativity or using intuition, for example, they can always get it back.

In fact, many management sources speak eloquently to the need for more nonlinear thinking to balance analytical, linear thinking (Agor, 1984a; Bennis & Nanus, 1985; Bright, 1985; Brown & Weiner, 1984; Garfield, 1986; Leavitt, 1986; Maddi & Kobasa, 1984). These responses can be explained and documented by reference to well-established sources in the field.

Negative Occurrences While Using the Technique

Any negative experience that occurs while using the technique (for example, if a participant becomes angry or sad) can be handled within the processing period when feelings are expressed. Because the techniques are presented as voluntary, the trainee can choose not to continue if the experience is too painful. If he wishes to continue and to express the feelings, he probably will receive support from the group. Of course, the trainer or consultant should be capable of and available for support (not therapy). Many other training techniques—role play, instrumentation, structured experiences, or even viewing a film—could produce the same potential problems. The profession has learned to handle these situations through competent processing.

RESULTS TO BE EXPECTED

If a trainer decides to use one or more of these New Age training techniques, certain results can be expected.

Benefits for Participants

Tangible results of New Age training technologies are discussed frequently and voluminously both in and outside training literature. Olympic athletes have used the techniques, with clear and internationally acclaimed results (Trachtenberg, 1987; Zilbergeld & Lazarus, 1987). The medical field cites positive results with more and more regularity (Benson, 1984; Siegel, 1987). Psychology continues to study the effects of these various techniques in normal healthy cases as well as abnormal ones (Burns, 1980; Carrington, 1977; Helmstetter, 1986; Romen, 1981; Zilbergeld & Lazarus, 1987).

Although no quantitative evaluative studies have been published, human resource development specialists use these techniques to produce results in the following areas:

- Whole-brain training (Herrmann, 1987);
- Learning skills (Meier, 1985);
- Program design (Chalofsky, 1987);

- Featuring skills (Gentilman & Nelson, 1983);
- Stress management (Jenner, 1986);
- Influencing subordinates' performance (Sandler, 1986);
- Changing the organization's future (Lynch, 1986);
- Improving performance (Friedrich, 1987);
- Motivating teamwork (Carlson, 1987); and
- Transforming large organizations (Veltrop, 1987).

Discussing results as the rewards of "mental training" (a combination of the technologies of visualization, affirmation, relaxation, and self-hypnosis), Zilbergeld & Lazarus (1987) conclude the following:

> There is hardly any situation in life that mental training can't help you deal with in a better, more constructive, and healthier way. No matter what you do, your mind is going to deal with every situation in one manner or another. Why not take steps to ensure that it works to your best advantage? (p. 216)

Benefits and Drawbacks for the Organization

Most of the results mentioned above can be seen as benefits to the employee and to the organization; if the employees learn all the skills New Age training technologies are being used to support, both they and the organization will surely profit. By learning to use relaxation, affirmation, and visualization as skills in their own right, employees may accrue some additional benefits:

1. *Employees will be more open to change,* knowing that they have some control over their own attitudes, options, actions, and reactions.

2. *Employees will be more able to concentrate,* focusing on the tasks before them.

3. *Employees will be more creative,* having greater resources for generating ideas and alternatives.

4. *Employees will be more responsible,* knowing that what happens is, at least in part, a result of how they manage their mental life.

5. *Employees will deal with others more effectively;* they will be more flexible and adaptable and know better how to control and to choose their actions and reactions.

6. *Employees will improve their personal lives,* which will in turn improve the work environment.

These techniques empower employees; empowered employees are more satisfied with themselves, and their work is more efficient, effective, and productive. New Age training techniques are available at a time when more organizations are being urged to empower their employees (Bennis, 1982; Bennis & Nanus, 1985; Bradford & Cohen, 1984; Bright, 1985; Garfield, 1986; Naisbitt & Aburdene, 1985; Pascarella, 1984).

Drawbacks to New Age training technologies are common to most training and development efforts. Some typical drawbacks are the following:

- Training takes time to deliver, reinforce, and support.
- Training costs money.
- Training may meet resistance.
- Training may stimulate certain individuals to take action of which management does not approve.

Although the last drawback can occur with any kind of training, empowered employees may feel more comfortable with confrontation. (Assertiveness training could have the same result.) They may also be more comfortable in leaving a situation they find untenable. (Problem solving and decision making could have the same result.) Finally, they may choose to make life choices that the organization would not deem beneficial, such as not working overtime or not doing the work required for a promotion. (Stress management could have the same result.) However, these outcomes are unlikely, because empowerment expands one's options rather than limiting them.

Impact on the Trainer

Knowing, using, and teaching these skills have the potential to produce the benefits all trainers desire, "If you truly want to reach [employees], work first with their self-talk" (Helmstetter, 1986, p. 96). By promoting more and longer term change, as well as leaving employees with flexible and adaptable skills for any situation, trainers will gain credibility, reputation, and influence. Expressed more forcefully, "The term *professional development* can never again denote only the acquisition of external skills and knowledge, but must include developing the full range of internal mental and spiritual skills as well" (Meier, 1984, p. 26).

Trainers will experience the same benefits as employees: They will feel more confident and competent and in more control of themselves and the situation. A list of ways trainers can use these techniques in training and development follows (Meier, 1984; Robinson, 1984):

- Learning factual material;
- Learning a system or a piece of equipment;
- Sorting and classifying data;
- Generating ideas;
- Solving problems;
- Resolving conflicts;
- Assessing "what-ifs;"
- Setting goals, planning for the future;
- Preparing for meetings;
- Determining organizational structure;
- Explaining concepts;
- Giving instructions;

- Devising changes in a physical setup;
- Sensing physical, mental, and emotional conditions;
- Establishing rapport;
- Designing curricula;
- Developing learning contracts;
- Tapping intuition;
- Patterning success; and
- Creating personal understanding and empowerment.

CONCLUSIONS

The best and safest of New Age training technologies are relaxation, affirmation, and visualization. Cutting edge literature such as *Leaders, Corporate Pathfinders, Managing for Excellence, Peak Performers, Super Managing, Gearing up for the Fast Lane, Reinventing the Corporation,* and *Thriving on Chaos* refer to these techniques as being or contributing to: intuition, imagineering, focusing, scanning, mental agility, self-confidence, self-nurturing, creativity, metanoia, vision, and empowerment. Although these techniques can be used for dysfunctional conditions and for spiritual growth, they also can be considered a series of techniques for "basically normal people who want to extend their capabilities" to whatever productive ends they wish (Zilbergeld & Lazarus, 1987, p. 15). New Age training technologies need not be attached to metaphysical, psychological, or spiritual theories; they can be presented in familiar language to avoid resistance and to become more workable. As accelerated learning techniques, they can be used as a means to many training ends and can be taught profitably alone. Trainers and consultants should be knowledgeable about these techniques for the same reasons as their clients: to expand their personal and professional boundaries.

REFERENCES AND BIBLIOGRAPHY

Adolph, J. (1988). What is new age? In F. Graves (Ed.), *The Guide to New Age Living.* Brighton, MA: Rising Star Associates.

Agor, W. (1984a). *Intuitive management.* Englewood Cliffs, NJ: Prentice-Hall.

Agor, W. (1984b). Using intuition to manage organizations in the future. *Business Horizons, 27*(4), 49-54.

Anderson, D. (1987). *Making personal transformation work in organizations.* Berkeley, CA: Optimal Performance Institute.

Bandler, R., & Grinder, J. (1979). *Frogs into princes.* Moab, UT: Real People Press.

Bennis, W., & Nanus, B. (1985). *Leaders: The strategies for taking charge.* New York: Harper & Row.

Bennis, W. (1982). Warren Bennis on leaders, vision, power. *Leading Edge Bulletin, 2*(10), 2.

Benson, H. (1975). *The relaxation response.* New York: Avon Books.

Benson, H. (1984). *Beyond the relaxation response.* New York: Harper & Row.

Bloomfield, H., Cain, M., Jaffe, D., & Kory, R. (1975). *TM* discovering inner energy and overcoming stress.* New York: Delacorte Press.

Bradford, D., & Cohen, A. (1984). *Managing for excellence.* New York: John Wiley.

Brena, S. (1972). *Yoga & medicine.* New York: Penguin Books.

Bright, D. (1985). *Gearing up for the fast lane.* New York: Random House.

Brown, A., & Weiner, E. (1984). *Supermanaging: How to harness change for personal and organizational success.* New York: McGraw-Hill.

Burns, D. (1980). *Feeling good: The new mood therapy.* New York: Signet.

Burrows, R. (1986). Americans get religion in the new age. *Christianity Today, 30*(5), 17-23.

Carlson, R. (1987). How can trainers minimize risks of new age training? *Training and Development Journal, 41*(12), 18.

Carrington, P. (1977). *Freedom in meditation.* Kendall Park, NJ: Pace Educational Systems.

Chalofsky, N. (1987, June). *Zen and the art of program design.* Paper presented at the American Society for Training and Development National Conference, Atlanta.

Deo, L. (1987). Sound the alarm. *Training and Development Journal, 41*(8), 6.

Fitzgerald, P. (1987a). Four by four: How can trainers minimize risks of new age training? *Training and Development Journal, 41*(12), 18-21.

Fitzgerald, P. (1987b). Issues. *Training and Development Journal, 41*(8), 6-10.

Friedrich, O. (1987, December 7). New age harmonies. *Time,* pp. 62-72.

Garfield, C. (1986). *Peak performers.* New York: William Morrow.

Garvey, K. (1987). Sound the alarm. *Training and Development Journal, 41*(8), 8.

Gawain, S. (1982). *Creative visualization.* Toronto: Bantam Books.

Gentilman, R. (1984). Inner professional development. *Training and Development Journal, 38*(5), 24-25.

Gentilman, R., & Nelson, B. (1983). Futuring: The process and implications for training & development practitioners. *Training and Development Journal, 37*(6), 31-38.

Gordon, J. (1985). The woo woo factor. *Training: The Magazine of Human Resources Development, 22*(5), 26-42.

Hackett, G., & Abramson, P. (1986, December 15). Ramtha, a voice from beyond. *Newsweek,* p. 42.

Helmstetter, S. (1986). *What to say when you talk to your self.* New York: Pocket Books.

Henderson, C. (1975). *Awakening: Ways to psycho-spiritual growth.* Englewood Cliffs, NJ: Prentice-Hall.

Herrmann, N. (1987, June). *What does the brain have to do with me, anyway?* Paper presented at the American Society for Training and Development National Conference, Atlanta.

Hubbard, L. (1978). *Dianetics: The modern science of mental health.* Los Angeles, CA: Bridge Publications.

Jacobson, E. (1938). *Progressive relaxation.* Chicago: University of Chicago Press.

Jenner, J. (1986). On the way to stress resistance. *Training and Development Journal, 40*(5), 112-114.

Leavitt, H. (1986). *Corporate pathfinders.* Homewood, IL: Dow Jones-Irwin.

Leonard, J., & Laut, P. (1983). *Rebirthing: The science of enjoying all of your life.* Hollywood: Trinity Publications.

LeShan, L. (1974). *How to meditate.* New York: Bantam Books.

Letters to the editor. (1987). *Training: The Magazine of Human Resources Development, 24*(12), 23.

Lozanov, G. (1978). *Suggestology and outlines of suggestopedy.* New York: Gordon and Breach.

Ludwig, J., & Menendez, D. (1985). Effective communication through neurolinguistics. *Training and Development Journal, 39*(3), 44-48.

Lynch, D. (1986). Is the brain stuff still the right (or left) stuff? *Training and Development Journal, 40*(2), 23-26.

Maddi, S., & Kobasa, S. (1984). *The hardy executive:Health under stress.* New York: Macmillan Executive Summary Program, 1, 3.

Marcer, D. (1986). *Biofeedback and related therapies in clinical practice.* Rockville, MD: Aspen Publishers.

Meier, D. (1984). Imagine that. *Training and Development Journal, 38*(5), 26-29.

Meier, D. (1985). New age learning: From linear to geodesic. *Training and Development Journal, 39*(5), 39-43.

Miller, A., & Abramson, P. (1987, May 4). Corporate mind control. *Newsweek,* pp. 38-39.

Murphy, J. (1963). *The power of your subconscious mind.* New York: Bantam Books.

Naisbitt, J., & Aburdene, P. (1985). *Re-inventing the corporation.* New York: Warner Books.

Oki, M. (1970). *Practical yoga.* Tokyo: Japan Publications.

Ornstein, R. (1986). *The psychology of consciousness.* New York: Penguin Books.

Ostrander, S., & Schroeder, L. (1979). *Super-learning.* New York: Delta Books.

Pascarella, P. (1984). *The new achievers: Creating a modern work ethic.* New York: Free Press.

Pelletier, K.R. (1980). *Holistic medicine.* New York: Delacorte Press.

Peters, T. (1988). *Thriving on chaos: Handbook for a management revolution.* New York: Alfred A. Knopf.

Peters, T., & Waterman, R. (1980). *In search of excellence.* New York: Harper & Row.

Phelan, N., & Volin, M. (1963). *Yoga for women.* New York: Funk & Wagnalls.

Ray, S. (1981). *The only diet there is.* Berkeley, CA: Celestial Arts Publishing.

Robbins, A. (1986). *Unlimited power.* New York: Fawcett Columbine.

Robinson, A. (1984). What you see is what you get. *Training and Development Journal, 38*(5), 34-39.

Robinson, A. (1985). How to have a safe trip to the cutting edge. *Training and Development Journal, 39*(5), 45-48.

Romen, A. (1981). *Self-suggestion and its influence on the human organism.* Armonk, NY: M.E. Sharpe.

Sandler, L. (1986). Self-fulfilling prophecy: Better management by magic. *Training: The Magazine of Human Resources Development, 23*(2), 60-64.

Schwartz, M. (1987). *Biofeedback: A practitioner's guide.* New York: Guilford Press.

Shealy, C.N. (1977). *Ninety days to self-health: Biogenics: How to control all types of stress by yourself through a complete health program of autogenics, diet, vitamins, and exercise.* New York: Dial Press.

Showers, J. (1987). The point between two extremes. *Training and Development Journal, 41*(8), 9.

Siegel, B. (1987). *Love, medicine & miracles.* New York: Harper & Row.

Silva, J., and Stone, R.B. (1983). *The Silva mind control method for business managers.* Englewood Cliffs, NJ: Prentice-Hall.

Simonton, O., Matthews-Simonton, S., & Creighton, J. (1978). *Getting well again.* Los Angeles, CA: Jeremy P. Tarcher.

Smith, A. (1975). *Powers of mind.* New York: Random House.

Spice, M., & Kopperl, S. (1984). Are your trainees willing? *Training and Development Journal, 38*(5), 30-32.

Trachtenberg, J. (1987, June 1). Mainstream metaphysics. *Forbes,* pp. 156-158.

The training zone awards. (1986). *Training: The Magazine of Human Resources Development, 23*(1), 37-41.

The training zone awards. (1987). *Training: The Magazine of Human Resources Development, 24*(1), 20-29.

The training zone awards. (1988). *Training: The Magazine of Human Resources Development, 25*(1), 22-30.

Trends in training. (1986). *Training and Development Journal, 40*(12), 6.

Udupa, K. (1978). *Stress and its management by yoga.* Delhi, India: Motilal Banarsidass.

Veltrop, B. (1987). How can trainers minimize risks of new age training? *Training and Development Journal, 41*(12), 21.

Watring, R. (1987). Issues. *Training and Development Journal, 41*(4), 8.

Wilson, L. (1987, June). *Changing the game.* Paper presented at the American Society for Training and Development National Conference, Atlanta.

Zemke, R. (1987). What's new in the new age? *Training: The Magazine of Human Resources Development, 24*(9), 25-33.

Zilbergeld, B., & Lazarus, A. (1987). *Mind power.* Boston, MA: Little, Brown and Company.

Beverly Byrum, Ph.D., is both a professor of communication at Wright State University, Ohio, and the president of her own company, The Communication Connection. Dr. Byrum conducts seminars on topics such as conflict management, team building, stress and time management, and assertiveness. As a consultant, she facilitates team-building sessions in organizations. She has written one book, coauthored three others, and has published articles on interpersonal and group communication and training.

CREATIVE RISK TAKING

Richard E. Byrd and Jacqueline L. Byrd

UNCERTAINTY AND RISK TAKING

Risk taking has become a necessity for individual and corporate success in a changing world. Surviving in the current business environment is analogous to standing in the surf; as the sand seeps away, those who stand still lose their footing. Restructuring in such fundamental industries as health, transportation, communications, and finance adds to the prevailing uneasiness. If mergers and acquisitions are not enough to disrupt a sense of equilibrium, companies in the United States are reorganizing on the average of every eighteen months; in the past, a five-year time frame was more typical. Many managers as well as employees feel their careers and their companies have one foot in the boat and the other foot on shore. All, in fact, share the paradoxes that come with change.

This erosion of business and community infrastructures has increased the sense of anomie and has loosened the bonds of employee loyalty to career corporations. Furthermore, consumers have lost allegiance to brand names, often because these brands failed to deliver value as manufacturers rushed production to increase profits. Crime has invaded even small towns with waves of burglaries, rapes, and robberies. The numbers of people installing security systems is itself a statement about changing times.

Will the stock market regain stability, or will it continue to be volatile, with a life of its own, apart from the classic drivers of the economy, interest rates, or the value of the dollar? Will mortgage rates ever again be predictable? Will product-development cycles continue to be shortened, and will these tougher demands cause neglect of human values and increase burnout in the name of corporate success—or survival? More and faster change means greater uncertainty for all. Rules for success are increasingly unclear and a person's true capacities are often untested when confronted by choices.

Uncertainty is an opportunity for those not afraid to take risks, but it is an enemy to those dominated by fear of failure. Change creates uncertainty; uncertainty leads to possible risk because of unfamiliar choices; and risk fires people up, making them lightheaded or exhilarated, making their adrenaline run faster. Risk creates that special kind of fear that causes the hair to stand up on the back of one's neck. Change creates the opportunity to experience new situations, but people differ in how comfortable and how prepared they feel to take the required personal risks (Moore & Gergen, 1985).

Fear is the major inhibitor of creative risk taking and each person reacts individually to fear. Keyes (1985) says some people avoid and deny feeling fear; others abuse it for the sake of excitement and self-mastery; and still others try to control it directly in order to put its energy to work. Every reasonable person experiences fear on occasion.

This article describes the nature of personal risk taking. It compares the creative risk taker with the addicted risk taker and addresses the organization's expectations about risk as well as the human resource development (HRD) professional's use of risk taking.

Taking Personal Risks

Personal risk taking is not gambling. In personal risk taking, outcomes are affected by the individual's skill, talent, judgment, physical condition, and experience. Thus, most managers who are positive about taking risks are not enamored of gambling (March & Shapira, 1987). Personal risk taking then involves individual acts or decisions that exceed ordinary expectations. These may be the expectations of one's family, of co-workers, or even those of society. Personal risk involves more than money; it might involve rejection, career threat, loss of self-esteem, or physical disability. When someone says of the local hero who jumped into freezing waters to save a stranger, "How could he have done that?", it is clear that the boundaries of ordinary expectations were exceeded.

Individuals who generally take greater personal risks than other people are betting on a level of happiness, achievement, love, justice, self-esteem, or satisfaction that promises exponentially greater gains than the potential loss. Examples of such people include Olympic athlete Mary Lou Retton, entrepreneur Donald Trump, intrapreneur Lee Iacocca, politician Jesse Jackson, and Secretary of State George Schultz. Less visible people also risk life, limb, and personal happiness for causes larger than themselves. All of these people are personal risk takers. Some of them are creative risk takers.

Assessing Risk Taking

Risk taking is in the eye of the beholder. What appears to be an incredible risk to one person may seem to another to be a natural response to a given set of circumstances. Two recent situations illustrate this point. After discovering that Tylenol packages had been tampered with, executives of Johnson & Johnson pulled all Tylenol from stores, lest the tampering recur and endanger even one more life. They took a short-term high risk for the potential gain of keeping faith with their customers and saving the reputation of a very profitable product. On the other hand, Beechnut executives, after discovering that their apple juice formula for infants lacked apple juice, permitted lawyers to persuade them to ignore the facts and stonewall. They took the long-term risk of losing credibility with their customers in exchange for short-term profits. Who took more risk?

Each person observes and judges risk-taking styles, measuring others by his or her own personal standards. To a reserved person, openness may be seen as high risk taking. Yet a person's lack of openness might limit spontaneous, trusting relationships—something considered high risk to another person.

Consider the case of a vendor who does not let the customer know that the schedule is in trouble. Is that vendor taking a risk? How large a risk? What might happen if the customer were told? One can quickly see that not only are short- and long-term risks pitted against each other, but the perceived degree of either risk will depend on the observer's judgment of the potential to modify the odds against success.

The subjective character of risk taking can be seen in an experiment in which Rowe (1983) sought to determine what words connote what level of risk to whom (Figure 1). Participants were asked to assign a percentage figure to each of the words, quantifying the *certainty* the word suggested to them. The results of this research are shown in Figure 1, with the numbers representing the mean percent value of the responses.

Even people with similar backgrounds differ on the meanings of the words in the list, yet they use these words with others to describe the levels of risk being taken. Differences among participants, friends, and colleagues demonstrate the subjectivity of risk assessment. This phenomenon is supported by the work of March and Shapira (1987), who state that most managers portray themselves as judicious risk takers and less risk averse than their colleagues or their supervisors. On the other hand, their supervisors considered themselves greater risk takers. Risk taking again is subjectively measured in the eye of the beholder.

RISK TAKING IN INDIVIDUALS

Personal Risk Taking As a Trait

Some investigators believe that risk taking is a partly stable aspect of personality (March & Shapira, 1987). However, more evidence points to the conclusion that risk taking is not a personal trait (Wallach & Kogan, 1964).

WORD/PHRASE	LEVEL OF CERTAINTY
1. Almost certainly	90
2. Highly likely	84
3. Very good chance	74
4. Doubtless	82
5. Probable	66
6. Likely	67
7. Believed to	60
8. Doubtful	33
9. Probably	64
10. Improbable	18
11. Unlikely	21
12. Probably not	23
13. Little chance	13
14. Almost no chance	6
15. Could be	51

Figure 1. Levels of Certainty

A trait is a genetic characteristic or predisposition, something with which a person is born. It is predictable and consistent. What might be considered a risk taking trait would cause a person to react to all situations in a predictable and consistent manner. Yet each situation faced is unique; one's individual characteristics, combined with the particular factors present in a given situation, create a once-in-a-lifetime event. Consistent and predictable risk taking then is not a trait; it is more accurately termed *addicted risk taking*.

Addicted risk taking is more obvious in those who take risks for thrill, for the excitement engendered by the unknown or dangerous. Who wants to work for a manager who takes personal or organizational risks for thrills? On the other hand, few want a supervisor who, when feeling the thrill, consistently backs away. Consistency thus is the hobgoblin of risk taking. It proves only that a person is not considering all the facts. Addicts—whether they are addicted to sex, drugs, money, caution, or thrills—are dangerous to everyone. Creative risk takers, on the other hand, consider the facts and trust their intuition.

Creative Risk Takers

Creative risk takers are those who do not pursue risk for its own sake, but rather invest their resources, their lives, and their companies for an appropriate return, an accomplishment of value to them. They are not gamblers; they take risks only when they have some control over the outcome.

Research has shown that intelligence, ability to handle stress, strong religious faith, personal security, and high self-esteem are common attributes of creative risk takers (Byrd, 1974; Skrzycki, Horn, Moore, Golden, Linnon, & Dworkin, 1987). These characteristics seem to fortify individuals to cope with uncertainty. Creative risk takers are less controlled than others by irrational levels of fear. They seldom see failure as something from which they cannot recover. They are self-directed enough to tolerate rejection, albeit painfully at times. These are people who take responsibility for their actions and seldom are afraid of true success with its continual burden of decision making.

Creative risk takers are more likely to have honed their judgment on previous experiences from which they truly learned. For this reason, corporations rarely leap-frog employees from lower to higher positions, even in exceptional cases. Bypassing the development process increases risks for the inexperienced, almost assuring failure.

Creative risk takers also tend to control the odds. They set limits on their losses, not risking more than they can afford to lose (Byrd, 1982). Realizing that stress distorts judgment, creative risk takers seek input from knowledgeable people; they weigh risks on the scale of their own fears before taking action (Keyes, 1985). Although stress creates pressure and affects judgment, creative risk takers are less likely to have delusions. These are not people who believe winning is always "just around the corner." They do not volunteer for the toughest job regardless of its chances for success. In acting or deciding to act, creative risk takers are realistic in appraising people and circumstances, including themselves.

High- and Low-Risk Takers

All people have a certain risk-taking propensity; their decisions and acts tend to be higher or lower in risk within a relatively consistent range. For example, a person who risked changing employers once is more likely to take the chance again. The person who has worked for the same company for twenty years is unlikely to seek employment elsewhere unless the pain of staying outweighs the risk of leaving. Some people change jobs every few years, considering it part of their growth process;[1] for these people, new jobs bring opportunities to meet people, to learn, and to experience other challenges and responsibilities. To other people, changing jobs may mean loss of self-esteem, feelings of incompetence, and a loss of friends and predictability. One person's challenge is another's threat.

The following diagram (Figure 2) illustrates the differences between the *addicted* high-risk taker and the *creative* high-risk taker. An addicted high-risk taker, as represented in the upper part of the figure, is consistent in the level of risk taken. A creative high-risk taker, as represented in the lower part of the figure, chooses a level of risk based on circumstances, rewards, punishment, and odds. Both addicted and creative high-risk takers have central tendencies, as depicted by the line through each diagram.

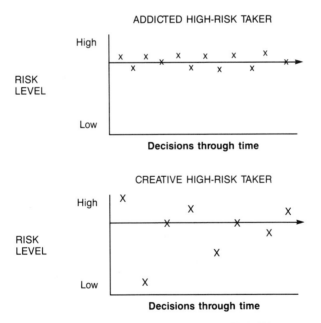

Figure 2. Addicted Vs. Creative High-Risk Takers

---

[1]For further exploration of the power of planned personal growth, see *Creating Your Future* by G.A. Ford & G.L. Lippitt, published by and available from University Associates, 8517 Production Avenue, San Diego, California 92121 (619-578-5900).

The same principle applies when one considers the addicted low-risk taker and creative low-risk taker (Figure 3).

Addicted high- or low-risk takers venture the same personal risk in every situation. On the other hand, the creative risk taker—high or low—will almost never choose the same level of personal risk. Individuals who are creative risk takers have a general bias toward or against greater risk taking; the same holds true for organizations. For example, Federal Express takes a variety of risks in the name of progress, inventing new services, products, or distribution methods. In contrast, the U.S. Postal Service is bound by conservative rules, traditions, and labor agreements and thus cannot and does not take comparable risks.

RISK TAKING IN ORGANIZATIONS

Organizations with Risky Missions

One could make a case that people either are attracted to or repelled by organizations with risky missions. Are those organizations or people necessarily addicted to risk? Think about tightrope walkers, aerial-steel connectors working on high bridges, emergency workers in electrical companies, local rescue squads, or police and fire departments. Although some higher-order motivation is served by choosing such occupations, most of these people know that working with people who are consistently

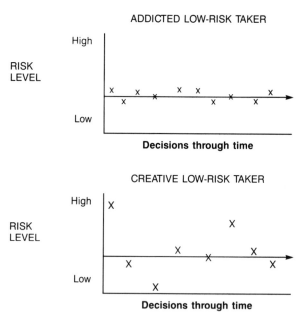

Figure 3. Addicted Vs. Creative Low-Risk Takers

high- or low-risk takers could be hazardous to their health. No policeman wants a trigger-happy partner. No high-bridge worker wants a fearless supervisor.

Authors such as Keyes (1985) accept thrill seekers as a legitimate category of risk takers. They describe these people as motivated by their fears, abusing fear for the sake of action, change, excitement, freedom, intensity, speed, and variety. However, these people also can be seen as risk addicts who place themselves and their organizations in jeopardy for the satisfaction of feeding their addiction.

The Need for Greater Risk Taking

Many corporate culture change processes have demanded, both explicitly and implicitly, greater personal risk taking from managers. Such newly aggressive companies include IDS Financial Services under its new owner, American Express; First Bank Systems in its centralization process; and Minnesota's largest hospital company, the newly merged Health One Corporation. These examples represent only a smattering of what has happened to American business and industry. In recent times, ordinary employees and managers live in a shifting paradigm, that of change versus status quo. They no longer have implicitly understood criteria to assess the degree of personal risk taking that their managers will tolerate from them on behalf of the company. The old rules were easier to follow (or to deviate from) because everyone knew them: stay within budget, squeeze for short-term profit, and be predictable.

In the past, government regulations inhibited risk taking in some industries (see Figure 4). Today's picture is changing, however, to one of deregulation, in which survival depends on the introduction of new or timely products of better quality and lower cost, as well as on better distribution or a unique market position. Greater risks are being demanded; the matrix box of low regulation and higher competition increasingly is the home of the many rather than the few (Figure 5).

These diagrams (Figures 4 and 5) point out the changing situation and the new demands on the ordinary worker and manager. If industries are to compete successfully

| | COMPETITION | |
	Low	High
REGULATED High	Communications Airlines Utilities Hospital/Health Government	Banks Alcohol and tobacco Trucking Insurance Securities Drugs
REGULATED Low	Smokestack Medical profession Legal profession Architects After-market companies	Computer Defense contractors Consumer products Automobiles

Figure 4. Regulation and Competition in the Past

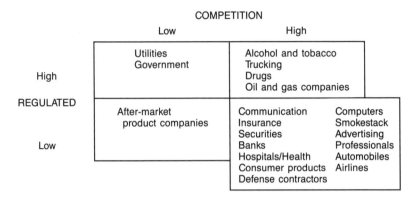

COMPETITION

	Low	High	
High REGULATED Low	Utilities Government	Alcohol and tobacco Trucking Drugs Oil and gas companies	
	After-market product companies	Communication Insurance Securities Banks Hospitals/Health Consumer products Defense contractors	Computers Smokestack Advertising Professionals Automobiles Airlines

Figure 5. Regulation and Competition in the Present

in the United States, not to mention in world markets, they must take more short-term risks for long-term gains. Some companies are talking a good game; others are doing it. The "Big Board" is keeping score.

TRANSFORMING THE ORGANIZATION

Individual/Organization Relationships

Why people work; what they believe about people; and their attitudes toward ethics, achievement, and teamwork are rooted in their personal and educational histories before they begin work. Later shaping and honing are accomplished through experiences, both negative and positive, that motivate them. Corporations also condition or shape values and expectations. What have organizations shaped people to do—to risk or not to risk?

In the past, no business book with the title *Thriving on Chaos* (Peters, 1987) would have made the best-seller list. However, modern corporations need to deal with uncertainty as well as to adapt and to innovate. It is clear that reasonable, creative risks to master uncertainty produce positive results for individuals and for their corporations. Managers can build strong self-esteem, especially if their results are positive at least 50 percent of the time. Fewer tasks are neglected, fewer self-serving games are tolerated, and questionable ethics is less a problem (Byrd, 1974). Schedules are met, promises are kept, and customers are better served.

Although all people have certain propensities for personal risk taking, empirical studies indicate that preference varies with context. Therefore, organizations that expect managers to "make things happen" must create an environment that supports and fosters risk taking (March & Shapira, 1987). Creative risk taking is encouraged in an environment that does not punish people who try and fail, one that expects and accepts mistakes, one that values differences in perspectives, one that provides the resources necessary to create success (Moore & Gergen, 1985).

Creative risk taking is a crucial element in change, transition, and intrapreneurship.[2] In turn, fear of risks is a key factor in resistance to change, both for managers who need to decide whether or not to initiate change as well as for employees required to adapt to change (Byrd, 1974). Therefore, the question arises as to whether intrapreneurship actually can be created in organizations or if it requires waiting for the few natural, internal entrepreneurs to come along (Moore & Gergen, 1985).

Fostering Risk Taking in Organizations

Matching an individual's propensity to take personal risk with an organization's willingness to support risk is a delicate matter. As a first step, managers must understand their own risk-taking styles and those of the people who work for them. People differ in their comfort levels and readiness to take risks. The sensitive manager knows and accepts these differences by promoting an environment that allows people to feel secure and accepted as they confront the riskiness of change or choice.

In 1971, Richard Byrd developed the Creativity and Risk Taking (C&RT) Creatrix Inventory[3] to help individuals explore their own risk-taking tendencies and how these tendencies affect the organization. This questionnaire has helped both managers and employees to understand one another better and to create an environment that nurtures creativity in the midst of change. The instrument has been used by over seventy-five companies, government agencies, and not-for-profit organizations in the United States and Canada.

Questionnaire data project the respondent into one of eight zones on a matrix, each representing a risk taking/creativity style. Assessing the risk-taking and creativity style of individuals in organizations can help to explain why some organizations stagnate and die, others take excessive risks and end in bankruptcy, and still others succeed (Byrd, 1982).

The eight zones of the matrix are represented in Figure 6. The C&RT zones indicate general tendencies rather than a stable personality type. Although the instrument is continually in the process of re-evaluation and revalidation, thus far the zones have been more stable than expected.

If the first step in fostering creative risk taking is understanding one's own personal risk-taking style as a manager and the styles of one's subordinates, the next step is to put this understanding into action. Not all organizations can tolerate high-risk takers, even creative ones. Those who are in organizations that do not reward or forgive employees who take reasonable risks should not take many risks if they want to remain with that organization. Often the unwritten rules determine the limits of risk possible. Creative risk takers assess situations realistically and take the greatest reasonable risk, realizing that corporate risks are essential in today's environment.

---

[2]For further discussion of intrapreneurship, see "Fostering Intrapreneurship in Organizations" by Gifford Pinchot III, in this *Annual*.

[3]*C&RT* (Creativity and Risk Taking): The Creatrix Inventory is published by and available from University Associates, 8517 Production Avenue, San Diego, California 92121 (619-578-5900).

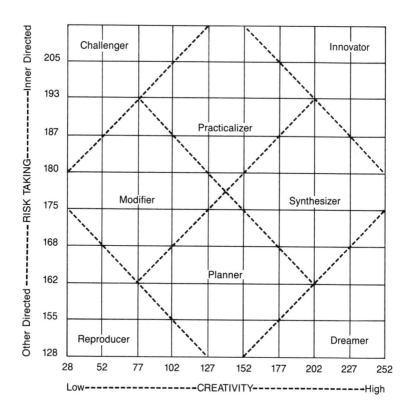

Figure 6. The Creatrix

Personal Initiatives

Personal initiative is the key to the following seven strategies, designed to help employees encourage their organizations to move toward a greater level of creative risk taking. Regardless of one's individual style according to the C&RT, a person can take these steps:

Personal initiative 1. Diagnose the unwritten rules of the organization, as well as one's own rules, to determine tolerable limits on personal risk taking.

Personal initiative 2. Build a power base; for example, become more competent technically, more skilled interpersonally, or more connected to the power network.

Personal initiative 3. Be prepared to exceed expectations of acceptable organization behavior. A low personal risk taker must assume "immaculate perception" on major issues until proven wrong. This action will compensate for any self-doubt; at most, such a person will appear to others to be modestly self-confident.

Personal initiative 4. Know when to admit defeat and cut losses. However, beware of the predilection toward built-in fear (Jeffers, 1987). Owning up is rarely a true risk; rather it is a short-term risk for long-term potential gain of building trust.

Personal initiative 5. Take short-term loss for long-term gain. For instance, tell customers the truth; lose face if necessary to preserve the relationship; or work with someone who grabs credit if it gets the job done.

Personal initiative 6. Observe the obvious. Delusion of self and the organization may be the worst enemies of success in today's business world. Saying the unsayable often prevents disaster even though it causes some immediate pain.

Personal initiative 7. Break rules to get the job done. However, breaking the spirit of corporate policy should be approached very carefully. Individuals should never risk more than they, their supervisors, or their companies can afford to lose.

THE ROLE OF THE CONSULTANT IN CHANGE

A trainer or consultant is always involved in the process of change. Regardless of the object of change, the change agent is the primary tool. Books, techniques, role plays, simulations, and team-building skills are all part of the process. More than twenty years of organization development experience confirms that trust begets trust, candor begets candor, seeking feedback begets reciprocal requests, and a lack of defensiveness begets self-examination. In other words, the consultant must model the desired behavior. He or she must know, be, and do what others are being asked to become. Thus the change agent, by definition, must take more personal risk than the ordinary manager or individual contributor.

Consultants therefore take tremendous risks by not risking. They may lose contracts by being perceived as not value added. Avoiding personal risk can undermine long-term goals of real change; if the consultants do not "walk their talk," they will not establish credibility. Such inconsistencies make the consultant/trainer role that of entertainer rather than change agent.

Not being risk averse is also risky. As change agents, taking totally unnecessary risks may defeat the change-agent role. Such things as doing one's homework with regard to the client, managing the environment toward a positive outcome, getting as much information from the client as is needed, preparing carefully, considering alternatives and developing one's approach with the client are all risk-averse behaviors. They serve as the net beneath the high wire. Once on the wire or in the situation, the consultant must take all personal risks necessary to achieve the objective.

However, consultants need to be wary of taking more risk than the clients can handle. As an esteemed associate once said, "You can't exceed the system's openness norms more than .5 and still be seen as credible." Highly overt expressions of trust, openness, candor, and vulnerability can appear to be false or manipulative. The change agent has to behave at a level of personal risk that the client system can tolerate. As a client once complained, "You mainline on this stuff. Give me a chance to catch up. Right now I'm just scared to death." Such a reaction can undermine the consultant's efforts; it is best therefore not to risk more than the client can afford to lose or the consultant might lose the client.

SUMMARY

The nature of personal risk taking is situational, not a gamble, not genetic, and always in the eye of the beholder. This application of the concept of risk taking has been limited to a narrow but significant area—that of the work place that shapes values by rewarding, protecting, and giving a relative sense of making a contribution. This sense of contributing is threatened by the speed of change and the lack of a clear and obvious direction in most enterprises. Uncertainty creates a need for creative risk-taking norms that are higher than American business and industry ever has sought or rewarded in the past. Industries are beginning to address the need for greater personal risk taking and to use instruments such as the C&RT to match individual and corporate styles. The personal initiatives outlined are designed to promote creative risk taking in organizations. These same initiatives, combined with the usual consultant skills, ethics, and willingness will increase a consultant's effectiveness as an agent of transformation or change.

REFERENCES

Byrd, R.E. (1974). *A guide to personal risk taking.* New York: AMACOM.

Byrd, R.E. (1982). *Managing risks in changing times.* Basking Ridge, NJ: AT&T Management and Education Methods.

Jeffers, S. (1987). *Feel the fear and do it anyway.* New York: Fawcett, Columbine.

Keyes, R. (1985). *Chancing it.* Toronto, Canada: Little, Brown.

March, J.M., & Shapira, Z. (1987). Managerial perspectives on risk and risk taking. *Management Science, 33*(11), 1404-1418.

Moore, M., & Gergen, P. (1985). Risk taking and organization change. *Training and Development Journal, 39*(6), 72-76.

Rowe, A.J. (1983, July). Paper presented at the Defense and Risk Uncertainty Workshop, Fort Belvoir, VA.

Skrzycki, C., Horn, M., Moore, L. Golden, S., Linnon, N., & Dworkin, P. (1987, January 26). Risk takers. *U.S. News & World Report,* pp. 60-67.

Wallach, M.A., & Kogan, N. (1964). *Risk taking.* New York: Holt, Rinehart and Winston.

Richard E. Byrd, Ph.D., *is the president of The Richard E. Byrd Company, a private consulting firm. He works mostly with senior management in such areas as team building, reshaping organizational values, and strategic planning. A clergyman as well as a consultant, Dr. Byrd stresses the need for humanistic and caring environments in organizations. He has been published in over fifty books, articles, video- and audiotapes.*

Jacqueline L. Byrd, Ph.D., *is the director of policy analysis/research and planning for Ramsey County, St. Paul, Minnesota. She is also an assistant professor in the Human and Health Services Administration graduate program at St. Mary's College. Dr. Byrd is the author of several policy reports and is a consultant in the areas of policy research, planning, and administration. She and her father, Richard E. Byrd, Ph.D., collaborated on this article.*

EVALUATION: ISSUES FIRST, METHODOLOGY SECOND

Phyliss Cooke and Ralph R. Bates

Many organizations require evaluation of training in terms of the "bottom line" in order to make judgments about future resource allocations to human resource development (HRD) efforts. The problem is that complex, bottom-line indicators are not the same types of data or couched in the same language as the behavioral criteria used in training. It would be virtually impossible to design, conduct, and control a research project that could account for and "evaluate" all forms of organizational and behavioral change. However, this is what would have to be done in order to assess the true impact of training on the bottom line. Professionals in HRD continually are forced to respond to the challenge of trying to assess training effects and to provide useful data to the decision makers in organizations. Yet few organizations are willing to invest the dollars, time, and talent needed to engage in complex cause-and-effect evaluation projects; and many trainers seem reluctant to advocate more easily attainable but "soft" evaluation data such as participants' and trainers' self-reports, test scores of accuracy on discrete tasks, observations during training sessions, retention scores on performance tasks, and so on.

Although most of us believe that providing training ultimately results in higher productivity and job satisfaction, we know how difficult it would be to have to try to "justify" training costs exclusively on the basis of return on investment (ROI) analysis. Few researchers who have written about training evaluation have proposed strategies for viewing training effects strictly on the basis of financial analysis. Those who have proposed strategies have cautioned that establishing direct links between training and complex organizational factors *can* be misleading. We practitioners need to help our organizations come to grips with that reality.

We can and should be promoting more appropriate guidance in terms of training evaluation. We should be working to find ways to support our conviction that we are necessary to the accomplishment of our organizations' long-term objectives. What we should not do is be caught in the trap of trying to justify our existence by using inappropriate indicators or promise increased productivity outcomes when much of our training is not primarily designed to provide technical-skills acquisition. Because the primary function of most training is to provide opportunities for people to learn potentially useful ideas; to practice and acquire relevant skills (that are the basis of improved performance); and to explore attitudes toward themselves, others, and their work that ultimately affect their on-the-job performance, we need to operate and evaluate within these boundaries. We can and should educate the users of our services about appropriate strategies for evaluating our contributions.

This article proposes a sequence and a structure for the dialog that needs to take place when one is considering a training-evaluation project. In addition, a model is proposed for guiding the planning of the project.

STEP 1: DECIDE WHETHER TO EVALUATE

The first step for HRD practitioners is to help all who are involved to gain greater clarity about the purpose of a proposed training and evaluation effort—what it is realistic to expect from the data once they have been generated. The HRD person can explore a number of questions with the intended users of the assessed data in order to determine the true purpose of the evaluation project. The first question to be discussed is whether the training should be evaluated. Then, and only then, should questions concerning the appropriate methodological approach be addressed. Beginning with the question of whether or not training should be evaluated suggests that there are several legitimate reasons not to evaluate. This question should be explored carefully, because once an evaluation project has been started it begins to take on a life of its own.

It is important to remember that even the most sophisticated and well-implemented evaluation process can provide only information. The practitioner, or the people who ultimately will be using the information, must decide ahead of time the questions to be answered or the decisions to be made once the data have been generated. If the intended users of the data do not know specifically why the data are being generated, it might be better to rethink the decision to evaluate.

Other questions to be addressed at this point are as follows:

- What resources (time, money, access, personnel, materials) are needed and/or available to support the evaluation?

- Does it seem likely that there will be a commitment to actually use the data for the original purpose once they have been generated?

If the answer to either of these questions is negative, one should advise against proceeding. If the answers are positive, proceed to Step 2.

Ideally, the planning of the evaluation procedure should take place in the sequence shown in Figure 1.

STEP 2: CLARIFY THE TYPE OF EVALUATION PROJECT DESIRED

Once the decision has been made that the effects of training are to be evaluated and there is commitment to use the data, the next step is to decide the type of evaluation desired, that is, whether the evaluation is being undertaken for purposes of justification or determination.

1. *Justification.* Purposes having to do with justification include the following:

- Demonstrating through the use of carefully thought-out criteria and assessment strategies that situations or events occurred;

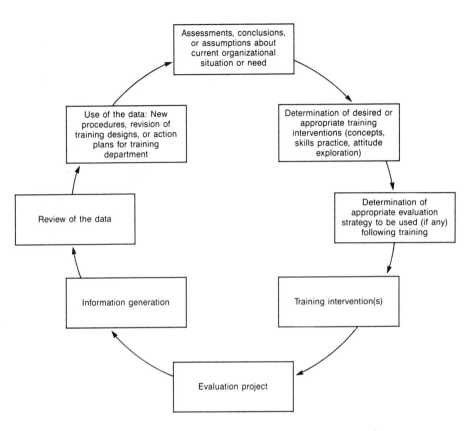

Figure 1. The Sequence for Planning an Evaluation Procedure

- Verifying that a specific outcome was reached;
- Supporting a predetermined conclusion or expectation; and
- Establishing the supportive documentation for a positional statement.

In other words, evaluation for purposes of justification assumes that one is planning to generate a predetermined type of information that will support a desired interpretation, conclusion, or objective. This is not unethical; it simply differs from generating information that will be used for purposes of determining if something occurred or was experienced. It is intended to show a relationship between training efforts and a desired or predetermined outcome. For example, one could set out to document that a predetermined number of hours of training had been delivered, or that the training delivered had been requested by a certain percentage of the participants.

2. *Determination.* Determination purposes are those in which the information provided is to be used as a factor to aid in future decision making. Typically, this type of data is viewed as more objective than justification data, although it is recognized that even these more "objective" data always must be interpreted and that some subjectivity is inherent in using data for decision making. To enhance objectivity, these evaluation designs typically utilize preset levels in response categories so that decision makers will not be unduly swayed by the data during the decision-making process.

For example, a typical evaluation-for-determination format might request that participants rate the perceived value of a training session by assessing it as good, fair, or poor, or by providing a numerical rating on a scale of 1 to 10. Data reviewers then decide if trainees' needs were met based on a preset level of expressed satisfaction such as "A mean of seven on a ten-point scale will indicate satisfaction." Another example is a post-course examination in which items on a test are answered either correctly or incorrectly. From these answers, one could determine the content areas that need additional attention. The design of this type of evaluation project also could begin by establishing pretraining skill levels or concept familiarity in order to compare these data with post-training measurements to determine whether or not learning occurred. By determining participant satisfaction with the trainer, and/or participants' perceptions of the job applicability of the skills taught, trainers, designers, and training managers could make decisions about future training content; future skill emphasis; changes in trainers or trainer style; changes in learning methods; or changes in materials, design, selection, and so forth.

Each of these two main types of evaluation purposes is legitimate; each requires behavioral-science methodological sophistication. It simply is different to construct an evaluation for purposes of generating data that will be used to determine something in the future than it is to construct an evaluation in which the data will be used to justify a predetermined or desired outcome. Clarity of purpose is essential because it directs the evaluation strategy and the design and construction of the evaluation project.

STEP 3: CLARIFY THE SPECIFIC INFORMATION NEEDED

Not only is this important to the ultimate effectiveness of the evaluation project; it also eases the burden of planning the evaluation methodology and design. If one's purpose is to justify a particular point of view or action, one will find it much easier to plan an effective evaluation design; also, it will be much easier to utilize the data than if one merely collects some data and later tries to manipulate them to serve the purpose. Similarly, if one is trying to generate information to be used in making decisions (determination), it will be much easier to plan an effective evaluation if one knows what specific decisions are to be made; how the evaluation data are to be used in that process; what types of data might be useful; what data sources might be best; what levels of quantity, quality, and accuracy are needed in the data; and what might be the best way to compile the data for effective review. When the question to be answered or the kind of data needed is unclear, it is unlikely that an appropriate data-generation format will be used in the evaluation process; consequently, the data are likely to be inaccurate, irrelevant, or misleading and may be a hindrance rather than a help.

At this point the evaluation project designers should clarify these issues:

- What should be assessed?

- For whom are the data being generated? Who will be involved in the decision-making process for which the data will be used? Might there be different purposes to be served if there are to be several users of the data? Might separate evaluations be needed for different users?

- Who should collect the data? Who has the necessary skill, credibility, access, and objectivity?

- From whom should the data be collected? How many sources of data are needed to generate the quantity and/or quality of data needed?

- When should the evaluation take place? How many samples will be needed and over what period?

- How should the data be collected? Should the collection procedure include interviews, paper-and-pencil questionnaires, surveys, tests, observation(s)?

- Where should the evaluation (observations, interviews, and so forth) take place (in a private room, an on-the-job setting, a lunch room)?

All these factors must be coordinated so as to yield the quantity and quality of data needed in order to serve the intended purpose. The model in Figure 2 may be useful in conceptualizing these points and the other steps to be taken in planning the evaluation project.

The sampled data become more complex as the sources of the data expand and/or comparative data are introduced into the analysis plan. Should the design of the evaluation project call for an assessment of behavioral or attitudinal change(s), adequate time must be allowed to elapse for post-training sampling and/or for change(s) in the sampled criteria to become apparent.

In cases in which the intent of the evaluation project is to determine whether or not training and changes in behavior or attitudes on the job are related, control-group data would have to be generated. Although this adds to the complexity of the evaluation effort, it definitely enriches the quality of the data that can be used to determine causal effects. Training is not typically designed with clear and measurable enough criteria to account for complex organizational impacts such as improved morale or fewer customer complaints. But training can help to improve performance in these areas when and if the pretraining organizational need can be linked logically and directly to the participants' lack of relevant knowledge or lack of opportunities to practice necessary skills or to examine attitudes relevant to on-the-job performance variables. Just as importantly, these positive impacts occur when and if the concepts learned, the skills enhanced, and the attitudes revised are actively supported and reinforced when the participants return to their work settings. This point should be emphasized when it seems that the ultimate users of the evaluation data will be attempting to determine if training had the desired impact on very complex organizational factors.

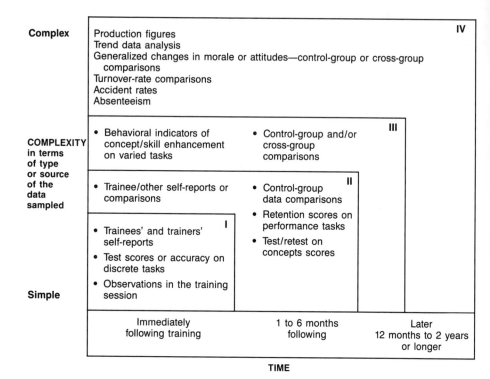

| | Immediately following training | 1 to 6 months following | Later 12 months to 2 years or longer |

Complex

Production figures
Trend data analysis
Generalized changes in morale or attitudes—control-group or cross-group
   comparisons
Turnover-rate comparisons
Accident rates
Absenteeism

COMPLEXITY in terms of type or source of the data sampled

III
- Behavioral indicators of concept/skill enhancement on varied tasks
- Control-group and/or cross-group comparisons

II
- Trainee/other self-reports or comparisons
- Control-group data comparisons
- Retention scores on performance tasks
- Test/retest on concepts scores

I
- Trainees' and trainers' self-reports
- Test scores or accuracy on discrete tasks
- Observations in the training session

Simple

IV

Immediately following training   1 to 6 months following   Later 12 months to 2 years or longer

TIME

Figure 2. A Model for Planning Evaluations

STEP 4: DETERMINE HOW BEST TO PREPARE DATA FOR INTERPRETATION

One can strive for objectivity in design and administrative procedures, format, statistical models, and so forth; but the numbers obtained in evaluation have no meaning in and of themselves. People give numbers their meaning, and doing so involves subjective decision making and interpretation. For example, even if a rating scale of one to ten is used to measure participant satisfaction, someone must determine the cutoff score of the lowest rating acceptable.

It is important for the designers of evaluation projects to acknowledge the inherent subjectivity of numerical data and to guard against its potentially negative influence. One way to do this is to predetermine decisions or actions that will follow the review of the information—especially when using numerical data. For example, interpretative limits or categories could be established prior to gathering data. Project designers could arbitrarily say that they would count as relevant only the first three items in a survey. Or, when using a survey employing a ten-point scale, they could view the data on satisfaction levels in relationship to a desired, preset satisfaction level such as "8." Or it could be decided that if actual satisfaction levels fell below 8, decision makers would interpret it to mean that participants were not sufficiently satisfied and that revisions to the training should be made.

Additional questions to be addressed during this step in the planning are as follows:

- Who should prepare the data for feedback and in what format?
- Who should provide feedback of the data? How, when, and in what format should it be provided?
- Who should distribute the data? How should the data be stored and for how long? Who should have access to the data? What should be done about confidentiality?

Once the evaluation-project designers are clear on these points, the actual design of an effective and useful data-generation process can be accomplished.

As depicted in Figure 1, The Sequence for Planning an Evaluation Procedure, the steps "review of the data" and "use of the data" set up the next round in the cycle of assessing, diagnosing, and planning action steps for improving current situations through training interventions. The human factors always are the ones that are critical to enhanced productivity, so human resource development—training—matters to managers and workers who want to see their organizations prosper.

Because HRD is a support function, it typically has no clear position power within an organization. Therefore, it seems advantageous to depict it as outside the management level yet deriving its authority from the CEO level (see Figure 3). Human resource development personnel can learn to use that fact to their advantage and press for authorization and role and function clarity from the authorizing source so that there will be less anxiety within our ranks. We can help our users to decide what they need to know in order to make sound decisions and then help them to obtain the information they need through sound evaluation processes.

THE ORGANIZATION/SYSTEM

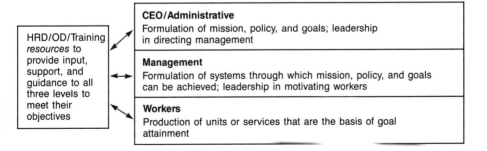

Figure 3. Model of Typical Levels Within Organizations

SUGGESTED ACTIONS FOR HRD PRACTITIONERS

Suggested actions are as follows:

1. *Know something about evaluation, its uses and abuses, and what data can and cannot do.* One can learn by reading books or by taking courses in research methodology. Develop skills and familiarity with the language of behavioral-science research design.

2. *When key decision makers begin to sound serious about evaluation, engage them in a discussion of their purposes and expectations before agreeing to execute their instructions regarding evaluation.* Find out what information they need in order to make what decisions; also explore with them their expectations about the effects of training.

3. *Help the key decision makers to explore other options for answering their questions.* For example, have them attend courses as full participants. Experiencing the training firsthand may give them all the data they need to evaluate it.

4. *Educate the key decision makers.* Explore with them the types of evaluation possible and the costs/benefits of each. See what they are willing to spend in terms of time, money, documentation, and so forth.

5. *Try to negotiate and clarify who makes decisions about the evaluation process.* If this responsibility is given to others, join the evaluators in order to learn from or even influence the scope and design of the evaluation.

6. *If the key decision makers are concerned with establishing cause-and-effect impacts, take charge by informing them of the cost of various evaluation strategies and what longitudinal evaluation data can and cannot demonstrate.* (If necessary, go back to Item 1.)

7. *Promote the notion of bringing in a carefully chosen evaluation expert who will not try only to "sell" his or her services, but who will be an ally in educating everyone about the process.* Another alternative is to distribute brief articles like this one to the key decision makers and to discuss their reactions to the points presented. Demonstrate an interest in the issues.

8. *If it seems that a decision is being made on political grounds to proceed with a "hard" evaluation and/or that someone is trying to make training efforts look bad, take a political approach.* Rally supporters and lobby the skeptics. Go on the offensive by declaring "This will be a great opportunity to evaluate all the conditions that need to exist within the system in support of training to help organizations to achieve their missions and goals." Support this position by bringing in experts in systems theory who can talk convincingly about the need for reinforcement throughout the system to promote and maintain behavioral changes that are initiated through training.

9. *Always be prepared to decline an offer of funds for evaluation projects unless key decision makers are committed to using the data and agree to accept their responsibility to support the changes that they decide to make.*

10. *If faced with certain defeat, knowing that the proposed evaluation process will not yield useful and relevant data, declare loudly and vigorously that this is one of those times when "there is no good reason to evaluate; it would waste the organization's time and money."* It is better to state an unpopular but supportable position than to keep quiet and have to live with a lie that one has helped to manufacture.

It is extremely important that HRD professionals be well educated in the subject of evaluation, so that they do not promise something (in terms of evaluation) that they cannot deliver and so that they can deliver what they set out to. If an adequate evaluation design cannot be created or implemented, if the cost of the evaluation would be greater than its benefit, or if there is no expectation that the evaluation will be used to indicate needed change, it would be wise not to evaluate. If evaluation is required, however, prior to designing the evaluation project, the HRD professional must be able to help the decision makers in the organization to determine the specific purpose of the evaluation, the methodology to be used, the resources required, the way in which the data will be prepared, and the way in which the data will be used. With these expectations clearly understood, there is an increased chance of conducting an evaluation that will be both appropriate and useful to the organization.

BIBLIOGRAPHY

Evaluation Design and Methodology

Brinkerhoff, R.O. (1987). *Achieving results from training.* San Francisco: Jossey-Bass.

Brinkerhoff, R.O. (1988, February). An integrated evaluation model for HRD. *Training and Development Journal.*

Campbell, D.T., & Stanley, J.C. (1966). *Experimental and quasi-experimental designs for research.* Chicago: Rand McNally.

Connolly, S.M. (1988, February). Integrating evaluation design and implementation. *Training and Development Journal.*

Fink, A., & Kosecoff, J. (1978). *An evaluation primer.* Washington, DC: Capitol Publications.

Flanagan, J.C. (1949). *Critical requirements for research personnel.* Pittsburgh, PA: American Institute for Research.

Hamblin, A.C. (1974). *Evaluation and control of training.* London: McGraw-Hill.

Isaac, S., & Michael, W.B. (1971). *Handbook in research and evaluation.* San Diego, CA: Edits Publications.

Kirkpatrick, D.L. (1967). Evaluation of Training. In R.L. Craig & L.R. Bittel (Eds.), *Training and development handbook.* New York: McGraw-Hill.

Lockwood, D.L., & Luthans, F. (1980). Multiple measures to assess the impact of organization development interventions. In J.W. Pfeiffer & J.E. Jones (Eds.), *The 1980 annual handbook for group facilitators.* San Diego, CA: University Associates, pp. 233-246.

Merwin, S. (1986). *Effective evaluation strategies and techniques: A key to successful training.* San Diego, CA: University Associates.

Morris, L.L. (Ed.). (1978). *Program evaluation kit.* Beverly Hills, CA: Sage Publications.

Patton, M.Q. (1978). *Utilization-focused evaluation.* Beverly Hills, CA: Sage Publications.

Richards, A. (Ed.). (1980). *Evaluation handbook.* San Francisco: Public Management Institute.

U.S. Office of Personnel Management. *Report of the training evaluation demonstration project.* Washington, DC: Author, March, 1979.[1]

---

[1]May be obtained by writing to Training Information Branch, Room 7453, Office of Personnel Management, 19th and E Streets, N.W., Washington, DC 20415.

Performance Analysis

Harless, J.H. (1970). *An ounce of analysis (is worth a pound of objectives)*. Newnan, GA: Guild V Publications.

Mager, R.F., & Pipe, P. (1970). *Analyzing performance problems (or you really oughta wanna)*. Belmont, CA: Lear Siegler/Fearon Publishers.

Rummler, G.A. (1976). The performance audit. In R. Craig (Ed.), *ASTD training and development handbook* (2nd ed.). New York: McGraw-Hill.

Cost-Benefit Analysis

Deming, B.S. (1982). *Evaluating job-related training*. Washington, DC: American Society for Training and Development, and Englewood Cliffs, NJ: Prentice-Hall.

Flamholtz, E.G. (1985). *Human resource accounting*. San Francisco: Jossey-Bass.

Paquet, B., et al. (1987, May). The bottom line. *Training and Development Journal*.

Seppala, G.R. (1979). An approach to determining the value of managerial training. In Peterson (Ed.), *ASTD research series: Determining the payoff of managerial training*, pp. 180-202. Madison, WI: ASTD.

Swanson, R.A., & Geroy, G.D. (1987). Forecasting the economic benefits of training. In J.W. Pfeiffer (Ed.), *The 1987 annual: Developing human resources*, pp. 213-223. San Diego, CA: University Associates.

U.S. Civil Service Commission. *A training cost model*. Washington, DC: Author, 1972.[2]

Phyliss Cooke, Ph.D., is a senior consultant with UA Consulting and Training Services, a subsidiary of University Associates, Inc., in San Diego, California. She specializes in coaching managers in communication and leadership style, the design of training programs, the training of trainers, management-development training in how to facilitate, leadership development, conflict management, and assertiveness training. She has had extensive experience in consulting with Pacific Rim groups and enjoys working with cross-cultural issues. At Kent State University, Dr. Cooke taught graduate courses in group development, organization development, assertiveness training, and personal development. She also served as administrative director of the Cleveland Institute for Rational Living, where she had a private clinical practice, and served as a psychologist for the Cleveland Board of Education.

Ralph R. Bates is a senior trainer with UA Consulting and Training Services. He specializes in the training of trainers, organization development, and management development. His main areas of emphasis are training design and facilitation, team building, strategic planning, conflict management, performance appraisal, problem solving, and leadership. He recently returned to private practice after seven years as vice president of OD and Personnel for TransCentury Corporation, an international consulting firm. He has done extensive consulting and training in Latin America and in Africa.

---

[2]May be obtained by writing to Training Information Branch, Room 7453, Office of Personnel Management, 19th and E Streets, N.W., Washington, DC 20415.

LEADERSHIP IS IN
THE EYE OF THE FOLLOWER

James M. Kouzes and Barry Z. Posner

What you have heard about leadership is only half the story. Leadership is not just about leaders; it is also about followers. Leadership is a reciprocal process. It occurs *between* people. It is not done by one person to another.

Successful leadership depends far more on the follower's *perception* of the leader than on the leader's abilities. Followers, not the leader, determine when someone possesses the qualities of leadership. In other words, leadership is in the eye of the follower.

LEADERSHIP CHARACTERISTICS

During a five-year period we investigated the perceptions that followers have of leaders. We asked more than 10,000 managers nationwide from a wide range of private and public organizations to tell us what they look for or admire in their leaders. The results from these surveys have been striking in their regularity. It seems there are several essential tests a leader must pass before we are willing to grant him or her the title of "leader."

According to our research, the majority of us admire leaders who are honest, competent, forward-looking, inspiring, and, ultimately, *credible*.

Honesty

In every survey we conducted, honesty was selected more often than any other leadership characteristic. After all, if we are to willingly follow someone, whether into battle or into the boardroom, we first want to assure ourselves that the person is worthy of our trust. We will ask, "Is that person truthful? Ethical? Principled? Of high integrity? Does he or she have character?" These are not simple questions to answer. It is not easy to measure such subjective characteristics. In our discussions with

Adapted from James M. Kouzes and Barry Z. Posner, "Eye of the Follower" (*Administrative Radiology,* April 1986, pp. 55-56, 58, 63-64); *The Leadership Challenge: How To Get Extraordinary Things Done in Organizations* (San Francisco, CA: Jossey-Bass Publishers, 1987); and the *Leadership Practices Inventory* (San Diego, CA: University Associates, 1988). Used with permission.

The Leadership Challenge and the *Leadership Practices Inventory* are available from University Associates.

respondents we found that it was the *leader's behavior* that provided the evidence. In other words, regardless of what leaders say about their integrity, followers wait to be shown.

Leaders are considered honest by followers if they do what they say they are going to do. Agreements not followed through, false promises, cover-ups, and inconsistencies between word and deed are all indicators that an ostensible leader is not honest. On the other hand, if a leader behaves in ways consistent with his or her stated values and beliefs, then we can entrust to that person our careers, our security, and ultimately even our lives.

This element of trustworthiness is supported in another study we conducted of leadership practices. In that study we found that of all behaviors describing leadership, the most important single item was the leader's display of trust in others. Irwin Federman, venture capitalist and former president and CEO (chief executive officer) of chip-maker Monolithic Memories, says it best: "Trust is a risk game. The leader must ante up first." If leaders want to be seen as trustworthy, they must first give evidence of their own trust in others.

Sam Walton, founder and chairman of Wal-Mart Stores, Inc., provides an excellent example of trustworthiness and "anteing up first" in leadership: In 1983 Walton—rated by *Forbes* to be the richest man in the United States—made a wager. Concerned that the company might have a disappointing year, he bet Wal-Mart employees that if they achieved a greater profit than in previous years he would don a hula skirt and hula down Wall Street. They did. And he did. He kept his word and did what he said he would do. He showed he had integrity, even if it meant public embarrassment. But imagine what would have happened had Sam not kept his word. You can believe that his employees would not have anted up for the next bet!

Competence

The leadership attribute chosen next most frequently is competence. To enlist in another's cause, we must believe that person knows what he or she is doing. We must see the person as capable and effective. If we doubt the leader's abilities, we are unlikely to enlist in the crusade. Leadership competence does not necessarily refer to the leader's technical abilities. Rather the competence followers look for varies with the leader's position and the condition of the company. For example, the higher the rank of the leader, the more people demand to see demonstrations of abilities in strategic planning and policy making. If a company desperately needs to clarify its corporate strategy, a CEO with savvy in competitive marketing may be seen as a fine leader. But at the line functional level, where subordinates expect guidance in technical areas, these same managerial abilities will not be enough.

We have come to refer to the kind of competence needed by leaders as *value-added competence*. Functional competence may be necessary, but it is insufficient. The leader must bring some *added value* to the position. Tom Melohn, president of North American Tool and Die (NATD) in San Leandro, California, is a good case in point. Tom, along with a partner, bought NATD several years ago. A former consumer-products executive, Tom knows nothing about how to run a drill press or a stamping machine. He claims he cannot even screw the license plates on his car. Yet, in the nine years since he bought the company, NATD has excelled in every possible measure in its industry, whereas under the original founder—an experienced toolmaker—NATD achieved only average or below-average results.

If Tom brings no industry, company, or technical expertise to NATD, what has enabled him to lead the firm to its astounding results? Our answer: Tom added to the firm what it most needed at the time—the abilities to motivate and sell. Tom entrusted the skilled employees with the work they knew well; and for his part, he applied the selling skills he had learned from a quarter-century in marketing consumer products. He also rewarded and recognized the NATD "gang" for their accomplishments, increasing their financial and emotional sense of ownership in the firm.

Being Forward-Looking

Over half of our respondents selected "forward-looking" as their third most sought-after leadership trait. We expect our leaders to have a sense of direction and a concern for the future of the company. Some use the word "vision"; others, the word "dream." Still others refer to this sense of direction as a "calling" or "personal agenda." Whatever the word, the message is clear: True leaders must know where they are going.

Two other surveys that we conducted with top executives reinforced the importance of clarity of purpose and direction. In one study, 284 senior executives rated "developing a strategic planning and forecasting capability" as the most critical concern. These same senior managers, when asked to select the most important characteristics in a CEO, cited "a leadership style of honesty and integrity" first, followed by "a long-term vision and direction for the company."

By "forward-looking" we do not mean the magical power of a prescient visionary. The reality is far more down to earth: It is the ability to set or select a desirable destination toward which the organization should head. The vision of a leader is the compass that sets the course of the company. Followers ask that a leader have a well-defined orientation to the future. A leader's "vision" is, in this way, similar to an architect's model of a new building or an engineer's prototype of a new product.

Think of it another way. Suppose you wanted to take a trip to a place where you had never been before—say Nairobi, Kenya. What would you do over the next few days if you knew you were going there in six months? Probably get a map, read a book about the city, look at pictures, talk to someone who had been there. You would find out what sights to see, what the weather is like, what to wear, and where to eat, shop, and stay. Followers ask nothing more from a leader than a similar kind of orientation: "What will the company look like, feel like, be like when it arrives at its goal in six months or six years? Describe it to us. Tell us in rich detail so we can select the proper route and know when we have arrived."

Inspiration

We expect our leaders to be enthusiastic, energetic, and positive about the future—a bit like cheerleaders. It is not enough for a leader to have a dream about the future. He or she must be able to communicate the vision in ways that encourage us to sign on for the duration. As Apple Computer manager Dave Patterson puts it, "The leader is the evangelist for the dream."

Some people react with discomfort to the idea that being inspiring is an essential leadership quality. One chief executive officer of a large corporation even told us, "I don't trust people who are inspiring"—no doubt in response to past crusaders who led their followers to death or destruction. Other executives are skeptical of their ability to inspire others. Both are making a mistake. It is absolutely essential that leaders inspire our confidence in the validity of the goal. Enthusiasm and excitement signal the leader's personal conviction to pursuing that dream. If a leader displays no passion for a cause, why should others?

Credibility

Three of these four attributes—honesty, competence, and being inspiring—comprise what communications experts refer to as "credibility." We found, quite unexpectedly, in our investigation of admired leadership qualities that more than anything else people want leaders who are *credible*. Credibility is the foundation on which inspiring leadership visions are built. When we believe a leader is credible, then we somehow feel more secure around him or her. This sense of security enables us to let go of our reservations and release enormous personal energy on behalf of the common vision. Credibility and an attractive image of the future are the very essence of leadership.

However, credibility is extremely fragile. It takes years to earn it, an instant to lose it. Credibility grows minute by minute, hour by hour, day by day, through persistent, consistent, and patient demonstration that one is worthy of followers' trust and respect. It is lost with one false step, one thoughtless remark, one inconsistent act, one broken agreement, one lie, one cover-up.

LEADERSHIP PRACTICES

Leaders establish and maintain their credibility by their actions, and in our research we uncovered five fundamental practices that enabled leaders to earn followers' confidence and to get extraordinary things done. When at their best, leaders (1) challenge the process, (2) inspire a shared vision, (3) enable others to act, (4) model the way, and (5) encourage the heart.[1]

---

[1]The *Leadership Practices Inventory* measures these five practices.

Challenging the Process

Leaders are pioneers—people who seek out new opportunities and are willing to change the status quo. They innovate, experiment, and explore ways to improve the organization. They treat mistakes as learning experiences. Leaders also stay prepared to meet whatever challenges may confront them.

Inspiring a Shared Vision

Leaders look toward and beyond the horizon. They envision the future with a positive and hopeful outlook. Leaders are expressive and attract followers through their genuineness and skillful communications. They show others how mutual interests can be met through commitment to a common purpose.

Enabling Others to Act

Leaders infuse people with spirit-developing relationships based on mutual trust. They stress collaborative goals. They actively involve others in planning, giving them discretion to make their own decisions. Leaders ensure that people feel strong and capable.

Modeling the Way

Leaders are clear about their business values and beliefs. They keep people and projects on course by behaving consistently with these values and modeling how they expect others to act. Leaders also plan and break projects down into achievable steps, creating opportunities for small wins. They make it easier for others to achieve goals by focusing on key priorities.

Encouraging the Heart

Leaders encourage people to persist in their efforts by linking recognition with accomplishments, visibly recognizing contributions to the common vision. They let others know that their efforts are appreciated and express pride in the team's accomplishments. Leaders also find ways to celebrate achievements. They nurture a team spirit that enables people to sustain continued efforts.

UNIQUE RELATIONSHIP

Leadership is a relationship, a unique and special trust between the leader and followers. The development of this trusting relationship requires our full and caring attention as leaders. Below are five prerequisites to building and maintaining this bond of trust.

1. *Know your followers.* Building any relationship begins with getting to know those we desire to lead. Get to know their hopes, their fears, their values, their biases, their dreams, their nightmares, their aspirations, and their disappointments. Find out what is important to your followers. Come to know what they seek. Only in this way can you show them how their interests can be served by aligning with yours.

2. *Stand up for your beliefs.* In our culture we appreciate people who take a stand. We resolutely refuse to follow people who lack confidence in their own values and decisions. Confusion among your followers over your stand creates stress; not knowing what you believe leads to conflict, indecision, and political rivalry. There is, however, a danger in always standing on principle; it can make one rigid and insensitive. The key to escaping rigidity is to remain open to others. Listen; understand; empathize. We respect leaders who can listen to and understand our points of view, yet believe in their own hearts that other viewpoints are superior. If your beliefs are strongly held, ethical, and based on sound thinking, followers will find ways to align themselves with you.

3. *Speak with passion.* Managers constantly talk about motivating their people, of lighting a fire under them. If the leader is a wet match, there will be no spark to ignite passion in others. Enthusiasm, energy, and commitment begin with the leader. To gain the commitment of others you must communicate your excitement about the dream. Paint word pictures. Tell stories. Relate anecdotes. Weave metaphors. Enable others to see, hear, taste, smell, and feel what you experience. When the dream lives inside others, it lives forever.

4. *Lead by example.* Leaders are role models. We look to them for clues on how we should behave. We always believe their actions over their words. We will never forget the story told to us by a young manager, John Schultz, about his days as a high-school football player:

> When I played high-school football, I had three coaches. The first two were exactly alike. Each said, "Men, while you are in training I don't want you to smoke, drink, stay up late, or fool around with girls. Got that?" Then we would watch our coaches during the season. They would smoke, drink, stay up late, and fool around with women. So what do you suppose we did? Boys will be boys, after all.
> My third coach was the best I ever had. At the beginning of the season we had the same locker-room sermon as with the other coaches. Except this coach just said, "I have only one rule. You can do anything I do. If I smoke, drink, stay up late, or fool around with women, then I would expect you to do the same. But if I don't, you'd better not!"

If leaders ask followers to observe certain standards, then the leaders need to live by the same rules. That is exactly what we were told many times by exemplary leaders. You can only lead by example. Leadership is not a spectator sport. Leaders do not sit in the stands and watch. Hero myths aside, neither are leaders in the game substituting for the players. Leaders coach. They show others how to behave.

5. *Conquer yourself.* Jim Whittaker, the first American to reach the summit of Mt. Everest, learned that he could not conquer a mountain, because mountains cannot be conquered. He had to conquer himself—his hopes, his fears. It might brighten

our heroic image of leaders to believe that they conquer organizations, communities, states, nations, the world. It might make good cinema to picture the leader riding into town on a white horse and single-handedly destroying the villains. But this Lone Ranger portrait of great leaders only perpetuates a falsehood. The real struggle of leadership is internal. The everyday struggles of leaders include internal questions such as: Do you understand what is going on in the company and the world in which it operates? Are you prepared to handle the problems the company is facing? Did you make the right decision? Did you do the right thing? Where do you think the company should be headed? Are you the right one to lead others there?

This inner struggle places enormous stress on the leader. Followers do not want to see that their leaders lack self-confidence. Certainly they like to know their leaders are human, that they can laugh and cry and have a good time; but followers will not place their confidence in someone who appears weak, uncertain, or lacking in resolve. Followers need to sense that the leader's internal struggle has been fought and won. Conquering yourself begins with determining your value system. Strongly held beliefs compel you to take a stand.

THE EYE OF THE FOLLOWER

These characteristics, these practices, these relationships are tough measures for the leader. It may not seem right to be judged so harshly, but followers perceive leadership in their own terms, and those terms are not always fair. After all, the leader is not a leader unless there are followers; and there are no true followers unless the leader is a leader in the eye of the follower.

James M. Kouzes is the president of TPG/Learning Systems and a partner in The Tom Peters Group. He is the former director of the Executive Development Center (EDC) in the Leavey School of Business and Administration at Santa Clara University. In addition, he was the founder of the Joint Center for Human Services Development at San Jose State University, which he managed from 1972 to 1980. He is the author of numerous publications and the co-author of the Leadership Practices Inventory.

Barry Z. Posner, Ph.D., is an associate professor of management and the director of graduate programs at the Leavey School of Business and Administration at Santa Clara University. He is an internationally recognized scholar and educator and has received his university's Distinguished Faculty Award. Dr. Posner is currently the president of the Western Academy of Management, serves on the boards of directors of two companies, and is a frequent conference speaker. He is the author of many publications and the co-author of the Leadership Practices Inventory.

FOSTERING INTRAPRENEURSHIP IN ORGANIZATIONS

Gifford Pinchot III

Intrapreneur: Any of the "dreamers who do." Those who take hands-on responsibility for creating innovation of any kind within an organization. The intrapreneur may be the creator or inventor but is always the dreamer who figures out how to turn an idea into a profitable reality.

Gifford Pinchot III, 1985
Intrapreneuring: Why You Don't Have to Leave the Corporation to Become an Entrepreneur, p. ix

Entrepreneurism is alive and well in America. It is generated by the American spirit of adventure, the desire to try new things. Americans are known for this spirit, and it shows up in their approach to business and organizational life. Americans do not want to be just cogs in a machine; they want to contribute, to make names for themselves, to do something new and different. This desire is not exclusive to entrepreneurs, who branch out on their own and start new businesses; it is also characteristic of *intrapreneurs,* those heroes inside existing organizations who are driven to innovate. In fact, it is unusual for innovation to happen in a large organization without one or more such individuals who are totally dedicated to making it happen.

Unfortunately, the systems of control in many organizations, particularly in very large ones, often make innovation difficult if not impossible. Intrapreneurs often have to battle tedious bureaucracies to see their "intraprises"—those innovations to which they dedicate themselves—become reality. Yet innovation still happens, despite such systems of control. There is almost no stopping intrapreneurs in pursuit of their dreams, even when they have to leave their organizations to realize those dreams. The tragedy of this phenomenon is that when intrapreneurs leave to become entrepreneurs, it is their parent organizations that suffer from the loss of some of their best employees; often these employees start businesses that later become competitors of the organizations left behind.

Based on and adapted from *Intrapreneuring: Why You Don't Have to Leave the Corporation to Become an Entrepreneur* by G. Pinchot III, 1985, New York: Harper & Row. Copyright © 1985 by Gifford Pinchot III. Used with the permission of the author. The hardcover book is available from Pinchot & Company, 409 Orange Street, New Haven, CT 06511, phone (203) 624-5355. The price is $15.00 (includes shipping and handling in the U.S.).

Halting the exit of dedicated intrapreneurs poses an enormous challenge to today's organizations. Despite the systems of control they have created, most organizations do not want to lose these people. Consequently, they need to find ways to encourage rather than discourage the development of intraprises. A number of organizations are successfully accomplishing this objective (Pinchot, 1985)—for example, 3M, General Electric, IBM, Tektronix, Ore-Ida, Texas Instruments, Du Pont—and much can be learned from their experiences. This article addresses two important issues: (1) the ways in which an organization can encourage innovation and empower intrapreneurs and (2) the roles that an HRD practitioner can assume to help in this process.

WAYS TO ENCOURAGE INNOVATION
AND EMPOWER INTRAPRENEURS

1. Encourage Self-Appointed Intrapreneurs

The traditional organizational approach to job assignments is paternalistic. The manager decides which subordinate would be right for a particular task and then delegates the task to that person. But intrapreneurs are not typical subordinates; they come up with intraprises on their own and cling to them steadfastly, doing whatever is necessary to be allowed to execute those intraprises.

Although the idea of allowing a subordinate to choose his or her own projects may seem unusual, it fits with one of the primary objectives of any manager: to get subordinates to engage their minds and hearts in tasks that fulfill corporate objectives. Managers may have difficulty in letting go of the notion that they know best how tasks should be delegated and that only the traditional tasks associated with their subordinates' jobs are appropriate. The critical test for accepting or rejecting an intraprise about which an intrapreneurial subordinate feels passionately is whether that intraprise helps to fulfill corporate objectives. The intrapreneur has almost a sixth sense about the services and products that clients and customers need, and the wise manager will recognize and make use of this sense.

Intrapreneurs cannot be appointed and told to bring their zeal to bear on specific intraprises. Instead, managers should watch for subordinates who express passionate beliefs in specific projects; then these subordinates can be empowered to act on these beliefs. What often happens is that intrapreneurs are so convinced of the rightness of their intraprises that they proceed without permission. The system that recognizes and fosters intrapreneurship may only be legitimizing what is already happening. Managers need to recognize another potential benefit of encouraging intrapreneurship: the intrapreneur's commitment to an intraprise in which he or she deeply believes can shave weeks or months from the time required to execute that intraprise. When an intrapreneur gets going, the speed of work can be astonishing.

2. Allow the Intrapreneur to Follow Through to Completion

In many large organizations, new ideas are handed from group to group during the course of development. Part of this practice stems from the specialization of work that often develops in big companies. However, it is not natural for an idea to be formed by researchers, then developed in the form of a prototype by people in advanced development, then designed by engineers, then executed by people in manufacturing, and finally sold by marketing people. Such a system does not work because (1) people want to work on ideas of their own choosing and are most committed to those ideas, and (2) no one can transfer everything he or she knows about something to another person, regardless of the extent to which that knowledge is documented. Thus, taking intraprises from intrapreneurs and reassigning those intraprises to others can result in the loss of two elements that are critical to success: commitment and knowledge.

Finding ways for intrapreneurs to stay with their intraprises is an important challenge for managers. The source of the intrapreneur's satisfaction is commercial success and social contribution. Consequently, the intrapreneur will not be content until the idea that he or she is committed to has reached the market and started to sell well; this commitment extends to seeing the idea fulfill its promise in commercial terms. Keeping the intrapreneur assigned to an intraprise past the point of market introduction is important not only in terms of the intrapreneur's own satisfaction but also in terms of protecting the organization's market position. Very often the intrapreneur and the members of the intrapreneurial team are the only ones capable of altering the idea quickly enough to keep up with market demands and/or competitor efforts.

3. Let the Intrapreneur Decide and Act

Intrapreneurs need to feel that they are in control of their intraprises. They like to be their own bosses and to do their work as they see fit. One of the surest ways to quell innovation in an organization is to subject intrapreneurs to a cumbersome process that keeps them from making their own decisions and acting quickly in accordance with those decisions. Tying an intrapreneur's hands with bureaucratic red tape not only causes frustration; it also may preclude action to such an extent that the entire intraprise is jeopardized.

A number of large organizations place the authority for making decisions about intraprises with people at several hierarchical levels above the intrapreneur. Often these people cannot or do not communicate with the intrapreneur and, therefore, do not have access to critical information about decisions. Also, the thinking accompanying a potential innovation is usually so complex that those who are not intimately involved cannot hope to grasp it fully. As a result of this dilemma, many intrapreneurs break corporate rules on purpose by simply announcing what they plan to do and proceeding without permission.

Occasionally it may be necessary to let the decision-making authority reside with people other than the intrapreneur, and on these occasions it is essential that the intrapreneur be able to communicate face to face with these people. Most of the time, however, the intrapreneur knows the intraprise best and is in the best position to decide and act as he or she sees fit. This is not to say that intrapreneurs should not be given feedback about their intraprises; on the contrary, they care so deeply about the ultimate success of their innovations that they generally welcome feedback.

4. Provide the Freedom and Resources to Experiment

An organization that commits all of its resources to planned activities cannot foster intrapreneurship. Innovation cannot be planned; when an intrapreneur becomes committed to an innovation, he or she must have access to organizational resources in order to turn the idea into reality. Asking an intrapreneur to predict in advance what resources he or she will need to follow through on an as-yet-unthought-of innovative idea is ludicrous; nevertheless, those resources must exist when the intrapreneur adopts such an idea.

The necessary resources take three forms:

1. *Discretionary time.* In the absence of discretionary time, the intrapreneur's ideas die. This time is needed to prove the viability of an idea without putting that idea under someone else's critical scrutiny. An intrapreneur generally goes through a series of actions aimed at turning an idea into successful reality; the first time is rarely the charm. That is the nature of innovating. But if the first is expected to be the last and experimentation is outlawed, innovation eventually goes by the wayside.

2. *Discretionary funds.* Beyond simple tinkering, experimenting with innovations cannot take place without money. Many organizations slash discretionary funds from their budgets without considering the effect that this policy might have on employees' future intraprises that could either save money or bring in unanticipated funds.

The authority for discretionary spending—and for deciding specifically how to spend money earmarked for a particular experiment—should lie with the people who will work on innovations. It may seem that intrapreneurs tend to spend their allocated funds in unorthodox ways, but it is important to remember that innovations are themselves unorthodox. The course of experimentation often requires a change in plans, which in turn necessitates substituting one expense for another. The system that requires justification of such substitutions or that demands inflexibility in how the experimenter spends allotted money hinders intrapreneurship. Another important point is that even a small amount of money can encourage employees to innovate and can convey an important message about the organization's support of experimentation as well as its belief in its people.

3. *Discretionary help.* Turning innovative ideas into reality generally requires the efforts of at least several people. Yet discretionary help in the form of fellow employees that intrapreneurs can call on when needed is often more difficult to obtain than discretionary money. The practice of freezing numbers of employees in units, departments, or divisions, which is fairly common in large organizations, can seriously undermine

intrapreneurial efforts. Organizations should be aware that intrapreneurs generally need to recruit fellow employees and should create ways to override freezing policies if necessary so that promising innovations can be pursued.

It has long been true that most organizational innovation takes place in a sort of corporate underground that exists beneath the confines of formal systems. Tenacious intrapreneurs frequently find ways to obtain what they need to pursue their dreams, regardless of whether they have official approval. However, when an organization makes it possible for the intrapreneur to obtain discretionary resources by using official systems rather than the underground, innovation is much more likely to occur.

5. Avoid the Grandiose Approach

Some organizations—particularly large ones—make the mistake of assuming that every intraprise that receives the go-ahead should or will result in enormous economic success and, therefore, is worthy of enormous investment. This viewpoint ignores a couple of important facts: (1) many smaller successes can equal one large one; and (2) huge financial investments at the outset can deplete funds that may be more critically needed later, after an innovation has taken hold and achieved some degree of success.

A better approach—one that allows an organization to grasp more opportunities—is to encourage and sponsor a number of small intraprises, each of which offers some short-term promise and several possibilities for the future. This approach fits better with the successful pattern of innovation—a series of corrected mistakes eventually leading to success, followed by rapid expansion. Also, a policy of pursuing a number of small intraprises rather than saving resources only for huge ones gives an organization a better chance of getting in on the ground floor of new industries. Intraprises have a way of becoming new lines of business with their own managements headed by the intrapreneurs who initiated them, and such developments enable a large organization to diversify and to become as responsive to clients and customers as small companies characteristically are.

6. Tolerate Risk, Mistakes, and Failures

Innovation is inherently risky; the organization that encourages innovation is an environment in which people are conditioned to failure and mistakes as an everyday part of their jobs. Most organizations, if polled on the subject, would say that they encourage innovation. However, although they might also claim to encourage risk taking, the opposite is more often true. Part of the problem is that managers often trust themselves to take risks but do not trust subordinates or those in lower organizational levels to do the same, probably because managers are the ones who take much of the flack if risks taken at lower levels result in failure. Consequently, the tolerance of risk, mistakes, and failures must come from the top of the organization, must be communicated downward, and must be genuine. Simple lip service is not enough; when employees actually do fail in innovative efforts, the response of top management must bear out this tolerance.

When failure is not accepted in a system, employees eventually stop taking risks, which means that they stop innovating. Also, it is important to remember that the organization that refuses to tolerate failure is not immune to it. Failures happen, despite people's best efforts to avoid them; thus, a policy against risk taking on the basis that it might result in failure does not make sense.

The benefits of tolerating risk and failures are great:

1. *Learning.* At the very least, people learn from their failures and can apply what they have learned to future efforts. This learning is not exclusive to the person who experiences the failure; co-workers and others frequently share in the learning.

2. *Generation of other innovations.* It is often the case that the failure of the originally conceived intraprise leads to the success of a different but related innovation.

3. *Market exploration.* Not all market discoveries can be made on the basis of information extrapolated from past experience. The organization that tries to gauge future moves exclusively on the basis of history relies on ideas whose time has passed—a policy that is dangerous in turbulent times. All markets are fraught with unknowns that can be uncovered only through experimentation. Intrapreneurs who are passionately dedicated to their intraprises are tenacious in developing customers for their innovations.

7. Be Patient

One of the most formidable barriers to innovation is not giving innovative intraprises time to reach maturity. In some industries it takes a long time to achieve success. Some organizations become impatient with intraprises and pull the plug on their financial backing before giving an intraprise a reasonable amount of time to achieve a degree of success. In many organizations personnel changes wreak havoc with intraprises; for example, the intrapreneur's manager or sponsor may move up or out and leave the intrapreneur out of favor with the powers that be and/or without the help and encouragement needed to proceed.

The problem of assigning a limited time frame for achieving innovative success can be addressed in several ways:

1. *Slow the pace of job transfers.* These days managers move up the corporate ladder with such speed that they seldom stay around to see the completion of intraprises begun in their areas. Consequently, they may tend to favor intraprises that promise quick success—and an accompanying positive image—rather than risky, long-term innovations. The elimination of layers of middle management, as suggested in *In Search of Excellence: Lessons from America's Best Run Companies* (Peters & Waterman, 1982), will help to alleviate this problem. A manager will have fewer steps to take in reaching the top; will spend more time in each position; and may, as a result, be more inclined to encourage long-term intraprises.

2. *Reward the individual steps of innovation, not just the achievement of the final goal.* Waiting for the success of an innovation can be frustrating even to the intrapreneur. When the ultimate reward is far in the distance, it is important to celebrate the achievement of each step along the way.

3. *Make managers' rewards dependent on what happens in their areas after they have moved on.* This approach would encourage managers to focus on long-term success and the innovations that make it happen. The same approach can be taken with CEOs by paying them bonuses after their tenure for successful innovations that were begun under them.

4. *Encourage all employees to consider the long run.* Traditionally only managers have been expected to consider the good of the company in the long run, but all employees should be encouraged to consider the future consequences of their actions. This process is an important part of an employee-involvement program in which people at all organizational levels are taught to be involved, to make good decisions, and to focus on such long-term issues as quality and turning first-time buyers into loyal customers. One way to do this is to promote the survival of intrapreneurial teams that are assembled to work on innovations; these teams should be kept intact through the succesful introduction of the innovation and for some time thereafter to ensure that each team will face the consequences of its members' actions.

5. *Promote a sense of ownership among employees.* An organization can encourage intrapreneurs by offering them the ability to earn a sort of "ownership" of their intraprises that would simulate that of the actual organizational owners. This ownership would include the responsibility not only for completing the innovative intraprise but also for administering the necessary "intracapital"—the discretionary budget allotted to the intrapreneur to fund the innovation. The feeling of ownership generated by this responsibility leads to a sense of security akin to that which owners feel, which, in turn, leads to a consideration of the long run.

6. *Promote the relationship between intrapreneurs and their sponsors.* Organizations that want to foster intrapreneurship must honor this relationship and ensure that intrapreneurs are not separated from their sponsors through events like promotions, transfers, and reorganizations. Sponsors need to maintain contact with intrapreneurs, perhaps even after those sponsors have retired. Offering senior executives a chance to serve as sponsors after retirement, thereby affording them a chance to continue participating in organizational life and earning money, would be an excellent incentive to innovation.

8. Discourage Obsession with Turf

As managers climb the organizational ladder, they sometimes are overconcerned with getting to the top more quickly than their peers. This attitude can lead to an obsession with turf, a struggle for position that can overshadow the importance of striving for results and looking ahead to the future. Because the intrapreneur's responsibility entails crossing turf boundaries and integrating disciplines in the interest of doing something new, obsession with turf can make life difficult for the intrapreneur.

Obsession with turf is contagious; when managers play one group against another, nonmanagerial employees start manifesting the same obsession. Another factor that can exacerbate the problem is the practice of comparing employees during the process of performance review. Also, in larger organizations, separate functions such as accounting sometimes develop a sense of loyalty that leads to snobbery, unhealthy competition between functions, and rigid territorial boundaries.

To eliminate or circumvent this problem, managers can take several actions:

1. *Stay focused on results.* When managers maintain this focus, nonmanagerial employees tend to do the same and are more willing to help intrapreneurs than they might otherwise be.

2. *Emphasize win/win rather than win/lose solutions.* The traditional win/lose attitude is based on the view of an organizational pie that consists of a fixed amount of resources, and this attitude fosters obsession with turf. However, when all employees are productive, the organization as a whole wins and the actual size of the pie increases. When everyone has access to more resources, concern with turf is less likely to develop.

3. *Build small teams whose members represent different functions.* Such a team is particularly appropriate for pursuing an intrapreneurial intraprise because its members operate in the interest of the innovation rather than in the interest of the individual functions they represent (see "9. Form Cross-Functional Teams").

4. *Help people to feel secure in their individual turfs.* When employees are insecure, they often see intrapreneurial ventures as threats and tend to react by entrenching themselves in their individual territories. Employees need to feel that they have their own small kingdoms within the organization; once they feel secure in those kingdoms, it becomes easier for them to be generous and to cooperate with intrapreneurs. To engender security, managers should ensure that people have sufficient control in their own areas to pursue their own dreams; when people feel in control in this way, they are less inclined to deny intrapreneurs access to needed resources.

9. Form Cross-Functional Teams

The best approach to pursuing innovation is to form cross-functional teams expressly for that purpose. When such a team is assembled, the members are recruited and actually taken away from their usual job responsibilities. Then they are assigned exclusively to the intraprise.

This approach offers a number of advantages that tend to foster innovation:

1. *The members of the team identify with the intraprise rather than with their individual functions.* Therefore, it is easy for team members representing different functions to let go of any functional loyalty that might otherwise hamper progress on their innovation.

2. *The team can concentrate exclusively on the intraprise.* Team members do not have to divide their attention between the intraprise and other job responsibilities.

3. *The team members possess enough knowledge and skills for superior problem solving.* Because all functional areas involved in the development and marketing of the intraprise are represented on the team,[1] the members are better able to see a problem from all different aspects, to identify possible ramifications, and to generate effective solutions.

---

[1]This does not necessarily mean that each of these functions has donated someone to serve as a member of the team. Instead, it means that someone on the team either knows or learns how to perform each of the functions necessary to the intraprise. Often team members learn how to do tasks that have nothing to do with their regular job assignments.

4. *The team can act quickly.* It is an autonomous, functionally complete group, and it can move with great speed because of its control over its innovation and because of the commitment of its members. With innovation it is often true that speed makes the difference between success and failure.

5. *There is continuity in team membership.* All members are assigned to the intraprise at least until it has been completed and preferably until sometime after the intraprise service or product has been successfully introduced. The continuity of knowledge, skill, and commitment afforded by this approach offers a distinct advantage over the situation created by changing personnel during the period of the intraprise.

6. *The team is responsible to a single leader, who is also a team member.* The important point is that the leader be in a position to determine the performance of team members, including his or her own. If this is not the case and individual members continue to report to their functional supervisors, the team members experience mixed loyalties, which, in turn, can cause delays, confusion, and so on.

7. *Commitment and ownership are fostered by recruiting rather than appointing team members.* Only people who are interested in an intraprise and volunteer to serve on an intrapreneurial team should be members. If no one volunteers, this is an indication that the intraprise is not a good idea.

10. Let the Intrapreneur Choose from Multiple Options

In pursuing an intraprise, the best policy is to leave many options open to the intrapreneur and to let him or her make all the choices. Requiring an intrapreneur to use exclusively internal resources, for example, may hinder the development of the intraprise.

Putting the intrapreneur in charge offers several advantages. For example, the intrapreneur who is allowed to choose where and how to get the job done can take advantage of the best deals in terms of both price and speed of delivery; often the best deals are not available from internal suppliers who do not have to be as competitive as external ones. Also, both internal and external vendors find it easier to deal with only one person who can evaluate products and services and then has the authority to buy what he or she wants. The intrapreneur can respond quickly when time is important and can avoid the tedium of waiting for approval of purchases. With this approach, innovations become reality sooner.

The principle of allowing the intrapreneur to make major choices should extend to selling the innovation as well. Often companies go through the entire innovative process and then assign responsibility to sell their innovations to the regular sales force. What frequently happens in such situations is that the sales force is not as committed to an innovation as are the members of the intrapreneurial team that developed it; consequently, the salespeople may ignore or give improper attention to the new product or service in favor of selling existing ones with which they are more familiar and more comfortable. For these reasons some people believe it is better for the intrapreneurial team to have its own sales force dedicated exclusively to selling the innovation.

THE ROLES OF THE HRD PRACTITIONER
IN FOSTERING INTRAPRENEURSHIP

The most important function that an HRD practitioner can perform in helping an organization to foster intrapreneurship is that of consciousness raising. It may be that an organization's personnel, both managerial and nonmanagerial, are totally unaware of the concept of intrapreneurship and its benefits; even if some employees are familiar with the concept, it is quite likely that the organization is not actively encouraging intrapreneurs. The practitioner's job is to turn this situation around. There are several roles that the HRD practitioner can assume in connection with the responsibility of raising people's consciousness: consultant, promoter, educator, trainer, and facilitator. These roles and the associated activities are discussed in the following paragraphs.

Consultant/Promoter

By keeping in close contact with managers and their needs and objectives, the HRD practitioner will be in a better position to advise intrapreneurs who seek the practitioner's help in promoting particular intraprises. The practitioner also should keep an eye out for appropriate people within the organization who can serve as sponsors of intrapreneurs and should be prepared to put intrapreneurs in touch with these sponsors.

Another way in which the HRD practitioner can serve as a promoter is to emphasize the importance of supporting the intrapreneur's idea from inception through entry into the market. No idea becomes organizational reality without the sponsorship of key organizational members. The intrapreneur, his or her immediate supervisor, and at least one or two members of a management level above the supervisor's should understand the importance of sponsorship to the success of the intrapreneur's idea. The practitioner can make this importance known, help to recruit sponsors, and perhaps even serve as an advocate of the idea.

When an intraprise succeeds, the practitioner should point out the need to recognize and reward the intrapreneurial team. Sometimes there is a tendency to heap glory exclusively on the intrapreneur who originally pursued the idea, but the reality is that all the members of the team are intrapreneurs. They all take the risks involved in turning a new idea into reality, and they all should be rewarded. The practitioner can be instrumental in seeing that this happens.

On the other hand, when an intraprise fails, there is a potential for career setbacks, not only for the intrapreneur but for the entire intrapreneurial team. If these setbacks occur, the practitioner should be ready to provide encouragement, to point out options, and to coach members of the team as appropriate. If the intrapreneur is inclined to accept the total responsibility for failure, the practitioner should work with the intrapreneur to ensure that this negative experience does not permanently damage his or her innovative spirit.

Educator/Trainer/Facilitator

Working with the Intrapreneur,
the Intrapreneurial Team, and Sponsors

Often an intrapreneur is made the leader of an intrapreneurial team whose task is to bring a particular intraprise to fruition. However, if the intrapreneur has no leadership experience, he or she may be at a loss as to how to fulfill this role. The HRD practitioner should be able to help find or even conduct appropriate training for the intrapreneur and should be willing to serve as a source of further information on the subject of leadership.

Also, lack of experience on the part of the intrapreneur and other members of the intrapreneurial team may mean that they will need help in setting achievable milestones for their intraprise. If this is the case, the practitioner should be prepared to train the team in goal setting and action planning. It may be that the members of the team will need help with team building and with solving problems having to do with team-member interactions. The practitioner may find it helpful to teach the team some of the basics of group process and development as well as some tools that they can use to help group work flow more smoothly. Attending some team meetings as a facilitator may also be appropriate, especially during the early stages of the team's existence.

Intrapreneurs also may lack experience in dealing with organizational politics. Their zeal can sometimes serve to their political disadvantage. Consequently, when working with intrapreneurs, the practitioner should remain on the lookout for political pitfalls that might spell disaster for intraprises. Educating intrapreneurs and their sponsors with regard to these pitfalls and to potential enemies behind the scenes is one of the more valuable services that the practitioner can provide. With knowledge of barriers that might be faced, the intrapreneur and his or her sponsor can plan an effective strategy for by-passing these barriers or at least mitigating their potency.

One political issue that an intrapreneur may not be prepared to handle is the possibility that the innovation might be stolen if it is a success. As discussed previously, it is important, both for intrapreneurs and for the organization's interests, to keep intraprises in the hands of their creators. However, connection with successful intraprises is a strong enticement to those who might want to steal the idea if it is particularly desirable to competitors. Even if it seems unlikely that the idea could be stolen, some individuals might attempt to steal the limelight, the credit, or other rewards that rightfully belong to intrapreneurs. The practitioner should keep intrapreneurs and their sponsors informed about such possibilities and should be prepared to give advice for dealing with threats or actual thefts. This may entail putting intrapreneurs in touch with legal counsel or others who will be able to advise them about patents, copyright issues, and so on.

Working with Management

Battling long-established systems of control may be the HRD practitioner's greatest challenge in helping to foster intrapreneurship. For example, the notion of granting decision-making authority to intrapreneurs may be totally foreign to established organizational policy. An important point to stress to top management is that innovation cannot wait; when it is put on hold, the competitive edge may be lost. The practitioner can also help managers to realize that even though they may be unable to fathom a particular decision or its urgency, their faith in the intrapreneur and his or her profound commitment to the intraprise should convince them to grant the authority to follow through on that commitment.

Similarly, if managers are skeptical about providing resources for the purpose of experimenting, the practitioner should stress that people who are not encouraged to experiment may eventually lose the inclination, if not the ability, to innovate. Also, employees who are never trusted to handle money, as would be required during the process of experimentation, may become indifferent to it and never learn to spend it fruitfully yet prudently. Because the process of experimentation requires responsibility in using resources, responsibility is what employees who experiment learn— along with an enhanced appreciation of scarce resources. The practitioner may be able to use these principles effectively as selling points.

It also may be useful for the practitioner to cite precedents for fostering intrapreneurship along with examples of bottom-line results (Pinchot, 1985). Many large companies—IBM, Tektronix, Ore-Ida, 3M, and DuPont, among others—allow their employees to spend between 5 and 15 percent of their time exploring ideas of their own choosing. The results of providing employees with discretionary resources in this way have been impressive. Ore-Ida, for example, reported savings of more than two million dollars from the outcome of an experimental project that the company funded for $15,000. Ore-Ida and Texas Instruments offer employees different funding sources as ways to finance their experiments, and both companies have reported benefits.

On the other hand, an inclination to spend too much in the initial stages of innovation may be the problem in a large organization. In this case the practitioner should emphasize the advantages of financial restraint, pointing to the fact that greater funds may be necessary once the innovation has achieved a degree of success and goes into full swing as a viable line of business. As discussed previously, management sometimes loses sight of the fact that a number of small intraprises can equal one large one. Another useful selling point for investing relatively small amounts in several small intraprises is that this approach gives the organization an opportunity to capitalize on new trends.

If management seems reluctant to support a number of intraprises, the practitioner might suggest a policy of encouraging competition among intrapreneurial teams. With this policy several teams develop intraprises with the understanding that the best design, developed with the least expenditure of resources, will be the one that the organization ultimately supports. This approach gives rise to superior innovations but can work only if intrapreneurs are allowed to determine how to get the job done. In contrast, one sure way to discourage innovation is to take the all-too-frequent approach of always supporting the design that is developed by the people who have the formal authority and resources—such as the design of the engineering division as opposed to that of an eager intrapreneur from marketing. Performance—not politics—should be the basis for evaluating intraprises; using resources creatively and effectively and generating the best design should be the criteria for judging intraprises. The practitioner should encourage top management to be open minded when evaluating intraprises and to let employees know that innovation, regardless of its source, is valued.

Despite intrapreneurs' best efforts—and those of the practitioner to provide sufficient support—intraprises frequently fail. How management treats such failures can go a long way toward encouraging or discouraging innovation. One advantage to failure that managers may tend to lose sight of is that it is rarely total; it almost always leads to valuable learning, not only on the part of the employee or group that has failed, but also on the part of those who learn from documentation as well as word-of-mouth information about that failure. The practitioner can stress this point to managers and can cite examples like that of Ore-Ida, whose management tries to encourage experimentation through its fellows program, whereby employees can receive grants for pet innovative projects (Pinchot, 1985). This program, for which there is no retribution whatsoever for failure, is, according to Ore-Ida's manager for research and development, intended to tell employees that they do not need to be afraid to fail and that all they need to do is learn from their efforts. Ore-Ida gives each intrapreneur who pursues an idea a certificate, even if the intraprise in question has failed. This policy says to employees that their learning is valued as much as their intraprise efforts.

Managers must be able to congratulate employees for what they have learned even when their intraprises have failed. People at all levels should be conditioned to take pride in the knowledge and skills acquired and the courage they have shown in pursuing intraprises. This may mean that the practitioner will have to work with management to establish and publicly acknowledge support of intelligent risk taking, creativity, and similar values. The knowledge that these values are organizational norms gives rise to security, which is a prerequisite to innovation.

CONCLUSION

Intrapreneurs are the people of courage and conviction within our organizations. By pursuing innovation with total commitment, they are largely responsible for organizational growth and expansion; without them progress would be difficult, if not impossible. An organization can make it difficult or easy for intrapreneurs to pursue their intraprises. It can insist on adherence to rigid system controls; or it can encourage experimentation, risk taking, and the pioneering spirit. It can force its intrapreneurs to leave and start their own businesses, or it can make a purposeful effort to keep these people and to provide them with what they need in order to create. The challenge for the HRD practitioner is to guide intrapreneurs, intrapreneurial teams, their sponsors, and the organizational management toward behaviors that foster rather than hinder intrapreneurship.

REFERENCES

Peters, T.J., & Waterman, R.H., Jr. (1982). *In search of excellence: Lessons from America's best run companies.* New York: Harper & Row.

Pinchot, Gifford III. (1985). *Intrapreneuring: Why you don't have to leave the corporation to become an entrepreneur.* New York: Harper & Row.

Gifford Pinchot III is an author, speaker, and consultant on innovation management. His best-selling book, Intrapreneuring: Why You Don't Have to Leave the Corporation to Become an Entrepreneur *(Harper & Row, 1985) defined the ground rules for an emerging field of enterprise: the courageous pursuit of new ideas in established organizations. He is the chairman of Pinchot & Company, a firm based in New Haven, Connecticut, that helps companies to become more innovative. This firm diagnoses and helps to improve the environment for innovation, trains intrapreneurial teams to succeed, helps managers to be better sponsors of innovation, and designs reward systems more favorable to innovation and wise long-term management.*

A MODEL FOR THE EXECUTIVE MANAGEMENT OF TRANSFORMATIONAL CHANGE

Richard Beckhard

The focus of this article is the management of a transformational-change effort in a significant system or a complex organization. The management of this type of change is distinctly different in a number of ways from the management of change in many other arenas that concern HRD practitioners daily. A transformational change is orchestrated by the organization's executive managers, who must have access to a model that enables them to diagnose and manage the change process. In addition, employing such a model effectively is dependent on the managers' understanding of a number of important issues: the nature of transformation, the implications of transformational change, the organizational conditions and behavioral changes that are necessary for transformation to succeed, and the challenges and dilemmas that are likely to be encountered. This article presents a model for transformational change that HRD practitioners may suggest to managers facing this difficult task, and it provides useful information that practitioners can pass along to managers to help them develop the understanding of the process that is so critical to success.

THE NATURE OF TRANSFORMATION

The definition of transformation in Webster's is "A change in the shape, structure, nature of something." This definition coordinates well with the needs and practices of organizations involved in transformational change. There is no question that there is an increasing need for a complex organization in today's world to change its *shape* to accommodate changing demands; an organization faces a heavy responsibility in attempting to determine the shape, in terms of both size and complexity, that will allow it to function effectively in the dynamic world in which it operates. Merely altering the configuration or writing new job descriptions is an inadequate and possibly even inappropriate response, given the difficulty of the task.

Transformation in an organization can also address *structure,* or the basic parts of the organization that are responsible for its character or its *nature*. Structure includes values, beliefs, reward systems, ownership, patterns, and so on. Sometimes environmental factors change and necessitate significant reappraisals of the organization's nature: consumer interests and demands, work force, technology, telecommunication, and competition.

However, an in-depth assessment of shape, structure, character or nature, and environment—difficult and essential as that task may be—is insufficient of itself. Undertaking transformational change also necessitates re-examining the organization's mission and creating a vision or desired future state as well as the strategies by which the organization can move toward that vision. The strategic issues involved in formulating an organization's mission and vision are quite different from those involved in "running the store" or increasing profits in the short term, and HRD practitioners need to ensure that executive managers who attempt transformation are aware of these differences.

The types of organizational changes that can be called transformational are as follows:

1. *A change in what drives the organization.* For example, a change from being production driven or technology driven to being market driven is transformational.

2. *A fundamental change in the relationships between or among organizational parts.* Examples include redefining staff roles and moving from central management to decentralized management or from executive management to strategic management.

3. *A major change in the ways of doing work.* Such transformational changes include moving from low-technology to high-technology manufacturing systems, implementing computers and telecommunications, and redesigning the customer interface (for example, by providing salespeople with lap computers so that they can interact directly with both customers and suppliers).

4. *A basic cultural change in norms, values, or reward systems.* An example of a cultural change is moving from standardized incentive rewards to individualized ones.

ORGANIZATIONAL PREREQUISITES

The following ten conditions or elements, which are discussed in order of priority, must exist before transformational change can be achieved in an organization.

Prerequisite 1: Committed Top Leaders

One or more of the organization's top leaders, including the chief executive officer (CEO), must be committed champions of the change. In assisting executive managers with transformational change, the HRD practitioner cannot overemphasize the importance of top-level commitment and the visibility of that commitment. Those at lower organizational levels who will be responsible for implementing various aspects of the change cannot be expected to commit to the effort until they see for themselves that the organizational leadership is similarly committed. Although it is possible to achieve some degree of change without top-level commitment, that change is likely to be ephemeral at best.

Prerequisite 2: Written Description of the Changed Organization

It is essential to have a statement, written in behavioral terms, of how the changed organization will function. This statement should include a description of the basic organizational character, policies, values, and priorities that will exist as a result of the transformational change. The HRD practitioner should stress that this statement is not a list of short-term objectives and should monitor the writing process carefully to ensure that the statement is sufficiently detailed and focused on behavior.

Prerequisite 3: Conditions That Preclude Maintenance of the Status Quo

Another critical prerequisite is the existence of a set of external conditions that makes the choice of maintaining the status quo either unlikely or impossible. The HRD practitioner should explain to the executive managers that the transformation will not occur unless people are feeling so much pain in the present situation that they are motivated to change it; in the absence of such pain, resistance will take over and make the change difficult or even impossible.

Prerequisite 4: Likelihood of a Critical Mass of Support

The organizational situation should be studied carefully to determine the potential that a critical mass of support for the change will develop. The HRD practitioner can assist in this task through the use of such means as surveys and interviews. The key players involved in the change, both inside the hierarchical system and in the immediate environment, must be identified and their commitment to the change solicited and obtained.

Prerequisite 5: A Medium- to Long-Term Perspective

Transformational changes take years, not months; it is important that the executive managers understand and accept this time perspective. The HRD practitioner might want to cite examples from his or her own experience of the fact that ''quick-fix'' changes tend to be just that—first-aid treatments that do not have a base for perpetuation. However, it should also be stressed that it is sometimes necessary in the turbulent transitional environment to make quick, dramatic changes in the organization's character. When this is the case, a trap is to mistake such an event for the completion of the entire change effort; instead, it represents only the beginning of the change-management process. Executive managers may need help in discerning the difference between the individual changes that take place during transformation and the completion of the transformation itself. They also may need help in developing a clear strategy for managing the tension between the need for stability—the need to ''run the store''—and the need for change.

Prerequisite 6: Awareness of Resistance and the Need to Honor It

Those managing a transformational change need to be helped to understand and accept resistance to that change. It is essential to devise strategies for working with rather than against resistance. Many executive managers assume that resistance is a representation of "the enemy," whereas the reality is that no change can occur without it. Resistance is the process of internalizing, taking on and letting go, and moving into the new state. This process is totally normal, not neurotic. The tension between the status quo and change is an inherent part of transformation. The appropriate response is to set up ways to manage the resistance productively and to ensure that its effects further the organization's progress in its journey from here to there.

Prerequisite 7: Awareness of the Need for Education

The executive managers must develop awareness of the need to educate the people and groups involved in or affected by the change. This education may go well beyond simply fostering understanding of the change itself; it may include needs assessment and subsequent training in the skills and knowledge that are shown to be essential to functioning successfully in the changed environment. Education is also one of the best tools for reducing resistance and obtaining commitment to a change. The HRD practitioner can play a vital role in developing awareness of the need, pinpointing the kinds of education required, and providing such education through various training programs.

Prerequisite 8: The Conviction That the Change Must Be Tried

This conviction on the part of executive management should include willingness to sustain an experimental attitude throughout the change effort and to stick with the effort. Inherent in this willingness is the assumption that occasional failures will be experienced and will be accepted as a normal part of the learning process that accompanies change. Intolerance of such failures will convince those implementing the change that executive management is not, in fact, committed to the change process and that the old ways of doing things are safer. It is essential that management reward rather than punish the risk taking required in abandoning the old and trying the new. The HRD practitioner can assist in assessing people's orientations toward risk, fostering risk-taking behaviors, and developing an appropriate reward system.

Prerequisite 9: Willingness to Use Resources

Executive management must be willing to "put its money where its mouth is" and use all kinds of resources—technical, consultative, and expert—in support of the change effort. Those responsible for implementing the change will be thwarted in their efforts if they cannot have access to the resources they need. The HRD practitioner can provide useful assistance in specifying the resources that are needed, in serving as a resource, in identifying other internal and external resources, and in encouraging people to generate creative ways of using resources.

Prerequisite 10: Commitment to Maintaining the Flow of Information

From the outset of a transformational-change effort, information must flow freely between and among the different parts of the organization. All employees must receive explicit information about the vision, values, priorities, and rewards that will govern the new state or condition. This often means issuing such information before all of the details are complete. In addition, information about the progress of the effort and about what has worked and what has not worked is extremely valuable. When information is not shared appropriately, mistakes can be repeated and valuable time and other resources can be wasted. Inadequate information also can lead to morale problems. The HRD practitioner can help by stressing the importance of communication; by suggesting appropriate ways to communicate; and by recommending, setting up, and/or conducting training in communication if necessary.

A MODEL OF TRANSFORMATIONAL CHANGE

The process of transforming inputs (needs and raw materials) into outputs (goods and services) is the "work" of an organization. When an organization needs to transform itself, it is, in fact, transforming its work. In any such change, there are three states that must be dealt with: (1) the *present state,* which is things as they are; (2) the *future state,* which is what the changed condition will be; and (3) the *transitional state,* which is the one that exists when evolving from the present to the future—the state during which the actual changing takes place.

The author's model addresses the critical relationships among these three states as well as the ten prerequisites previously discussed. It consists of the following steps:

1. *Designing the future state.* The future state can be defined as the vision for the organization or the strategic objectives of the change. It includes not only the end state but also an intermediate state, which, for example, might be a year or two from the time during which the future state is being planned. The model assumes that for either the end state or the intermediate state, a scenario is needed—a written description of the envisioned behavior of the operation at some point in time. Generally the existing situation is seen as a problem and the future state as the solution to that problem.

2. *Diagnosing the present state.* This diagnosis is performed in the context of the future state. The model suggests that during this step the entire gamut of issues embedded in the defined change problem must be identified, analyzed, and prioritized in terms of any probable domino effects. This means determining whether the individual parts of the change process should or must be completed in a particular order.

3. *Extrapolating what is required to go from the present state to the transitional state.* This step consists of identifying in detail what is required to get from here to there: the activities that must be completed, the resources that must be allocated, the relationships that must be in place, the management structures that are necessary for the transition, and the rewards that must exist. These requirements should be listed in sequence and some time frame established for meeting them.

4. *Analyzing the work that occurs during the transitional state.* This step consists of formulating a complete picture of how the organization will function during the transitional state.

5. *Defining the system that is affecting the problem.* This step does not necessarily mean that everyone affected by the problem must be identified. What is essential is to identify a "critical mass" of people inside and directly outside the organization who must be committed to the change in order for it to succeed. The smallest number of people or groups is the optimum.

6. *Analyzing each of the members of the critical mass with regard to readiness and capability.* Readiness refers to an individual's attitude toward the change, and capability refers to an individual's capacity to do whatever the change requires of him or her. This step is important in that organizational transformation always necessitates the need for changes in the behavior of those who hold key roles in the organization. For example, the types of decision making that are appropriate for a functionally controlled organization are inappropriate for a matrix organization or an organization driven by business areas.

When managing a transformational change, the CEO must behave in ways that indicate commitment to the new state; demonstrating such commitment may be a new and unfamiliar form of behavior. In addition, the goals, priorities, and even activities of the human resource manager may require major modification as a result of transformational change; he or she may need to switch from controlling to facilitating, from providing services only to leading the change, and/or from simply implementing policies to actively initiating new mechanisms like improved reward systems. Finally, a transformation can involve agonizing changes in the power structure, expectations about performance, and the control wielded by heads of major staffs in their own functional areas. The staff heads may have to develop new relationships among themselves and with the business leaders; new rewards must be negotiated; and many questions must be answered. The staff heads, who are accustomed to functioning as "experts" in their particular functions, may need to become supporters, facilitators, and leaders in long-range thinking—a major change requiring behavioral modification. It is a good idea to know at the outset whether the members of the critical mass will be willing and able to respond appropriately to the change; then, if it is determined that certain members are unwilling or unable, that situation can be planned for and dealt with.

7. *Identifying the power relationships and resources necessary to ensure the perpetuation of the change.* It is not enough to carefully analyze what is required to get from here to there; it is equally important to analyze and provide what is necessary to make the change stick.

8. *Setting up an organization (or structure or system) to manage the transformation.* The company's executive managers are responsible for managing the organization that is set up, not necessarily for managing the change work itself. In the absence of such a setup, the transformational effort may deteriorate into a series of undocumented experiments from which people fail to learn.

EXAMPLES OF THE MODEL AT WORK

Case 1: A Cultural Change Initiated Within the Organization

The large, multinational chemical company that is the subject of Case 1 had facilities in over eighty countries and produced a variety of products from pharmaceuticals to heavy chemicals. It operated in many markets, and its competitors were all over the world. Its ownership relationships varied from a wholly owned territory to joint ventures to a partnership.

The company was organized in approximately ten areas of business, each of which had its own board of directors and its own CEO, but all of which were wholly owned by the parent company. The enterprise governance was achieved through a board of directors, half of whom were designated as *executive* directors who provided the company's active leadership and half of whom were designated as *nonexecutive* (external) directors who fulfilled the more traditional board functions. The organization had historically operated through executive management in which the executive directors were the CEOs of the individual businesses as well as the heads of the territories and the functions, such as finance and personnel.

This organization was a leading part of the economy of its home country. It was traditional, highly people oriented, somewhat paternalistic, and a comfortable place to work. Relations with the trade unions were excellent; the company was one of the first to start joint consultations many years ago.

Eventually it became apparent to several members of both the main board and the heads of the businesses that the technically controlled, decentralized divisions, which were primarily local in nature, were not appropriate for addressing the market of the future. Technical innovation had slipped; markets had been eroded in various ways; some of the products were too mature for growth.

Some of the members of the executive board decided to rethink the organizational culture with the following aims:

1. To focus on moving toward a world-wide business;

2. To place the authority for running the businesses with the heads of those businesses rather than with the central directors;

3. To reduce the central directorate to a small number of enterprise directors and to limit their influence; and

4. To revitalize research and development and relate it more to the businesses, replacing the highly centralized research effort with a smaller central effort.

For a number of years the efforts of those who were proponents of this vision were either contained or circumvented by the majority, who resisted such a massive change. The resistance followed classic patterns. For example, commissions and study groups were set up to study organizational changes and changes in board functioning. Through various tactics such as postponing, returning reports for further clarification, and stalling based on excuses like "bad timing," the change efforts were effectively squashed.

A few proponents of the change effort saw themselves as having to provide the executive leadership for the change and having to develop a strategy for doing so. Two or three of them who were on the main board solicited support from other board members; they worked even harder to obtain commitment from the heads of the businesses, who would soon be board members. Over a six-year period the board membership moved from a minority of three people who supported the change to a "critical mass" of individuals who were firmly committed to the change and concerned only about how to implement it.

As some of the leaders of this effort moved into top positions, they began to strengthen the division leadership and to exert their influence in various meetings of the leaders of the businesses around the world. They engaged in goal setting and envisioning for the enterprise and changed the methodology by which the business heads reported to control groups from the center. They began to institute the actual changes that were necessary:

1. They reduced the number of board members to seven and granted group control to all members.

2. They redefined the role of the business head to that of CEO with control over all of his or her resources.

3. They changed to a strategy-management mode in which each of the business heads met with the entire executive board once a year to define strategic objectives and once a year to establish a budget. No other contact with the board was required of the business heads, although each had a contact on the board who provided ongoing support.

4. They revised the budget process.

5. They significantly reduced overhead by combining various subheadquarters of related businesses, thereby eliminating well over twenty thousand overhead positions. With the new, smaller board, they were able to reduce the support staff. The smaller staff allowed them to move their headquarters to a building half the size, thus providing one more visual symbol of the change in the organizational culture.

Despite all of these changes, the leaders of the change effort consciously supported and maintained those values and ways of work that had been productive in the past, such as joint consultation with the unions. They set up specific change-management systems that were administered by committees, subgroups of board members, and special study groups and closely monitored the resulting efforts.

In this case the driving force for transformational change came from within the organization and was led by the top leadership. For the last several years the transformation has been led by one particular member of that leadership, who was designated as the "project manager" of the entire change effort. He used his position power to effect the critical mass that was necessary to make the change.

Case 2: A Change Induced by Competitor Activity

For many years the large, consumer-goods enterprise that is the subject of Case 2 had a virtual monopoly on its products. It sold world-wide, was a household name, and had virtually no competition. It was driven primarily by technology, the making of its products, and the quality of those products. Although there were stores all over the world, manufacturing and distribution were highly centralized; most of the products were made in one giant plant. The majority of the company's employees worked at this home plant, with relatively few workers located at other plants. The function of research and development was very active, constantly upgrading product quality and in recent years moving into related products.

The organization was humanistic, caring, and paternalistic. Employees were never fired; a job at the company was a career for life that paid very well, included excellent benefits, and afforded a nice place to work.

The organization's market share had been relatively stable for a long time and even growing in concert with the growth in the world economies. However, it suddenly began to erode as a result of the emergence of a Japanese competitor that managed to produce a product that was not only competitively priced but also of comparable or better quality. This situation had never existed before. For a time the company failed to acknowledge the problem until the numbers began to be serious, at which time management decided to "regroup, become leaner, and work differently." As is often the case, the first thing the management planned to do was to eliminate people. Programs were instituted to reduce 20 percent of the work force, and these programs were implemented in various ways—generally in a humanitarian manner.

At this point the manufacturing entity, which was the largest facet of the organization in terms of people, initiated a change effort that was very creatively managed. Although the starting point was the requirement of reducing numbers of employees, this requirement was translated into a productivity-improvement program that was implemented under the leadership of a transition-management team composed of high-potential managers. The team members solicited improvement suggestions from the entire organization, received several hundred, and culled these to approximately fifteen. Then they set up fifteen study groups, each of which was charged with designing a new state for one of the fifteen suggestions. When the study-group reports and recommendations had been submitted and approved by the hierarchy, transition teams were established to manage the process of implementing the recommendations. Finally the new states began to emerge.

This change process enabled the manufacturing entity to effect not only the required reduction in numbers of employees, but also an improvement in operation. With many fewer people, ideas that had been considered impossible, such as combinations of major functions, were now implemented successfully. For example, five levels of management were cut; this development sent a message to the work force that the required reductions were not to take place only at the lower levels of the hierarchy.

Other parts of the enterprise made cuts, but not as radically. However, top management became aware that all of the work-force reductions, although necessary, were not attacking the basic problem: the organization had been designed for another time in history rather than for the competitive world in which it now lived. The business was not driving the organization; instead, the organization was driving the business.

It became apparent that the company needed to reorganize fundamentally. After consultation and planning, the company set up the organization in approximately fifteen lines of business, each representing a separate product line and each with a general manager. Clusters of these general managers reported to three group vice presidents. The manufacturing, technical, sales, and other staffs were matrixed. Part of each functional staff was now dedicated to the new businesses, but significant parts were kept functional in order to achieve the synergy necessary for certain processes to occur.

As it is easy to imagine, these changes produced a whole new set of issues. It became necessary to develop a number of change-management organizations to cope with the various matrices and to move the company toward some of the major changes that were essential to the total transformation. Ultimately, the transition state led to several thousand new jobs, important shifts in management, and a test of top management's commitment.

To achieve the critical mass, it was necessary to accomplish the following:

1. Make changes among the key leaders in the organization;
2. Provide new, highly committed leadership that would coordinate all manufacturing efforts; and
3. Make changes in the leadership of the various parts of the manufacturing process, the sales process, the advertising process, and so on.

It took a year to train a group of people to function as the general managers. A task force was set up to provide the training, most of which occurred on the job.

This case presents a situation in which the commitment for change was high at the top; but the methods for achieving the change were confused at first, and not enough effort was expended to infuse the total organizational environment with commitment. Each of the organizational parts was working on its specific concerns, and no one analyzed the domino effect. Subsequently the organization centralized the management of the change effort and instituted information linkages among the parts. Today the change tends to be managed in a more system-wide way than it was previously. The critical dimensions of this transformational effort were starting with a vision that was at first unclear or at least insufficiently communicated, focusing too much on cost reduction and not enough on developing a new state, trying to function without adequate transition-management structures, and consciously intervening in the matrix-management issues until they became acute.

THE CHALLENGES OF TRANSFORMATIONAL CHANGE

As discussed in this paper, a number of challenges must be met any time a transformational change is attempted:

1. Ensuring the commitment of the CEO and key leaders;
2. Ensuring that adequate resources are allocated to support the change and to maintain it once it has been achieved;
3. Reaching an appropriate balance between managing the change and managing the stability of the organization;
4. Ensuring appropriate use of special roles, temporary systems, study groups, consultants, and transition teams;

5. Continually evaluating both the total effort and its individual parts in terms of planning improvement;

6. Establishing and maintaining continuity of leadership during the change process;

7. Appropriately allocating rewards (and punishments) consistent with the priority of the change effort;

8. Ensuring adequate information flow among various parts of the organization; and

9. Constantly monitoring the system to ensure that people know what is happening during the change, understand their roles in the process, and comprehend the total effort rather than only isolated elements of it.

This impressive list could be quite intimidating to any executive managers faced with planning and implementing an organizational transformation. Consequently, the HRD practitioner's role in helping managers meet these challenges can be extremely useful and challenging in its own way.

Richard Beckhard has been consulting with organizations in the private and public sectors for thirty years. For more than twenty years he was a professor of management and organization behavior in the Sloan School of Management at the Massachusetts Institute of Technology in Cambridge. In addition, he has served on the faculties of the London Graduate School of Business, Columbia University Teachers College, and Pepperdine University. He has written several books and numerous articles and has created videotape and film programs on organizational change, organization development, and managing complexity.

MODEL A: A DESIGN, ASSESSMENT, AND FACILITATION TEMPLATE IN THE PURSUIT OF EXCELLENCE

Gerard Egan

I often ask people who manage the corporations, businesses, institutions, and agencies for which I provide consultancy services the following question: "Would it be useful to have a relatively simple and straightforward shared model, framework, or template that could be used by everyone within your enterprise to assess how things are going, to facilitate their work, and to design new projects?" Although they inevitably answer, "Yes," they are usually hard put to describe any kind of shared framework actually in place. This paper is about such a framework.

Many models deal with organizational change; far fewer deal with system design, functioning, and assessment. What is needed is a comprehensive model that is not too complex—one that can be used as a guide in designing, facilitating, and assessing an entire company or institution or any of its parts. Such a model must touch all the bases—business in both its strategic and operational dimensions, organization in terms of both structure and the deployment and utilization of human resources within that structure, guidance and facilitation in terms of both management and leadership, and the "shadow-side" realities that pervade every organization.

The focus of this article—Model A—is a template that touches all these bases. It can be used to design, assess, or facilitate the functioning of an entire company or institution, a division of the company, a department of the division, or a unit within the department. It can also be used for any project or program undertaken by any of these.

Outputs—whether products or services—that meet the needs and wants of clients or customers are the focal point of the model. Model A is *dynamic* because it portrays system members as transforming inputs into outputs (see Figure 1).

Model A has four major parts: business dimensions, organizational dimensions, management and leadership, and managing the shadow side of the organization. The elements of these dimensions are identified in the following paragraphs. In the pursuit of excellence, this model takes a "no-formula" approach. That is, in each of these

This article is based on Gerard Egan's new book *Change-Agent Skills A: Assessing and Designing Excellence,* which explores Egan's Model A and addresses the question of *what* to do in assessing and designing excellence in companies and institutions. Dr. Egan's book also provides examples to show *how* the job can be done. His companion book is entitled *Change-Agent Skills B: Managing Innovation and Change.* Both books were published in 1988 by University Associates.

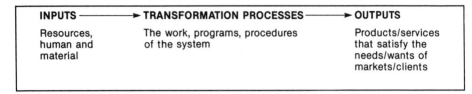

INPUTS ────────▶	TRANSFORMATION PROCESSES ────────▶	OUTPUTS
Resources, human and material	The work, programs, procedures of the system	Products/services that satisfy the needs/wants of markets/clients

Figure 1. Transforming Inputs into Outputs

four areas, the model suggests *principles* of effectiveness. But each company or institution must take these principles and tailor them to its own circumstances. Each must find its own formula. Figure 2 indicates how each of the areas of Model A can contribute to the ongoing pursuit of excellence.

Model A applies to all systems—for-profit, not-for-profit, large, small, start-ups, institutions in need of reform—but applies to each in its own way.

I. BUSINESS DIMENSIONS

The business dimensions of Model A focus on the exploration and establishment of markets and the delivery of quality products or services to clients or customers. There are both strategic and operational business dimensions.

Strategic Business Elements

The strategic business elements give direction and purpose to the company or institution. They include the following:

- *Markets, Customers, Clients.* Viable markets need to be identified; customer needs and wants within these markets need to be explored.

- *Business Environment.* The business environment—competition, economic and social trends, new markets, emerging technology, relevant government regulations, and so forth—needs to be scanned frequently for both threats and opportunities.

- *Mission.* A business mission or overall purpose needs to be developed together with a parallel and integrated *people* mission.

- *Business Philosophy.* An integrated set of values and policies needs to be formulated to govern the conduct of business.

- *Major Business Categories.* The major categories of products or services to be delivered to customers in selected markets need to be determined.

- *Basic Financing.* The system needs to be established on a solid financial foundation. Many enterprises, poorly capitalized, fail before they really get off the ground.

- *Strategy.* All these elements need to be addressed and pulled together into a strategic plan that sets the longer-term direction and goals of the system.

1. *Strategy.* Get the overall purpose and direction of the system straight.

2. *Unit Performance Plans.* Drive the strategy down into the guts of the system.

3. *Operations.* Deliver valued products/services to customers cost effectively in markets of choice.

4. *Organization.* Design and construct the kind of organization needed to "deliver the goods" both strategically and operationally.

5. *Culture.* Develop the beliefs, values, and norms needed to give spirit to the organization.

6. *Management.* Develop a cadre of skilled managers and supervisors to provide direction, coordination, and support.

7. *Leadership.* Develop leaders at every level of the organization to provide institution-enhancing innovation and change.

THE PURSUIT OF EXCELLENCE

Figure 2. The Logic of the Pursuit of Excellence

Operational Business Elements

Operational business elements refer to the day-to-day business of the company or institution. They include the following:

- *Products/Services.* High-quality products and/or services that meet the needs and wants of customers have to be designed, manufactured, marketed, and delivered.

- *Work Programs.* Step-by-step work programs that assure the efficient production and delivery of high-quality products and/or services need to be developed.

- *Material Resources.* Effective programs for choosing and using the material resources, including financial resources, to be used in work programs need to be established.

- *Unit Performance Plan.* Each unit has its own set of operations that contribute directly or indirectly to the delivery of products and services to customers. The unit performance plan sets year-long operational priorities for the unit and links operations to the overall strategy of the enterprise. Linking operations to strategy is critical. Many strategic plans lie in drawers gathering dust because managers have not found ways of getting them into the guts of the system.

II. ORGANIZATIONAL DIMENSIONS

The organization is the way a system structures itself and pulls together its human resources in order to deliver business outcomes. The business should drive the organization. The organization should serve the business. Unfortunately, too many systems become preoccupied with organizational concerns at the expense of the business. That is part of the crisis in both primary and secondary education in the United States today.

The organizational dimensions include the structure of the organization, that is, functional units and subunits, and the deployment and utilization of human resources within these units:

- *Structure and the Division of Labor.* Functional work units need to be established. Within these units, roles with broad charters or clear-cut job descriptions and responsibilities—depending on the circumstances of each system and each unit within the system—need to be set up.

- *Competence.* The units and the people working in the units must be competent, that is, capable of achieving business outcomes. Once jobs with broad role charters or clear-cut job descriptions are established, competent and compatible people need to be hired into these jobs and effectively socialized into the culture of the organization.

- *Teamwork.* Processes need to be established to ensure that units and people within units work together in teams whenever working together will deliver better business outcomes.

- *Communication.* Since communication is the lifeblood of the system, the organizational culture must call for (and individuals must have the skills needed for) effective information sharing, feedback, appraisal, problem solving, innovation, and conflict management among both units and individuals in units.

- *Reward System.* Incentives to do all the above must be provided, disincentives must be controlled, and performance rather than nonperformance must be rewarded.

- *Individual Performance Plans.* A sense of strategy or direction must permeate the entire system. Individual performance plans, established through dialog between individuals and their supervisors, focus on yearly work priorities for each person in the system. These plans link individual efforts to the unit performance plan and—through this plan—to the overall strategy of the system. In my experience, if performance-management systems, however they may be named—management-by-objectives, results management, performance planning and appraisal—do not carry strategy, they tend to carry trivia. Then, instead of being an instrument in the pursuit of excellence, they become one more administrative burden.

III. MANAGEMENT AND LEADERSHIP

If all the above is to happen, companies, institutions, and agencies need both effective management and ongoing leadership.

Management

Managers are both managers of process and managers of people. As managers of process, they are responsible for seeing to it that the elements of Model A described above are in place in their companies or units. Effective managers coordinate and facilitate all the business and organizational elements of Model A. They make things happen. However, since they make things happen through others, they are also managers of people. They make sure workers know what is expected of them, create clear paths to goals, provide resources and support, give feedback, monitor progress, and reward performance. Two of the reasons why managers do not manage well are (1) they do not have models of managing either processes or people (Model A provides such models) and (2) they do not get much feedback. Model A emphasizes the importance of developing a "culture of feedback" within the system.

Leadership

Leadership is an interactive *process* involving the leader, team members or associates, and changing situations. Leadership goes beyond effective management to innovation and change. Effective leadership is not predicated on the *traits* of the leader but rather on what he or she actually *accomplishes*. Leadership means (a) developing visions, (b) turning visions into workable agendas or programs, (c) communicating these agendas to others in a way that results in excitement about and commitment to them, (d) creating a climate and ferment of problem solving and learning around the agendas, and (e) making sure that everyone persists until the agendas are actually accomplished. Leadership, in this sense, is at the heart of the unending quest for excellence.

Ideally, leadership can be found at all levels in a company or institution, even though it will take different forms at each level. In that sense, we can talk about:

- Executive leadership
- Managerial leadership
- Supervisory leadership
- Professional/Technical leadership
- Operator leadership

Take operator leadership. Some companies are currently pursuing participative-management programs because they find that some of the best business ideas come from hourly employees.

Managers who are leaders keep finding new ways of making the organization serve the business. Leadership does not necessarily mean change in the sense of dramatic breakthroughs. One of the 1988 Toyota models, I am told, had about 140 changes from the 1987 model. Not dramatic changes. Managers who are leaders pursue constant *incremental* change. These small changes constitute the never-ending pursuit of excellence found in Toyota and other Japanese automakers.

IV. MANAGING THE SHADOW SIDE OF THE ORGANIZATION

Although managing the shadow side is not covered in this article, it needs to be mentioned briefly at this point since it pervades everything else.

The shadow side of an organization includes the arational factors that affect the business, organizational, management, and leadership dimensions of the system. Smart managers know how to make both the business and organizational elements of Model A work. On the other hand, wise managers know how to deal with the following elements:

- *The Natural Messiness of Organizations.* Organizations are loosely coupled systems in which the kinds of rationality outlined in Sections I, II, and III of Model A are only approximated. For instance, strategy and operations are not always well integrated. Wise managers are aware of the loosely coupled nature of systems and know how to work with it. They understand not just the formal but also the informal system, knowing when to intervene in it and when to leave it alone.

- *Individual Differences.* Individuals working within systems have their differences, idiosyncrasies, and problems, all of which need to be addressed and managed. Research shows that people in leadership positions often imprint their traits, good or bad, on the organization. Wise managers design technology that people can use and structures within which people can live.

- *The Organization as a Social System.* Organizations are social systems with all the benefits and drawbacks of such systems. Internal relationships and cliques develop that can help or hinder the business of the system.

- *The Organization as a Political System.* Because most organizations must deal with such realities as power, authority, scarce resources, the protection of turf, and differences in ideology, they are by nature political systems. Some people pursue the politics of self-interest, putting personal agendas ahead of the business agendas of the company or institution. Others understand and manage the politics of the system at the service of system-enhancing agendas.

- *Organizational Culture.* Organizations tend to develop their own cultures and subcultures. The shared beliefs, values, and assumptions in an organization can either enhance or limit the system's effectiveness. The culture is the largest and most controlling of the systems, because it sets norms for what may or may not be done in all the other "shadow-side" areas.

The ability to manage the shadow side of the organization often makes the difference between a successful or unsuccessful manager or between a mediocre and an excellent manager.

THE USES OF MODEL A

Model A is a business, organizational, managerial, and leadership effectiveness model. If shared among all key players in the system, it can provide the following:

- An integrative framework for understanding companies, institutions, and their subunits;
- A template for designing and running a system or any of its parts, projects, or programs;
- An instrument for assessing the effectiveness of a system and for choosing remedial interventions;
- A common language for talking about systems; and
- A map for helping people to understand the *geography* of systems and to make their way around in them.

HOW THE MODEL WORKS

The model can be explained further by a discussion of how the organization can contribute to or stand in the way of business outcomes. If we look back at the overview of Model A, we see that one of the organizational dimensions is *teamwork,* which would be a vital component in the pursuit of excellence. Therefore, we might select teamwork to demonstrate how the model works.

As we have seen above, "processes need to be established to ensure that units and people within units work together in teams whenever working together will deliver better business outcomes." Note that teamwork for its own sake is not being pushed. Indeed, some things are done better by units or individuals in isolation. The effective manager knows when the members of the unit need to come together as a team and when it is better to work alone. Kanter (1983) suggests that one of the principal reasons that companies and institutions fall short of excellence is the "segmentalism" that plagues most organizations. Units are either indifferent to or even at war with one another. Teamwork is the opposite of and the antidote to segmentalism.

Isolationism and empire building—instead of system-enhancing integration in the subunits—constitute one of the main forms of corporate arationality. Some institutions have such a history of segmentalism that innovative teamwork between units is all but impossible. Universities, with their untouchable departmental system, are cases in point, as the following example shows:

> The psychology and sociology departments at a large urban university, goaded by a few faculty members in each department, had a historic meeting to review ways in which the two could cooperate. Speeches were made to the effect that the age of interdisciplinary research and projects was at hand. The only decision made before the meeting dissolved into a nice social gathering was to meet again "soon." It was the last meeting the two departments had, and that was over fifteen years ago.

On the other hand, an organizational studies department (OSD) at another university is proactive in establishing and cultivating relationships that will benefit itself, other departments, and the entire university. For example, OSD helped the foreign-student office streamline many of its procedures, which—in turn—reduced delays in getting information to foreign students and in processing papers for visas.

This encouraged foreign students to attend that program; foreign students on arrival did not have to face a range of bureaucratic hassles and could get on with the process of learning; students from the United States felt they benefited from the viewpoints of students from other countries.

The OSD director also met with the director of maintenance to determine how they could collaborate in planning for conferences and workshops. The director of maintenance was floored by the upbeat nature of the meeting. He had never before been asked about collaboration; up to that point, the relationship between maintenance and other units of the university had been either neutral or adversarial. This cut down on logistical problems that often interfere with learning at such meetings.

In trying to increase the effectiveness of interunit teamwork, the following questions can help uncover some importance aspects in a company or institution:

- How well do different units work with one another to increase productivity?
- What "empires" have developed and in what ways do they stand in the way of business outcomes?
- To what degree does interunit competition, jealousy, or politics interfere with productivity?
- To what degree does interunit behavior actually decrease productivity?
- What significant partnerships have been established by *this* unit with key units and what further partnerships need to be developed?
- In what ways does a spirit of interunit teamwork permeate the organization?
- What innovative forms of collaboration can be developed between functions?

Teamwork within units can also serve the business outcomes of both the unit and the entire institution. One disturbing study (Knaus et al., 1986) provides evidence that effective teamwork can, literally, make a difference between life and death, the "business" of hospitals. The focus of the study was the intensive-care units of thirteen hospitals. All hospitals had similar technical capabilities in these units but differed in organization, staffing, commitment to teaching, research, and education. During the period of study, forty-one deaths occurred in the intensive-care unit of one hospital, whereas sixty-nine deaths would have been "normal." This hospital showed a consistent, coordinated response to patients' needs and a division of responsibility among physicians and nurses that precluded many problems. The hospital on the opposite end of the continuum had 58 percent more deaths than expected. Not surprisingly, this hospital lacked direct coordination of staff capabilities with clinical demands. There were also frequent disagreements about the ability of the nursing staff to treat additional patients. In sum, leadership was poor, teamwork was poor, and an atmosphere of distrust prevailed.

An effective team is very much like an effective company, institution, department, or project. The following guidelines can help promote business-enhancing outcomes. Before embarking, however, one should make sure that the work will be done better by using a team approach.

1. Choose people who are compatible with the mission of the team and its members.

2. Remain focused on both internal and external customers and their needs; that is, adopt a business rather than an organizational approach.

3. Make sure that the business outcomes of group efforts (products or services to be delivered) are clear.

4. Establish a mode of operating; make sure the team knows how it is expected to work as a team.

5. Coordinate individual efforts.

6. Give teams both responsibilities and the authority needed to execute them.

7. Balance team effort with individual effort.

8. Do not squash individual contributions.

9. Foster the kind of supportive climate that contributes to both improved quality of outcomes and quality of work life.

10. Get expert help outside the team as needed; do not make the assumption that the team has all the resources within itself.

11. Engage in ongoing evaluation of both team outcomes and individual contributions to outcomes. In what way are business outcomes better because of team efforts?

REFERENCES

Kanter, R. M. (1983). *Change masters: Innovation for productivity in the American corporation.* New York: Simon & Schuster.

Knaus, W. A., Draper, E. A., Wagner, D. P., & Zimmerman, J. E. (1986). An evaluation of outcome from intensive care in major medical centers. *Annals of Internal Medicine, 104,* 410-418.

Gerard Egan, Ph.D., is a professor of psychology and organizational studies at Loyola University of Chicago. He is program coordinator for the M.A. in the Center for Organization Development. He has written over a dozen books, including Change-Agent Skills A: Assessing and Designing Excellence, *and* Change-Agent Skills B: Managing Innovation and Change. *He currently writes and teaches in the areas of counseling, counselor education, and management and organization development. Dr. Egan consults to a variety of organizations worldwide, currently including The World Bank, the International Agricultural Research Centers, Amoco Corporation, British Telecom, and British Airways.*

A CAUSAL MODEL
OF ORGANIZATIONAL PERFORMANCE

W. Warner Burke and George H. Litwin

One might argue that the world does not need yet another organizational model. However, the purpose of this paper is to argue the opposite: a functional-cause-and-effect model based on sound research, theory, and organizational consulting experience can contribute both to scholarly usefulness and to a general understanding of organizations.

Organizational models that do little more than describe or depict are frustrating, both from the perspective of research about organizations and from that of consultation to organizational clients. What is needed is a model that *predicts* behavior and performance consequences, one that deals with cause (organizational conditions) and effect (resultant performance).

Some existing organizational models that are largely descriptive do stipulate certain parameters. Weisbord (1976), for example, states that the role of the leadership box in his six-box model is to coordinate the remaining five. The Nadler-Tushman (1977) model is one of congruence. These authors argue that for effectiveness, the various boxes comprising their model should be congruent with one another; for example, organizational arrangements (structure) should be congruent with organizational strategy. However, most if not all of these models are largely descriptive, with limited, if any, causal features.

It is true that contingency models of organizations (Lawrence & Lorsch, 1969; Burns & Stalker, 1961) do have certain causal aspects. Organizational effectiveness is, in part, contingent on the degree of match between the organization's external environment (whether static or dynamic) and the organization's internal structure (either mechanistic or organic). But contingency models tend to present too many contingencies and few, if any, methods for sorting out their interrelationships.

In contrast, the subject of this article, the Burke-Litwin model, is more than merely descriptive and congruent; it serves as a guide not only for organizational diagnosis but also for planned, managed organizational change.

Two primary risks were inherent in developing this causal model of organizational performance. First, "what causes what" could ultimately be wrong (although substantive theory and some research evidence have been encouraging). Second, narrowing the choices of causal factors might ignore some significant organizational variables.

The concepts of organizational climate and culture and a description of the Burke-Litwin model will be described next, including suggestions for ways to use the model and some preliminary research support.

BACKGROUND: CLIMATE AND CULTURE

Climate

The original thinking underlying the model presented here came from George Litwin and others during the 1960s. In 1967 the Harvard Business School sponsored a conference on organizational climate. Results of this conference were subsequently published in two books (Litwin & Stringer, 1968; Tagiuri & Litwin, 1968). The concept of organizational climate that emerged from this series of studies and papers was that of a psychological state strongly affected by organizational conditions, such as systems, structure, and managerial behavior. In their theory paper, Tagiuri and Litwin (1968) emphasized that there could be no universal set of dimensions or properties for organizational climate. They argued that one could describe climate along different dimensions depending on what kind of organization was being studied and what aspects of human behavior were involved. They described climate as a molar, synthetic, or changeable construct. Further, the kind of climate construct they described was relatively malleable; it could be modified by managerial behavior and by systems and strongly influenced by more enduring group norms and values.

This early research and theory development regarding organizational climate clearly linked psychological and organizational variables in a cause-effect model that was empirically testable. Using the model, Litwin and Stringer (1968) were able to predict and to control the motivational and performance consequences of various organizational climates established in their research experiment.

Culture

The concept of organizational culture is drawn from anthropology and is used to describe the relatively enduring set of values and norms that underlie a social system. These underlying values and norms may not be entirely conscious. Rather they describe a "meaning system" that allows members of a social system to attribute meaning and value to the variety of external and internal events that they experience. Such underlying values and meaning systems change only as continued culture is applied to generations of individuals in that social system.

The distinction between climate and culture must be very explicit because this model attempts to describe both climate and culture in terms of their interactions with other organizational variables. Thus this model builds on earlier research and theory with regard to predicting motivation and performance effects.

In addition, the variables that influence and are influenced by climate need to be distinguished from those influenced by culture. Thus there are two distinct sets of organizational dynamics. One set primarily is associated with the transactional level of human behavior or the everyday interactions and exchanges that create the climate. The second set of dynamics is concerned with processes of human transformation, that is, sudden "leaps" in behavior; these transformational processes are required for genuine change in the culture of an organization. Efforts to distinguish transactional and transformational dynamics in organizations have been influenced by the writings of James McGregor Burns (1978) and by experiments in modern organizations.

THE MODEL

As noted in the preceding section, the Burke-Litwin model owes its original development to the work of Litwin and his associates (Litwin & Stringer, 1968; Tagiuri & Litwin, 1968); it has been refined through a series of studies directed by Burke (Bernstein & Burke, 1989; Michela, Boni, Manderlink, Bernstein, O'Malley, Burke, & Schechter, 1988). Recent collaboration has led to the current form of this model, which attempts the following:

1. To specify the interrelationships of organizational variables; and

2. To distinguish transformational and transactional dynamics in organizational behavior and change.

Figure 1 summarizes the model. In accordance with accepted thinking about organizations from general systems theory (Katz & Kahn, 1978), the external environment box represents the input and the individual and organizational performance box represents the output. Feedback loops go in both directions. The remaining boxes of the model represent the throughput aspect of general systems theory.

The model is complex, as is the rich intricacy of organizational phenomena. However, this model, exhibited two dimensionally, is still an oversimplification; a hologram would be a better representation.

Arrows in both directions convey the open-systems principle that change in one factor will eventually have an impact on the others. Moreover, if the model could be diagramed so that the arrows were circular (as they would be in a hologram), reality could be represented more accurately. Yet this is a *causal* model. For example, although culture and systems affect one another, culture has a stronger influence on systems than vice versa.

The model could be displayed differently. External environment could be on the left and performance on the right, with all throughput boxes in between. Or the model could be inverted, that is, performance on the top and external environment on the bottom. However, displaying it as shown makes a statement about organizational change: organizational change stems more from environmental impact than from any other factor. Moreover, with respect to organizational change, the variables of strategy, leadership, and culture have more "weight" than the variables of structure, management practices, and systems; that is, having leaders communicate the new strategy is not sufficient for effective change. Changing culture must be planned as well as aligned with strategy and leader behavior. How the model is displayed does not dictate where change could start; however, it does indicate the weighting of change dynamics. The reader can think of the model in terms of gravity, with the push toward performance being in the weighted order displayed in Figure 1.

In summary, the model, as shown in Figure 1, portrays the following:

- The primary variables that need to be considered in any attempt to predict and explain the total behavioral output of an organization;

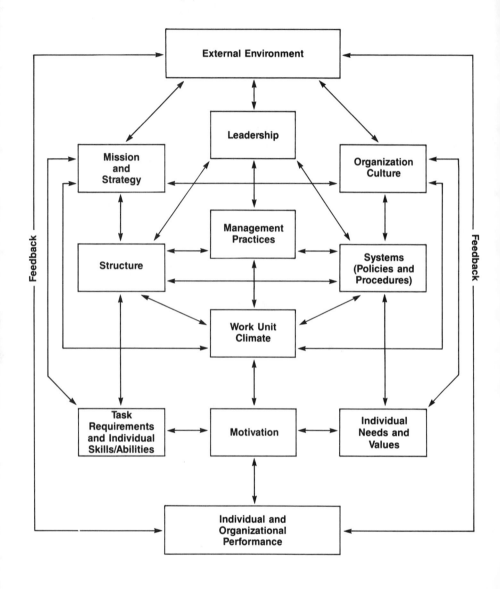

Figure 1. The Burke-Litwin Model
of Individual and Organizational Performance

- The most important interactions among these variables; and
- How the variables affect change.

TRANSFORMATIONAL AND TRANSACTIONAL DYNAMICS

The concept of transformational change in organizations is suggested in the writings of such people as Bass (1985), Burke (1986), Burns (1978), McClelland (1975), and Tichy and Devanna (1986). Figure 2 displays the transformational variables, those in the upper half of the model. *Transformational* refers to areas in which alteration is likely caused by interaction with environmental forces (both within and without) and which require entirely new behavior sets on the part of organizational members.

Figure 3 shows the transactional variables, those in the lower half of the model. These variables are very similar to those originally isolated by Litwin (1968) and later by Michela et al. (1988). They are *transactional* in that alteration occurs primarily via relatively short-term reciprocity among people and groups. In other words, "You do this for me and I'll do that for you."

Each category or box in the model can be described as follows:

External Environment. Any outside condition or situation that influences the performance of the organization. These conditions include such things as marketplaces, world financial conditions, political/governmental circumstances, and so on.

Mission and Strategy. What employees believe is the central purpose of the organization and how the organization intends to achieve that purpose over an extended time.

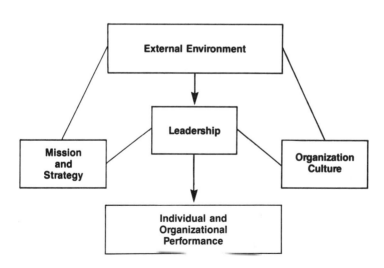

Figure 2. The Transformational Factors

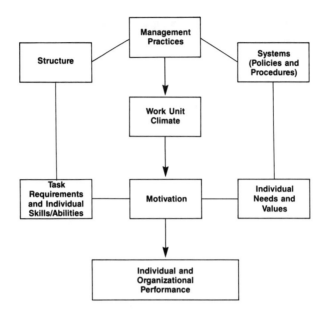

Figure 3. The Transactional Factors

Leadership. Executive behavior that encourages others to take needed actions. For purposes of data gathering, this box includes perceptions of executive practices and values.

Culture. "The way we do things around here." Culture is the collection of overt and covert rules, values, and principles that guide organizational behavior and that have been strongly influenced by history, custom, and practice.

Structure. The arrangement of functions and people into specific areas and levels of responsibility, decision-making authority, and relationships. Structure assures effective implementation of the organization's mission and strategy.

Management Practices. What managers do in the normal course of events to use the human and material resources at their disposal to carry out the organization's strategy.

Systems. Standardized policies and mechanisms that facilitate work. Systems primarily manifest themselves in the organization's reward systems and in control systems such as goal and budget development and human resource allocation.

Climate. The collective current impressions, expectations, and feelings of the members of local work units. These in turn affect members' relations with supervisors, with one another, and with other units.

Task Requirements and Individual Skills/Abilities. The behavior required for task effectiveness, including specific skills and knowledge required for people to accomplish the work assigned and for which they feel directly responsible. This box concerns what is often referred to as job-person match.

Individual Needs and Values. The specific psychological factors that provide desire and worth for individual actions or thoughts.

Motivation. Aroused behavioral tendencies to move toward goals, take needed action, and persist until satisfaction is attained. This is the net resultant motivation; that is, the resultant net energy generated by the sum of achievement, power, affection, discovery, and other important human motives.

Individual and Organizational Performance. The outcomes or results, with indicators of effort and achievement. Such indicators might include productivity, customer or staff satisfaction, profit, and service quality.

Climate Results from Transactions; Culture Change Requires Transformation

Organizational climate, as the concept originally evolved in the 1960s at the Harvard Business School and other centers of behavioral research, was a description of the immediate, short-term impact of the organizational environment on individual and group behavior. Of course, climate has long-term consequences, but these consequences develop as a result of a series of continuing, discrete day-to-day interactions and exchanges (transactions). The idea of climate evolved from the efforts of Litwin and others to describe the relatively fluid qualities of human behavior. Managers could establish a particular climate with a whole variety of consequences for motivation and organized performance.

In the causal model, day-to-day climate is a result of transactions related to issues such as:

- Sense of direction: the effect of mission clarity or lack thereof;
- Role and responsibility: the effect of structure, reinforced by managerial practice;
- Standards and commitment: the effect of managerial practice, reinforced by culture;
- Fairness of rewards: the effect of systems, reinforced by managerial practice;
- Focus on customer versus internal pressures or standards of excellence: the effect of culture, reinforced by other variables.

In contrast, the concept of organizational culture has to do with those underlying values and meaning systems that are difficult to manage, to alter, and even to be realized completely (Schein, 1985). Culture is not used to describe another way of understanding the short-term dynamics of the organization. Rather it provides a theoretical framework for delving into that which is continuing and more or less permanent. "More or less permanent" refers to the fact that change can be arranged or may come about as a result of uncontrolled outside forces but will involve substantial upheaval in all transactional level systems and will take time.

Instant change in culture seems to be a contradiction in terms. By definition, those things that can be changed quickly are not the underlying reward systems but the behaviors that are attached to the meaning systems. It is relatively easy to alter superficial human behavior; it is undoubtedly quite difficult to alter something unconscious that is hidden in symbols and mythology and that functions as the fabric helping an organization to remain together, intact, and viable.

To change something so deeply imbedded in organizational life does indeed require transformational experiences and events. New meaning is given to one's perceptions by such life-changing circumstances. Cataclysmic environmental changes shaped human evolution and produced the kind of internalized culture that people experience. Similarly, drastic environmental changes have shaped or will shape the culture of such organizations as Chrysler and General Motors.

Culture has enormous inertia. It takes drastic circumstances for leaders to question long-held assumptions. Walter Wriston, former chairman of Citicorp, is reported to have said, "You know when you change; when you run head-long into a brick wall, that's when you change!" Transformational experiences and events often result from environmental change, but other events may be critical, for example, the appointment of a new leader. Such transformational processes can provide the basis for "sudden leaps" in organizational behavior and performance because they provide new meaning to events such as cultural change and its interactions with other variables.

Using the Model: Data Gathering and Analysis

Distinguishing transformational and transactional thinking about organizations has implications for planning organizational change. Unless one is conducting an overall organizational diagnosis, preliminary interviews will result in enough information to construct a fairly targeted survey. Survey targets would be determined from the interviews and, most likely, would be focused on either transformational or transactional issues. Transformational issues call for a survey that probes mission and strategy, leadership, culture, and performance. Transactional issues need a focus on structure, systems, management practices, climate, and performance. Other transactional probes might involve motivation, including task requirements (job-person match) and individual needs and values. For example, parts or all of "The Job Diagnostic Survey" (Hackman & Oldham, 1980) might be appropriate.

A consultant helping to manage change would conduct preliminary interviews with fifteen to thirty representative individuals in the organization. If a summary of these interviews revealed that significant organizational change was needed, additional data would be collected related to the top or *transformational* part of Figure 1. Note that in major organizational change, transformational variables represent the primary levers, those areas in which change must be focused. The following examples represent transformational change (concentrated at the top of the model, as illustrated in Figure 2):

1. An acquisition in which the acquired organization's culture, leadership, and business strategy are dramatically different from those of the acquiring organization (even if both organizations are in the same industry), thereby necessitating a new, merged organization;

2. A Federal agency in which the mission has been modified and the structure and leadership changed significantly, yet the culture remains in the past; and

3. A high-tech firm whose leadership has changed recently and is perceived negatively, whose strategy is unclear, and whose internal politics have moved from minimal (before) to predominant (after). The hue and cry here is "We have no direction from our leaders and no culture to guide our behavior in the meantime."

For an organization in which the presenting problem is more a fine-tuning or improving process, the second layer of the model (shown in Figure 3) serves as the point of concentration. Examples include changes in the organization's structure; modification of the reward system; management development (perhaps in the form of a program that concentrates on behavioral practices); or the administration of a climate survey to measure job stratification, job clarity, degree of teamwork, and so on.

British Airways is a good example of an organization in which almost all of the model is used, providing a framework for executives and managers to understand the massive change they are attempting to manage. British Airways (BA) became a private corporation in February of 1987; changing from a government agency to a market-driven, customer-focused business enterprise is a significant change. All boxes in the model have been, and still are being, affected. Data have been gathered based on most of the boxes and summarized in a feedback report for each executive and manager. This feedback, organized according to the model, helps the executive or manager understand which of the boxes within his or her domain need attention.

It is also useful to consider the model in a vertical manner. For example, Bernstein and Burke (1989) examined the causal chain of culture, management practices, and climate in a large manufacturing organization. In this case, feedback to executives showed how and to what degree cultural variables influenced management practices and, in turn, work-unit climate (the dependent variable).

To summarize, considering the model in horizontal terms emphasizes that organizational change is either *transformational*—significant if not fundamental change— or *transactional*—fine-tuning and improving the organization rather than change that is significant in scope. Considering the model from a vertical perspective entails hypothesizing causal effects and assuming that the "weight" of change is top-down; that is, the heaviest or most influential organizational dimensions for change are external environment, first and foremost, and then mission-strategy, leadership, and culture.

It is interesting to note that executives and managers typically concern themselves with the left side of the model illustrated in Figure 1—mission and strategy, structure, task requirements and individual skills/abilities. In contrast, behavioral scientists are more likely to be concerned with the right side and middle of Figure 1—leadership, culture, systems (especially rewards), management practices, climate, individual needs and values, and motivation. One should be concerned with the entire model and with a more effective integration of purpose and practice.

Preliminary Support for the Model's Validity

One way to measure causal predictions is to stay with perceptions and beliefs, that is, how managers' beliefs about mission and strategy, for example, relate to and possibly predict their own perceptions and their subordinates' perceptions of work-unit climate. In the British Airways example, one of the performance indices used was perceived team effectiveness. In research designed and conducted by William M. Bernstein, data were collected from BA managers regarding their beliefs and perceptions about (1) team manager practices, for example, degree of empowering behavior toward subordinates; (2) the usefulness of BA's structure; (3) the clarity of BA's strategy; (4) the extent to which BA's culture supports change; and (5) the team's climate, for example, goal and role clarity. The data categorized according to just these five boxes from the model explained 54 percent of the variance in rating of team effectiveness. Figure 4 illustrates these relationships.

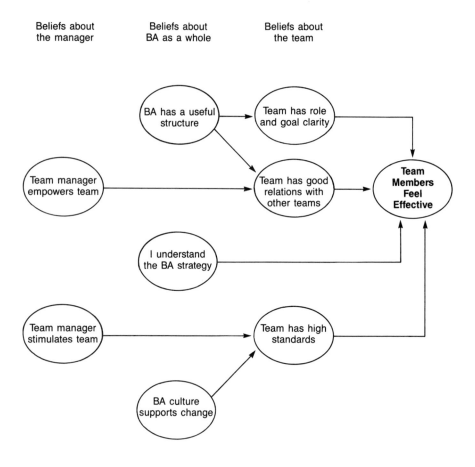

Figure 4. Beliefs Associated with Team Members' Feelings of Effectiveness

CONCLUSIONS

Data do not always support precisely the causal chain depicted in the model. For example, on occasion perceptions regarding strategy or structure explain more variance in ratings of climate or some index of performance than does the variable of management practices, which is usually a heavy predictor. These occasions are when the organization is in the midst of a change in strategy, a change in structure, or both. It may also be that national differences would affect the causal chain in ways not quite as the model would predict. In the United Kingdom, for example, beliefs about "the team" and what constitutes satisfaction may not be the same as American beliefs. When given the opportunity to complain or criticize, the British seem to attribute their feelings of dissatisfaction to more distant factors, such as the culture or the structure, than to factors close to home, such as one's teammates. Americans, on the other hand, are just as likely to criticize their teammates as they are to complain about the inadequate organizational structure.

Finding exceptions to the causal implications of the model does not necessarily detract from its usefulness. As a guide to what to look for and how to manage large-scale organizational change, the model is invaluable. Like any other model, however, it cannot determine exclusively what to diagnose or how to handle organizational change. It simply is one way of conceptualizing and helping organizations take another step forward, making the process more concrete, more testable, and more useful.

REFERENCES

Bass, B.M. (1985). *Leadership and performance beyond expectations*. New York: Free Press.

Bernstein, W.M., & Burke, W.W. (in press). Modeling organizational meaning systems. In R.W. Woodman and W.A. Pasmore (Eds.), *Research in organizational change and development* (Vol. 3). Greenwich, CT: JAI Press.

Burke, W.W. (1986). Leadership as empowering others. In S. Srivastva and Associates, *Executive power: How executives influence people and organizations* (pp. 51-77). San Francisco, CA: Jossey-Bass.

Burns, J.M. (1978). *Leadership*. New York: Harper & Row.

Burns, T. & Stalker, G. (1961). *The management of innovation*. London, England: Tavistock.

Hackman, J.R. & Oldham, G.R. (1980). *Work redesign*. Reading, MA: Addison-Wesley.

Katz, D., & Kahn, R.L. (1978). *The social psychology of organizations* (2nd ed.). New York: John Wiley.

Lawrence, P.R., & Lorsch, J.W. (1969). *Developing organizations: Diagnosis and action*. Reading, MA: Addison-Wesley.

Litwin, G.H., & Stringer, R.A. (1968). *Motivation and organizational climate*. Boston, MA: Harvard Business School.

McClelland, D.C. (1975). *Power: The inner experience*. New York: Irvington.

Michela, J.L., Boni, S.M., Manderlink, G., Bernstein, W.M., O'Malley, M., Burke, W.W., & Schecter, C. (1988). Perceptions of the work environment vary with organization and group membership and organizational position of the group. Working Paper. Unpublished manuscript, Teachers College, Columbia University, New York.

Nadler, D.A., & Tushman, M.L. (1977). A diagnostic model for organization behavior. In J.R. Hackman, E.E. Lawler, and L.W. Porter (Eds.), *Perspectives on behavior in organizations* (pp. 85-100). New York: McGraw-Hill.

Schein, E.H. (1985). *Organizational culture and leadership.* San Francisco, CA: Jossey-Bass.

Tagiuri, R., & Litwin, G.H. (Eds.) (1968). *Organizational climate: Explorations of a concept.* Cambridge, MA: Harvard University Press.

Tichy, N.M., & Devanna, M.A. (1986). *The transformational leader: Molding tomorrow's corporate winners.* New York: John Wiley.

Weisbord, M.R. (1976). Organizational diagnosis: Six places to look for trouble with or without a theory. *Group & Organization Studies, 1,* 430-447.

W. Warner Burke, Ph.D., *a psychology and education professor at Teachers College, Columbia University, is the coordinator of the graduate program in organizational psychology. He is also the president of W. Warner Burke Associates, Inc., a consulting firm. Dr. Burke is the editor of the* Academy of Management Executive, *and he is an active member of several professional associations. He has written extensively on organization development, training, social and organizational psychology, and conference planning.*

George H. Litwin, Ph.D., *is an organizational strategist with The Forum Corporation in Boston, Massachusetts. His specialties include large-scale organizational change, climate and culture, motivation and performance, and the dynamics of transformational and transactional change. Dr. Litwin has taught organizational behavior at Harvard University Graduate School of Business Administration, and served as an executive vice president of The Forum Corporation.*

CONTRIBUTORS

Jim Ballard
Developmental Editor
University Associates, Inc.
8517 Production Avenue
San Diego, CA 92121
(619) 578-5900

Ralph R. Bates
President
Bates and Associates
6818 Murray Lane
Annandale, VA 22003
(703) 354-0669

Richard Beckhard
Executive Director, RBA
320 Riverside Drive
New York, NY 10025
(212) 666-2222

Willa M. Bruce, Ph.D.
Assistant Professor of
    Public Administration
Department of Public Administration
University of Nebraska at Omaha
Omaha, NE 68182
(402) 554-2664

W. Warner Burke, Ph.D.
Columbia University
Teachers College
525 West 120th Street
New York, NY 10027
(212) 678-3249

Stephen C. Bushardt, D.B.A.
Professor of Management
Department of Management
College of Business Administration
University of Southern Mississippi
Southern Station Box 5077
Hattiesburg, MS 39406-5077
(601) 266-4673

Jacqueline L. Byrd, Ph.D.
Director of Policy Analysis/Research
    and Planning
Ramsey County Court House
Suite 28
St. Paul, MN 55102
(612) 298-5647

Richard E. Byrd, Ph.D.
President
The Richard E. Byrd Company
5200 Willson Road, Suite 402
Edina, MN 55424
(612) 925-1757

Beverly Byrum, Ph.D.
Professor of Communication
Wright State University
Dayton, OH 45435
(513) 873-2710
(513) 873-2145

Robert J. ("Jack") Cantwell
Training Officer
Personnel Office
DeKalb County Government
One Callaway Building, Room 408
120 W. Trinity Place
Decatur, GA 30030
(404) 371-2854
(404) 371-2332

Phyliss Cooke, Ph.D.
Senior Consultant
University Associates
    Consulting & Training Services
8380 Miramar Mall, Suite 232
San Diego, CA 92121
(619) 552-8901

Gerard Egan, Ph.D.
Professor
Department of Psychology
Loyola University of Chicago
820 North Michigan Avenue
Chicago, IL 60611
(312) 951-9182
(312) 670-3091

Judy H. Farr
Personnel Officer
Indiana National Bank
One Indiana Square, J100
Indianapolis, IN 46266
(317) 266-5690

Aubrey R. Fowler, Jr., Ph.D.
Department Chairman
and Associate Professor
Department of Marketing
and Management
University of Central Arkansas
Conway, AR 72032
(501) 450-3149

Tim Hildebrandt
Trainer/Coordinator
Employment Services and Economic
Security - New Careers Branch
500-213 Notre Dame Avenue
Winnipeg, Manitoba R3B 1N3
CANADA
(204) 778-4411

Sandra Hagner Howarth
Howarth Marketing, Inc.
4951 South Beeler Street
Greenwood Village, CO 80111
(303) 290-9468

Homer H. Johnson, Ph.D.
Director, Center for
Organization Development
Loyola University of Chicago
820 N. Michigan Avenue
Chicago, IL 60611
(312) 508-3027

Judith H. Katz, Ed.D.
Vice President
Kaleel Jamison Associates, Inc.
P.O. Box 30H
Cincinnati, OH 45230
(513) 231-1007

James M. Kouzes
President, TPG/Learning Systems
The Tom Peters Group
555 Hamilton Avenue
Palo Alto, CA 94301
(415) 326-5774

George H. Litwin
The Forum Corporation
One Exchange Place
Boston, MA 02109
(617) 241-5707

Lorna P. Martin, Ed.D.
Assistant Professor of Business Studies
Professional Studies Division
Stockton State College
Pomona, NJ 08240
(609) 652-4636

Frederick A. Miller
President
Kaleel Jamison Associates, Inc.
P.O. Box 30H
Cincinnati, OH 45230
(513) 231-1007

Udai Pareek, Ph.D.
1 Ganga Path
Suraj Nagar West
Jaipur 302006
INDIA

William N. Parker
Training Specialist
Virginia Power
4112 Innslake Drive
Glen Allen, VA 23060
(804) 273-3507

Will Phillips
Senior Consultant
The Small Business Advantage
9888 Carroll Center Road, Suite 225
San Diego, CA 92126
(619) 549-2001

Gifford Pinchot III
Chairman
Pinchot & Company
409 Orange Street
New Haven, CT 06511
(203) 624-5355

Barry Z. Posner, Ph.D.
225 Kenna Hall
Leavey School of Business
Santa Clara University
Santa Clara, CA 95053
(408) 554-4634

Ava Albert Schnidman
Deltech Consulting Group
51 Oakengates
Avon, CT 06001
(203) 673-3882

Bill Searle
Director, The Avrion Group
Professor of Management
  and Computer Science
Department of Business Administration
Asnuntuck Community College
Box 68
Enfield, CT 06082
(203) 745-1603

Charles H. Smith, Ph.D.
Assistant Professor of Management
School of Business
Hofstra University
Hempstead Turnpike
Hempstead, NY 11550
(516) 560-5726
(516) 560-5731